Casino

Martin Scorsese is one of the world's most acclaimed and provocative film-makers. He was assistant director on the Oscar-winning documentary *Woodstock* (1970) and went on to co-write and direct *Mean Streets* (1973). This was followed by *Alice Doesn't Live here Any More* (1974), *Taxi Driver* (1975), *New York, New York* (1977), *The Last Waltz* (1978), *Raging Bull* (1980), *After Hours* (1985), *The Color of Money* (1986), *The Last Temptation of Christ* (1988), *New York Stories: Life Lessons* (1989), *GoodFellas* (1990), *Cape Fear* (1991), *The Age of Innocence* (1993), *A Personal Journey with Martin Scorsese through American Movies* (1995), *Casino* (1995) and *Kundun* (1997).

Nicholas Pileggi worked as a reporter for the Associated Press from 1956 until 1968, covering crime, politics and corruption in New York. In 1968, he left the AP and joined *New York Magazine* during its first year and has remained there as a contributing editor, writing over 100 cover stories dealing with the city's underworld. His first book, *Blye, Private Eye*, was published in 1978. He took four years to research his second book, *Wiseguy*, from which he and Martin Scorsese wrote the screenplay *GoodFellas*. He spent another four years researching his non-fiction book, *Casino*, upon which, again, he and Martin Scorsese based their screenplay *Casino*. His screenplays include *GoodFellas* (1990), *Casino* (1995) and *City Hall* (1996), which he co-wrote with Paul Schrader.

NOTE

This edition represents the structure of the completed film rather than that of the shooting script.

*by the same authors*

**GOODFELLAS**

# Casino

## NICHOLAS PILEGGI & MARTIN SCORSESE

*faber and faber*
LONDON · BOSTON

First published in 1996
by Faber and Faber Limited
3 Queen Square London WC1N 3AU

Photoset by Parker Typesetting Service, Leicester
Printed in England by Clays Ltd, St Ives plc

Screenplay © 1995 Universal City Studios, Inc. and Syalis Droits Audiovisuels
Introduction by Ian Christie © *Sight and Sound*, 1996
Stills and photographs © 1995 Universal City Studios, Inc. except for portrait of
Nicholas Pileggi © Sigrid Estrada, 1996

Nicholas Pileggi, Martin Scorsese and Universal are hereby identified as authors
of this work in accordance with Section 77 of the Copyright, Designs and
Patents Act 1988

A CIP record for this book
is available from the British Library
ISBN 0–571–17992–4

4 6 8 10 9 7 5 3

# Contents

Nicholas Pileggi

Martin Scorsese

# Introduction: Stardust in Vegas

What do we expect from a Scorsese film? We know what the young Scorsese learned to expect from Powell and Pressburger after *The Red Shoes*, or from King Vidor after *Duel in the Sun*. He has talked eloquently about how these names became synonymous with an intensity and sheer rapture that shaped his passion for cinema. But what do we expect each time a new Scorsese is unveiled? Passionate commitment to a subject, consummate technical mastery, a masterpiece amid the opportunism and mediocrity of routine Hollywood production? Proof that the greatest living American film-maker is still – well, the greatest.

It's a tall order, like asking an athlete to break a record on every outing. Scorsese's films are not intended to be blockbusters, though they're hardly low-budget. So reviews and reputation are vital. His acknowledged artistry helps the studios feel like occasional patrons of the art they daily trade in. The equation is fragile, combining as it does studio pride, critical and industry respect, and audience response to what are often bewilderingly intense films in a bland era.

Here, the intensity is that of a Jacobean tragedy by Webster or Tourneur. Except this blood-spattered triangle of love and revenge isn't set in some renaissance court, but in a modern equivalent – the neon and rhinestone baroque of a Vegas casino. A Chicago gambler is given control of 'Paradise on Earth', in the shape of a new casino, by a murky cabal of Mafioso kingmakers. His realm flourishes, despite the arrival of a violent desperado from his past, and an unwise choice of consort from among the courtesans. Soon his friend and his wife form an adulterous alliance against him, using his child as a pawn in their game. But he survives a murder attempt, while both of them meet a degrading end.

There are other ways of telling the story of 'Ace' Rothstein, Nicky Santoro and Ginger McKenna. Scorsese's co-screenwriter, Nick Pileggi, who also collaborated on *GoodFellas*, has interviewed many of the survivors of this murderous period and chronicled the heyday of mob influence in Las Vegas during the seventies in his book, *Casino*, subtitled *Love and Honour in Las Vegas*. And Michael Mann drew on some of the same factual material for his impressive television series *Crime Story* in 1987. But in Scorsese's version, there are also echoes of a major American genre he has never directly tackled: the Western. *Casino* can be seen as a kind of *noir*-influenced Western, somewhere between Sturges's *The Law and Jake Wade* and Brando's brooding *One Eyed Jacks*, with Ace as a bad man who strikes lucky in the West and marries a saloon girl, before his past catches up with him in the shape of Nicky.

But isn't it, the sceptics will say, also *GoodFellas II*? Clearly the answer must be yes, in that it deals with the seventies after the sixties of *GoodFellas*, finding Las Vegas an ideal microcosm of that decade's false glamour. Yes, also insofar as Scorsese and Pileggi have mined another rich vein of America's parallel history of organized crime, and revel insolently in their findings. But this chapter is more varied in its hues, flecked with desert sunshine and extravagant neon; and more complex in its politics, as the traditional mafia seeks to extend its empire by remote control. It shows with a precision that no mere documentary could achieve how Vegas ruthlessly preyed on gamblers large and small to feed the insatiable appetite of the crime bosses. It shows a glittering, festering latterday Babylon surrounded by desert – like an obscene parody of the American myth of the Frontier-as-Promised Land – in which appearance is everything, and nothing is what it seems.

Most daring of all, in the midst of this decadence, shot through with the horrors of men clubbed to death, tortured and blown up, we're invited to laugh at its rulers' foibles, admire their wit and enterprise, and finally grieve over their destruction. The Rolling Stones and Bach's *St Matthew Passion* are juxtaposed on the soundtrack, as if *GoodFellas* were erupting into the drawing rooms of *The Age of Innocence*. Like Hans-Jurgen Syberberg 'tempting us' with the seductive appeal of the Führer in *Hitler, A Film from Germany*, or like Eisenstein lavishing his montage brilliance on the corruption of Romanov Russia in *October*, *Casino* challenges us with the lure of evil, the deep fascination of Lucifer and the fallen angels that Milton understood.

Eisenstein? Milton? Come on – surely it's only a gangster movie? Scorsese's work has a habit of ageing into classic status. Almost routinely, ever since the youthful triumphs of *Mean Streets* and *Taxi Driver*, each film has been found wanting by some; only to be reviewed and reconsidered, before being judged worthy additions to the canon. Philip Horne has already anticipated this process in his review of *Casino* for the *Times Literary Supplement*: 'This sad and brutal film grows richer and more sympathetic with attentive reviewing... Scorsese's pity – which has a religious dimension – finds human gravity in the deaths of bad men.' Only time will tell whether *Casino* is indeed another hard-won masterpiece.

IAN CHRISTIE: *What was the hook that persuaded you to tackle another mafia subject after* GoodFellas?

MARTIN SCORSESE: The first newspaper article Nick Pileggi showed me was about the police covering a domestic fight on a lawn in Las Vegas one Sunday morning. And in that article it slowly began to unravel – this incredible ten-year adventure that all these people were having – culminating in this husband and wife arguing on their lawn, with her smashing his car, the police arriving, and the FBI taking pictures. As you work back to the beginning, you find this incredible story with so many tangents and each is one more nail in their coffin. It could be the underboss of Kansas City, Artie Piscano, constantly complaining that he always had to spend his own money on trips to Las Vegas and never got reimbursed. Or it could be that unrelated homicide that made the police put a bug in the produce market that Piscano kept in Kansas City. Even they've forgotten about it, but it picks up all his complaining and alerts FBI men around the country to all these names. They're surprised to hear the names of the Vegas casinos being mentioned in a Kansas City produce market.

Then, quite separately, a court decrees that a woman should have her share of the money as a partner of the president of the Tangiers Hotel. But instead of settling with her, the mob shoot her. This then brings police attention to the president, although he was in no way involved in the decision to kill her. And then you have all these highly volatile characters involved. I just thought it would be a terrific story.

*Was Las Vegas unfamiliar territory for you?*

I'm pretty familiar with the characters around the tables and in the offices, but the actual place itself and the gaming was new to me. What interested me was the idea of excess, no limits. People become successful there like in no other city.

*So it's like the American dream carried to ridiculous lengths? You can go from rags to riches, and from riches to rags, in no time at all.*

Exactly, and that's what's happening right now in America. There's been a spread of new casinos all around the country, which reflects the desperation, when people think that with one throw of the die their whole life will be changed.

*It gives Ace a chance to create something, rather like an old-time prospector going west, who lands in a small town and by sheer hard work makes his fortune. But because he makes the classic mistake of loving without being loved, he falls.*

Well, it's his own fault . . . But as Nicky says at one point in the film, so long as they're 'earning with the prick' *they'll* never OK anything – the gods, that is – meaning they'll never authorize killing him. But Nicky likes to be prepared, so he orders two holes to be dug in the desert. That's the way they talk. This is the kind of dialogue you find from the witness protection programme.

*It's really Sodom and Gomorrah, surrounded by the desert, isn't it? There's a great fanfare of biblical language and images at the start of the film.*

Yes it is. We don't want to lay it on too heavily, but that was the idea. Gaining Paradise and losing it, through pride and through greed – it's the old-fashioned Old Testament story. He's given Paradise on Earth. In fact, he's there to keep everybody happy and keep everything in order, and to make as much money as possible so they can take more on the skim. But the problem is that he has to give way at times to certain people and certain pressures, which he won't do because of who he is.

*What about the whole country-club strand? Is this because he's Jewish and wants to be accepted socially?*

He says when he accepts that plaque, 'Anywhere else I'd be arrested for what I'm doing. Here they're giving me awards.' This is the only place he can use his expertise in a legitimate way, and so become a part of the American WASP community. That's why Nicky tells him in the desert, 'I'm what's real out here. Not your country clubs and your TV show.' I'm what's real: the dirt, the gutter, and the blood. That's what it's all about.

*It's a great scene in a classic Western setting.*

That's where they had to go to talk – in the middle of this desert. And Nicky had to change cars six times. I always imagined that the Joe Pesci character must be so angry, and getting angrier as he changes each car, until he gets out of the last one and De Niro can't say a word when he lashes right into him. But you know in this case I'm on Nicky's side. The rest *is* artifice, and if you buy into it it's hypocrisy. Know where it's coming from and know what the reality is. Don't think you're better than me, or than the people you grew up with.

*This creates the same moral dissonance that was so powerful in* GoodFellas, *where you want to see someone succeed, but it's the wrong business! The audience gets that taste for immorality, and you tempt them.*

Very often the people I portray can't help but be in that way of life. Yes, they're bad, they're doing bad things. And we condemn those aspects of them. But they're also human beings. And I find that often the people passing moral judgement on them may ultimately be worse. I know that here in England there were film-makers and critics who felt I was morally irresponsible to make a film like *GoodFellas*. Well, I'll make more of them if I can. Remember what happens at the end of the movie, where you see Nicky and his brother beaten and buried. That's all based on fact – I saw the pictures of the real bodies when they dug up the grave. Now it's shot in a certain way, very straight. And I happen to like those people. Nicky *is* horrible. He's a terrible man. But there's something that happens for me in watching them get beaten with the bats and then put into the hole. Ultimately it's a tragedy. It's the frailty of being human. I want to push audiences' emotional empathy with certain types of characters who are normally considered villains.

When I was growing up I was around many of these men, and most of them were very nice. They treated me and my family well, and they were attractive. I knew they were tough, and some were tougher than others. But it's a matter of the hypocrisy of those who condemn people, who often turn out to be twice as corrupt. I know it sounds like a cliché, but it's a cliché because it's real.

*You go to considerable lengths to make Nicky an attractive figure. He even comes home every morning and cooks breakfast for his son...*

Based on the real man, who did that. It's an interesting dilemma for both of them. They both buy into a situation and both overstep the line so badly that they destroy everything for everybody. A whole new city comes rising out of the ashes. What we show in this film is the end of the old way and how it ended. They got too full of pride, they wanted more. If you're gambling you want more, like the Japanese gambler Ichikawa, who bets less money than he normally would bet when he's tricked into coming back. But for him it's not a matter of winning ten thousand, it's losing ninety thousand, because normally he bets a hundred thousand.

*It's a neat little parable about gambling.*

We always had problems with where that scene was going to be placed in the structure. But I said it's very important to keep the move into Bob's face when he says, 'In the end we get it all.' They do, they really do. What an interesting place, because they're a bunch of cheats, watching cheats, watching cheats. Sam Rothstein and those guys know how to cheat, with handicapping and basketball games. They make it so natural that you wouldn't be able to tell whether the game is fixed. I'm sure he has that ability.

*There's a fantastic symphony of looks in the film, with everyone watching everyone, and you push it and push it until we reach...*

... the all-seeing eye. And that's when he sees Ginger for the first time. Before they had the video eye-in-the-sky, they hired men with binoculars who had been cheats to go up on the catwalks to try and find other cheats. I just thought it was really wonderful, with nobody trusting anybody.

*There's another great documentary thrust in the film: explaining how money gets skimmed and multiplied and diffused; and then how it gets distributed in equally bizarre ways.*

That was twenty years ago, before the old mob lost their control. At that time most casinos were 'owned' by some mob from a different part of the country. We combined four casinos – the Stardust, the Hacienda, the Frontier and the Marina – into the fictional Tangiers, which the Rothstein character controlled. So we just made them one giant hotel and combined all the elements. Where else could a great handicapper become the most important man in the city, with total control? We tried to show how far his control ran, even over the kitchen and the food. Insisting on an equal number of blueberries in each muffin may seem funny, but it's important because if the muffins and the steaks are good the people who are playing there will go and tell others. It's not just paranoia and obsessive behaviour – there's a reason: to make the Tangiers the best place on the Strip.

*And when Rothstein decides to go on television it reminds us of Rupert Pupkin in* King of Comedy.

Exactly. Rothstein thinks of it as a place to be heard.

*The bosses are seen in some highly stylized ways. When we see them round a table, they're like a group painted by Frans Hals.*

Yeah, they're definitely old-world.

*Then we see them in another mysterious nowhere place, with stark, almost silhouette lighting like a scene from Fritz Lang.*

That's the back of the garage, and Bob Richardson lit it like that. It's where Remo says, 'Go get them,' and they put the guy's head in a vice – not that they intended to do that. But after two days and nights of questioning they didn't know what else to do.

*This is so excessive that we know it's got to be real, because you wouldn't invent it. But it also seems to belong to a Jacobean horror tragedy.*

It really does. The incident actually occurred in Chicago in the sixties. There was a Young Turk argument which ended with guns and two brothers and a waitress were killed. It caused such outrage that they wanted the men who were with him also, and they finally got them and killed them all. But Joe found the human way of playing the scene: 'Please don't make me do this.' He's a soldier who has to take these orders, and he has to get that name, otherwise *his* head is in the vice.

*Although Ginger is as important a character as Ace and Nicky, we really only see her through their eyes and so she remains more of a mystery. Is she hustling him from the start, or does he kill whatever chance they had?*

She tells him exactly how things are in that scene where he proposes. Reaching the age of forty, if you find someone maybe you *try* to make it work in a reasonable way. I think they may have had a chance, if it wasn't for that city and what they were doing in it. Although I think there's something in Ace's character that ultimately destroys everything.

*Does it get worse as he gets more and more wrapped up in his role as casino boss? All intimacy between them seems to disappear.*

I think he's responsible for the emotional alienation. You get it when she goes to the restaurant and she says, 'I'm Mrs Rothstein' and the other lady says, 'Well you might as well get something out of it.' It's the way he treats her. He won't let her go. If he lets her go, he believes he'll just never see her again. He'll hear from her through a lawyer, but he'll never see her again.

Their daughter Amy is unfortunately just a pawn to be used. By the last third of the film, Ginger is definitely disturbed, she's no longer in her right mind. Whether it's from drugs or drink doesn't matter, she's completely gone. It doesn't excuse anything she does, but it does heighten the horror of what's going on – like tying the child up.

*Sharon Stone gives a very committed performance which shows she's got a range which hasn't always been called upon.*

I agree. De Niro really helped her through those scenes. He's very generous with her and you can see how he's always helping. It's a scary role, a tough one – like when she takes cocaine in front of the child: that was her choice.

*She has to spend nearly a third of the movie in a state of falling apart.*

Yes, and she did that with her whole body and with the clothes. She worked with the clothes, like that David Bowie-type gold lamé outfit she's wearing for the last third of the picture. It's a little baggy in places, because she tried to make herself look as bad, or as wasted, as she could. You could make ten films about each of those characters, all different, and I don't know if I did justice to any of them. I just wanted to get as much in as possible, plus I wanted to get all of Vegas in there as well. And also the whole climate of the time, the seventies – it was pretty ambitious for Nick and me to do.

*You shot the whole film in Las Vegas. Did you shoot in a real casino?*

Oh yes. And we shot during working hours. Barbara De Fina figured out that the extra time it could cost would probably be the same as to build one. And you won't have the electricity and the life around you, which is what we got. We would fill the foreground with extras dressed in seventies costumes, and the background would sort of fall off. Sometimes we shot at four in the morning. I really love the scene when Joe comes in with Frank Vincent and they're playing blackjack, even though he's banned from the place, and he's abusing the dealers. That was four o'clock in the morning, and you hear someone yelling in the background because he's winning at craps. The dealer went through the whole scene with Joe, who was improvising, throwing cards back at him and saying the worst possible things. Halfway through the scene, the dealer leaned over to me, and said, 'You know, the real guy was much tougher with me – he really was uncontrollable.'

*Why is the film so long?*

You have to work through the whole process of these three people who can't get away from each other. Every way they turn they're with each other. It's not even a story about infidelity. It's bad enough that they both were unfaithful to each other – the marriage was in terrible shape as it was – but worse that she starts with Nicky, because Nicky is the muscle. If anybody can get her money and jewels it's Nicky.

*The most remarkable thing about the film's structure is that you start with Sam being blown up. Was this how it started in your first script?*

In the very first script we started with the scene of them fighting on the lawn. Then we realized that it's too detailed and didn't create enough dramatic satisfaction at the end of the picture. So Nick and I figured we would start with the car exploding, and he goes up into the air and you see him in slow motion, flying over the flames – like a soul about to take a dive into hell.

*Did the internal structure of the film change a lot as you worked on it?*

Yes, it did, a lot. And that's where Thelma Schoonmaker came in very strongly, because she hadn't read the script, but just watched the footage come in and was able to take charge of elements that were in the middle, like the documentary aspects. Thelma and I used to edit documentaries twenty-five years ago, so she's very, very good at that. It is the most harrowing kind of editing you can do because you're never sure of the structure and you're not following a dramatic thread. There's no plot in this film: there's story, but no plot. So what you're following is the beginnings of Ace coming to Vegas, then the beginnings of Nicky in Vegas, and the beginning of Nicky and his wife in Vegas and their child. Then Ace is succeeding in Vegas, and what's Nicky doing? He's sandbagging guys. Ace's rise culminates with Nicky being banned. Then that takes us to Nicky rising, which is his montage of robbery – 'I'm staying here, you're not getting rid of me.' He creates his alternative empire. Then you start to bring the two tracks together. But up to the point at which Nicky builds his own empire we had a lot of reshuffling of scenes and rewriting of voice-over. At first we had split it up throughout the film, but it came a little too late, although on the page it looked all right. Finally, we put all the exposition at the beginning and we moved the explanation of the skim up front.

*You've become really interested in voice-over? What does it do for the spectator?*

There's something interesting about voice-over: it lets you in on the secret thoughts of the characters, or secret observations by an omniscient viewer. And for me it has a wonderful comforting tone of someone telling you a story. And then it has a kind of irony much of the time. Suppose you see two people saying goodnight, and the voice-over says, 'They had a wonderful time that evening, but that was the last time before so-and-so died.' You're still seeing the person, but the voice-over is telling you they died a week later, and it takes on a resonance, and for me a depth and a sadness, when used at moments like that. The voice-over in this particular film is also open to tirades by Nicky. If you listen to him complaining – about the bosses back home, how he's the one out here, the one in the trenches – then you begin to understand his point of view. Why should I have to work for somebody? Why don't I go into business for myself? You can see the kind of person he is from these tirades in voice-over.

*Did the change in visual style come from working with a new cinematographer, Robert Richardson, or from the subject's needs?*

Well, there are a lot of tracks and zooms; as well as pans and zip-pans. There are also more static angles, which are cut together very quickly, because of all the information that's being crammed into the frame. If you did too much moving you wouldn't be able to see what we're trying to show. So that became the style – a kind of documentary.

*You talked about excess as the keynote of Las Vegas, but the most excessive thing in the film is De Niro's wardrobe.*

That was Rita Ryack, who's done a number of films with me, and John Dunn also worked with her. We had fifty-two changes for Bob, which was a lot.

*It becomes a visible sign of him going off the rails.*

Absolutely. The mustard-yellow suit, the dark navy-blue silk shirt with navy-blue tie, with crimson jacket. We chose the colours very carefully. Our ritual in the morning, once we narrowed down the idea of which outfit, was to choose which shirt, then which tie, then which jewellery. If you look closely, the watch-faces usually match the clothes – even the watch he wears when he turns the ignition on. We were always rushed – I just needed a close-up of him turning on the ignition. Then we look at it through the camera, and we think, oh yes, the wristwatch. So we set the angle in order to show the watch as well as possible, for the short amount of time it's on. And if you look at the film again, or on laserdisc, you can see a lot of detail in the frames that we put there. Nicky didn't have that many changes, maybe twenty or twenty-five. And Ginger had about forty, I think.

*You've worked with Dante Feretti as production designer on a number of films. What kind of relationship do you have in terms of planning the overall look of a film?*

The casino we used, the Riviera, looked like the seventies, although it was only built in the late seventies. That was the centrepiece. Then we tried to find houses that were built in the late fifties or early sixties, which are very rare. There was one house which we finally got, and I laid all my shots there, rehearsed, and then about two weeks later we lost it. Then we had to find another house, and finally it all worked out for the best, because that was the best one we found. It was an era of glitz – a word I heard for the first time in the seventies – and I think you can tell what Dante brings to a film when you just look at the bedroom, especially in the wide shots, in the scene where she's taken too many pills and she's crying, and he's trying to help her. There's something about the way the bed is elevated; it looks like an imperial bed, a king's or a queen's bed. There's something about the wallpaper – everything, the dishes on the walls – that says a great deal about character. Dante made it regal, not just in bad taste – even though some of it is bad taste – but the quality is good, and that moiré silk headboard is just a backdrop for a battleground, like a silk battleground.

*I'm interested you say 'regal', because I also found myself thinking the film is about a court, with a king who chooses a consort, and what we see is the rise and fall of a little dynasty.*

Exactly. They're on display all the time. Appearance *is* everything, to the point where he didn't want people to smile at him or say hello. You can see it in the way he stands and looks around.

*The music for* Casino *uses the same general approach as* GoodFellas, *but the range is broader – like starting with the 'St Matthew Passion'.*

I guess for me it's the sense of something grand that's been lost. Whether we agree with the morality of it is another matter – I'm not asking you to agree with the morality – but there was the sense of an empire that had been lost, and it needed music worthy of that. The destruction of that city has to have the grandeur of Lucifer being expelled from heaven for being too proud. Those are all pretty obvious biblical references. But the viewer of the film should be moved by the music. Even though you may not like the people and what they did, they're still human beings and it's a tragedy as far as I'm concerned.

*In* Goodfellas *and again in* Casino *the music becomes another means of directing the viewer, like the voice-over. Every piece of music brings its own associations.*

That's right. There's Brenda Lee singing 'Hurt'; the Velvetones doing 'Glory of Love' – there's a lot, over fifty-five pieces, I think. Then there's the breakdown of style in 'Satisfaction' from the Stones to Devo. I was very lucky to be able to choose from over forty years of music and in most cases to be able to get it into the film.

*Is this all coming from you, setting the musical agenda of the film?*

Very much, yes. We did have one piece planned, but I decided to use it at the end instead of the beginning. Why waste it, because it has an almost religious quality.

*In fact, 'The House of the Rising Sun' encapsulates the moral of the film.*

Yes, it's a warning about telling your children not to do what you've done. We kept that for the end. And then lots of early Stones.

*Which you had wanted to use more in* Goodfellas*?*

I did, but I just couldn't fit in any more. It wasn't that we didn't have any room, but certain songs and pieces of music, when you play them against picture, change everything. So it's very, very delicate. In *GoodFellas* the sound is more Phil Spector, while in this picture it's more the Stones, especially 'Can't You Hear Me Knocking?', which is a key song in the film.

*You follow the same rule as in* GoodFellas *of keeping the music strictly in period?*

Yes, as far as possible. When Ace and Nicky need to talk, after the argument in the desert, they get into a car in the garage to have a private conversation. What would happen? They'd sit in the car and keep the radio on. And what's playing is 'Go Your Own Way' by Fleetwood Mac, which is a key song of the mid to late seventies. No matter what the mood of the conversation, that music is playing. So we were able to use music at that point that would take you further into the time. The sounds change from the beginning of the film from Louis Prima to Fleetwood Mac. You see, it's not so much the Bach that begins the film as the Louis Prima that cuts it off, creating a stong shock effect. I knew Louis Prima had to be in there, but we came to that later, and I remember the Bach was the first thing I had in mind.

*The Bach returns at the end, followed by Hoagy Carmichael.*

For the splendour of the destruction of this sin city it has to be

Bach. Because the old Vegas is being replaced by something that looks seductive, kiddie-friendly, but it's there to work on the very core of America, the family. Not just the gamblers and the hustlers and the relatively few gangsters who were around, but now it's Ma and Pa Kettle. While the kids watch the Pirate ride, we'll take your money.

*Why did you quote Georges Delerue's music from Godard's* Contempt?

I liked the sadness of it. And there are other movie themes in the film, like the theme from *Picnic*, over Mr Nance sashaying into the count room – the implication being that it was so easy you could waltz in and waltz right out with the money. The theme from *Picnic* was such a beautiful piece of music that it was played on jukeboxes and Top 40 all the time, so you would always hear it and you still do in Vegas. The other one was 'A Walk on the Wild Side' by Elmer Bernstein and Jimmy Smith. That has a nervous energy that's good, especially in that sequence where we use it, the killing of Anna Scott. Again, it was a very famous piece of music that was taken out of context from the film, and became a part of life in America at the time. Along with these, it seemed interesting to try the *Contempt* music and see what we could do.

*That's also a movie about a man who has a problem in his relationship with his wife.*

He certainly does! After the Bach you can't do anything. The only thing would be *Contempt* to wipe the slate clean. And then after that the only possible thing is one of the greatest songs ever written, 'Stardust' – the only piece that could sum up the emotions and thoughts about what you've seen.

Ian Christie
1996

*This introduction and interview appeared in a different form in* Sight and Sound, *January 1996*

*Casino* was released in the United States in November 1995, and in Great Britain in March 1996.

The cast and crew includes:

| | |
|---|---|
| SAM 'ACE' ROTHSTEIN | Robert De Niro |
| GINGER MCKENNA | Sharon Stone |
| NICKY SANTORO | Joe Pesci |
| LESTER DIAMOND | James Woods |
| BILLY SHERBERT | Don Rickles |
| ANDY STONE | Alan King |
| PHILIP GREEN | Kevin Pollak |
| PAT WEBB | L. Q. Jones |
| SENATOR | Dick Smothers |
| FRANK MARINO | Frank Vincent |
| DON WARD | John Bloom |
| | |
| *Director* | Martin Scorsese |
| *Producer* | Barbara De Fina |
| *Based on the book by* | Nicholas Pileggi |
| *Screenplay* | Nicholas Pileggi & Martin Scorsese |
| *Director of Photography* | Robert Richardson |
| *Production Designer* | Dante Ferretti |
| *Editor* | Thelma Schoonmaker |
| *Music Consultant* | Robbie Robertson |
| *Title sequence* | Saul and Elaine Bass |
| *Costume Designers* | Rita Ryack |
| | John Dunn |
| *Casting* | Ellen Lewis |

A De Fina/Cappa Production presented by Universal Pictures.

This edition would not have been possible without the heroic assistance of Alfonso Gomez-Rejon, who prepared the manuscript for publication, nor without the care and attention which Thelma Schoonmaker-Powell, with utmost generosity, dedicated to the project.

# Casino

*Adapted from a true story*

1983

SAM 'ACE' ROTHSTEIN, *a tall, lean, immaculately dressed man approaches his car, opens the door, and gets inside to turn on the ignition.*

ACE: (*Voice-over*) When you love someone, you've gotta trust them. There's no other way. You've got to give them the key to everything that's yours. Otherwise, what's the point? And, for a while . . . I believed that's the kind of love I had.

> (*Suddenly, the car explodes. Flames, smoke and metal rise into the sky covering the view of the Las Vegas casinos and their signs.*
> *Music in: J. S. Bach – 'St Matthew Passion'.*
> *Ace's body comes flying in – extreme slow motion. His body twists and turns through the frame like a soul about to tumble into the flames of damnation.*)

MAIN TITLE SEQUENCE.


INT. TANGIERS CASINO FLOOR – NIGHT

*Vignette of* ACE: *through rippling flames, we move in on* ACE ROTHSTEIN *overseeing the casino. He lights a cigarette.*

ACE: (*Voice-over*) Before I ever ran a casino or got myself blown up, Ace Rothstein was a hell of a handicapper, I can tell you that. I was so good, that whenever I bet, I could change the odds for every bookmaker in the country. I'm serious. I had it down so cold that I was given paradise on earth. I was given one of the biggest casinos in Las Vegas to run, the Tangiers . . .

3

INT. SAN MARINO ITALIAN GROCERY/BACK ROOM, KANSAS
CITY – NIGHT

*Vignette of* MOB BOSSES: *sitting at a table surrounded by food and wine like the gods of Olympus.*

ACE: (*Voice-over*) . . . by the only kind of guys that can actually get you that kind of money: sixty-two million, seven-hundred thousand dollars. I don't know all the details.

NICKY: (*Voice-over*) Matter of fact . . .


INT. BAR, LAS VEGAS – NIGHT

*Vignette of* NICKY SANTORO: *standing at a bar with* DOMINICK SANTORO, *his brother, and* FRANK MARINO, *his right-hand man.*

NICKY: (*Voice-over*) . . . nobody knew all the details, but it should'a been perfect. I mean, he had me, Nicky Santoro, his best friend, watching his ass . . .


INT. NIGHTCLUB – NIGHT

*Vignette of* GINGER MCKENNA: *a dazzling thirty-one-year-old blonde seated by a small fiery pool.*

NICKY: (*Voice-over*) . . . and he had Ginger, the woman he loved, on his arm. But in the end . . .


INT. TANGIERS SPORTSBOOK/ACE'S OFFICE – NIGHT

ACE *looks over the casino he rules.*

NICKY: (*Voice-over*) . . . we fucked it all up. It should'a been so sweet, too. But it turned out to be the last time that street guys like us were ever given anything that fuckin' valuable again.


EXT. LAS VEGAS – NIGHT

*Aerial shot coming down out of the clouds over the brightly lit Vegas Strip and off into the blackness of the desert night.*

ACE: (*Voice-over*) At that time, Vegas was a place where millions of suckers flew in every year on their own nickel, and left behind about a billion dollars. But at night, you couldn't see the desert that surrounds Las Vegas . . .

EXT. DESERT – DAWN

*Aerial shot swooping along desert floor, then rising above the mist to reveal mountains in the distance.*

ACE: (*Voice-over*) But it's in the desert where lots of the town's problems are solved.

NICKY: (*Voice-over*) Got a lot of holes in the desert, and a lot of problems are buried in those holes. Except you gotta do it right. I mean, you gotta have the hole already dug before you show up with a package in the trunk. Otherwise you're talkin' about a half-hour or forty-five minutes of diggin'. And who knows who's gonna be comin' along in that time? Before you know it, you gotta dig a few more holes. You could be there all fuckin' night.

EXT. LAS VEGAS STRIP, 1973 – NIGHT

TITLES IN: 'THE STRIP', 'LAS VEGAS', 'TEN YEARS EARLIER'

*ACE is greeted by a casino exec and walked through the brightly lit entrance to the Tangiers Casino.*

ACE: (*Voice-over*) Who could resist? Anywhere else in the country, I was a bookie, a gambler, always lookin' over my shoulder, hassled by cops, day and night. But here, I'm 'Mr Sam Rothstein'. I'm not only legitimate, but running a casino. And that's like selling dreams for cash.

INT. TANGIERS CASINO – NIGHT

*We see ACE enter alone. He is greeted by BILLY SHERBERT. They are joined by top executives RICHIE and RONNIE in suits and ties. They walk through the casino, past crowded and noisy craps tables,*

7

*spinning roulette wheels, blackjack tables, poker-faced players at poker tables, and elegant, cordoned-off, black-tie, baccarat tables.*

ACE: (*Voice-over*) I hired an old casino pal, Billy Sherbert, as my manager and I went to work.

SHERBERT: (*Introducing the* EXECS *to* ACE) . . . And this is Ronnie, who takes care of the card room . . .

ACE: (*Voice-over*) For guys like me, Las Vegas washes away your sins. It's like a morality car wash. It does for us what Lourdes does for humpbacks and cripples. And, along with making us legit . . .

INT. TANGIERS/HARD COUNT ROOM – NIGHT

*Dolly back from a wall of money. An employee pours a bucket full of coins into a trough. Camera follows progress as numerous coins move on a conveyor system, through a sorting machine. Camera reveals several rolls of coins on a lower conveyor as they move up a ladder towards an employee's hands, who then places the rolls on a rack.*

ACE: (*Voice-over*) . . . comes cash. Tons of it. I mean, what do you think we're doing out here in the middle of the desert?

It's all this money. This is the end result of all the bright lights and the comped trips, of all the champagne and free hotel suites, and all the broads and all the booze. It's all been arranged just for us to get *your* money. That's the truth about Las Vegas.

INT. TANGIERS/FLOOR/SOFT COUNT ROOM – DAY

*Camera follows* JOHN NANCE *carrying a small suitcase and walking through the casino to a door leading to the cashier's cage. The sign on the door reads 'Authorized Personnel Only'. He walks through the cage, to another door: 'Notice – Keep Out'.*

ACE: (*Voice-over*) We're the only winners. The players don't stand a chance. And their cash flows from the tables to our boxes . . . through the cage and into the most sacred room in the casino . . . the place where they add up all the money . . . the holy of holies . . . the count room.
(*He opens the door. We see inside the count room from* NANCE's *point of view. It looks like the area behind a teller's cage in a bank. A large room, windowless, decor-free. One side is a mesh cage, opened to reveal stacks of cash boxes. Several* COUNTERS *in white shirts are gathered around a glass table counting and sorting paper money.*)
Now this place was off limits.

COUNTER #1: Verify two thousand.

ACE: (*Voice-over*) Even I couldn't get inside, but it was my job to keep it filled with cash. That's for sure.

NICKY: (*Voice-over*) They had so much fuckin' money in there, you could build a house out of stacks of $100 bills. And the best part was that upstairs, the board of directors didn't know what the fuck was going on.

(*At one end of the room the clerks empty the metal boxes and rapidly count the cash at a counting table. The camera follows a cash 'drop box' being lifted from the stack by a clerk. He pours the cash on to the table and shows the empty box to a video camera.* COUNTER #2 *rapidly counts the cash and announces:*)

9

COUNTER #2: Five thousand.

NICKY: (*Voice-over*) I mean, to them everything looked on the up and up. Right? Wrong.

(*The first counter recounts the cash.*)
COUNTER #1: Verify five thousand.

NICKY: (*Voice-over*) The guys inside the counting room . . .

(*Stacks of bills lie nearby. The camera pans across the room to another table manned by a* COUNT ROOM EXECUTIVE *who repeats the figure and writes it down on a master list.*)
COUNT ROOM EXEC: Five thousand.
(*We move back to* NANCE *opening a cabinet full of stacks of $100 bills. He opens his suitcase and begins to fill it with cash. As he does this, the workers studiously look in other directions.*)

NICKY: (*Voice-over*) . . . were all slipped in there to skim the joint dry. They'd do short counts, they'd lose fill slips. They'd even take cash right out of the drop boxes. And it was up to this guy right here [NANCE], standin' in front of about two million dollars, to skim the cash off the top without anybody gettin' wise . . . the IRS or anybody.

COUNTER #1: Verify two hundred.
(NANCE *closes the case and walks out. One of the counters dumps another container of money on the table.*)

NICKY: (*Voice-over*) Now, notice how in the count room nobody ever seems to see anything. Somehow, somebody's always lookin' the other way. Now, look at these guys [COUNTERS]. They look busy, right? They're countin' money. Who wants to bother them? I mean, God forbid they should make a mistake and forget to steal. Meanwhile, you're in and you're out.
(NANCE *exits the count room and proceeds through the lobby of the casino, passing* ACE *and* SHERBERT, *to a side exit door.*)
Past the jag-off guard who gets an extra c-note a week just to watch the door. I mean, it's routine. Business as usual: in, out, hello, goodbye. And that's all there is to it. Just another fat fuck walkin' out of the casino with a suitcase.

Now, that suitcase was goin' straight to one place: right to Kansas City . . . which was as close to Las Vegas as the Midwest bosses could go without gettin' themselves arrested.

(NANCE *leaves the casino and gets into a cab parked at the curb.*)

EXT. KANSAS CITY AIRPORT – DAY

NANCE *arrives. He is greeted by* ARTIE PISCANO, *a gray-haired sixty-year-old underboss.*

TITLE IN: 'KANSAS CITY'

NICKY: (*Voice-over*) That suitcase was all the bosses ever wanted . . . and they wanted it every month.

PISCANO: Hey, John, how are you? How was your ride?

EXT. SAN MARINO ITALIAN GROCERY, KANSAS CITY – DAY

NANCE, *with suitcase, and* PISCANO *leave the car and enter the produce market.*

NICKY: (*Voice-over*) Now this old Mormon fuck here . . .

(*Cut to:* NANCE, *as he gets out of Piscano's car.*)

INT. SAN MARINO ITALIAN GROCERY, KANSAS CITY – DAY

NANCE *and* PISCANO *walk through the grocery store, through the warehouse, past various employees to a doorway leading into the back room, where they are greeted by five older men around a large wooden table with bowls of macaroni and old jelly glasses filled with red wine.*

NICKY: (*Voice-over*) . . . he had to fly in with suitcases once a month, nice and easy.

NANCE: Somethin' smells good.
PISCANO: Yeah, they made us somethin' to eat.

II

NICKY: (*Voice-over*) The bosses would come from all over the place: Detroit, Cleveland, Milwaukee. All over the Midwest. And they would meet in the back of this produce market in Kansas City. I mean, nobody even knew.

(NANCE *shakes hands with* AMERICO CAPELLI, *sixty-eight, a bald, affable Milwaukee entrepreneur and* ARTHUR CAPP, *his thirty-year-old yuppie lawyer son. Camera continues to pan around the room.*)

One of the guys made his mother do all the cooking.

(*On* VINCENT BORELLI, *seventy-year-old Kansas City boss.*)

BORELLI: Did you ever see that guy Jerry Steriano?

(*On* VINNY FORLANO, *mid-seventies, an old-timer who once drove for Capone and is now Remo Gaggi's right-hand man.*)

FORLANO: Jerry Steriano?

BORELLI: Yeah.

NICKY: (*Voice-over*) Now, these old greaseballs might not look it, but believe me, these are the guys who secretly controlled Las Vegas.

(PISCANO *joins his* MOTHER *and* DAUGHTER *by a stove.*)

PISCANO'S MOTHER: That man's here again.
(*Piscano dips a piece of bread into a pot of tomato sauce*).

NICKY: (*Voice-over*) Because they controlled the Teamsters' Union, and that's where you had to go if you wanted to borrow money to buy a casino.

BORELLI: (*Off-screen*) When you've finished with him, I want him.

PISCANO'S MOTHER: (*Carrying a plate of food to the table where* BORELLI *and* FORLANO *are seated.*) Here you are, gentlemen.

NICKY: (*Voice-over*) And nobody got a Teamsters' loan, unless the guys in this room knew they were gonna get their little suitcases.
(FORLANO *gets up from the table and walks toward* NANCE.)
Guys like this antique here [FORLANO], out of Detroit.
Or especially guys like Remo Gaggi, the outfit's top boss.
(NANCE *embraces* REMO GAGGI *who's seated on a couch, and sits across from him.*)

GAGGI: You got a round figure on it?

NICKY: (*Voice-over*) Definitely the most important guy in this room.

NANCE: (*Picking up the suitcase*) About twenty pounds.
GAGGI: So?
NANCE: That's around seven hundred thousand.
GAGGI: Uh-huh, good.
(NANCE *opens the case to reveal the money.*)
ANDY STONE: (*Off-screen, from following scene*) I know it's a little early for Las Vegas . . .


INT. TANGIERS EXECUTIVE OFFICE PRESS CONFERENCE/
BANQUET ROOM – DAY

*Camera tilts down a model of the Tangiers Hotel and Casino, then reveals the cover of* Business Week *magazine with a drawing of* PHILIP GREEN, *a young corporate type, smiling out under the headline: 'Philip Green, Vegas Wunderkind'.*

STONE: (*Off-screen*) . . . but I do want to welcome the ladies and gentlemen of the gaming industry.
(*On* ANDY STONE, *a middle-aged man at a podium giving a speech while* GREEN, *seated at a table, looks on.*
   PHOTOGRAPHERS *flash their cameras.* ACE *and* SHERBERT, *sitting next to* GREEN, *also watch the photo op ceremony.*)

ACE: (*Voice-over*) As far as the world was concerned Andy Stone, the head of the Teamsters' Pension Fund, was a legitimate guy.

STONE: This is a very auspicious occasion.

ACE: (*Voice-over*) A powerful man.

STONE: Philip, if you would rise.
(GREEN *stands up.*)

ACE: (*Voice-over*) He even played golf with the President.

STONE: On behalf of the Teamsters' Pension Fund, it is my pleasure to present to you . . .

ACE: (*Voice-over*) But Andy also took orders. And when he was told to give a pension fund loan to Philip Green . . .

STONE: (*Handing* GREEN *a large cardboard facsimile 'check'*) . . . this check for $62,700,000 for the new Tangiers.
GREEN: Thank you.

ACE: (*Voice-over*) . . . he did what he was told.

(PHILIP GREEN, *who is now head of the Tangiers Hotel and Casino Corporation, is standing at the podium giving a speech.*)

NICKY: (*Voice-over*) Now here was the perfect front man. I mean, what the fuck else could he be? He didn't know too much. He didn't want to know too much, especially that the bosses made the Teamsters lend him the money. He wanted to believe the Teamsters gave him all that fuckin' money 'cause he was smart.

(*An exploding flash bulb fills the screen.*)
GREEN: . . . I say that, knowing full well just how much competition we have in this great city.

14

EXT. CHEAP MOTEL OFF HIGHWAY – DAY

*We see a* MAN *and a* WOMAN *swimming underwater. Camera reveals they are in a motel swimming pool with glass portholes. Expensive cars are parked outside one of the rooms. Hoods stand around outside the door.*

NICKY: (*Voice-over*) And where they got Green from – who the fuck knows? All I know is that Green was an Arizona real estate hustler, who barely had enough gas money to come and pick up his own fuckin' check . . .

INT. TEAMSTERS' OFFICE – DAY

*A plaque on the wall reads:* 'Central States Teamster Pension Fund'. ANDY STONE *and* ARTIE CAPP (*Americo Capelli's son*) *stand over* GREEN *who is signing an agreement at a large desk under a Teamster Pension Fund banner in a large ornate office.*

NICKY: (*Voice-over*) And of course it was the bosses' man, Andy Stone, who gave all the orders . . . not the Chairman of the fuckin' Board, Philip Green.

GREEN: (*To Stone*) I understand. I understand. (GREEN *signs the document which reads:* 'Tangiers, Corp., a Nevada Corporation by: Philip Green'.)

INT. TANGIERS EXECUTIVE OFFICE PRESS CONFERENCE/
BANQUET ROOM – DAY

*We return to the press conference. Photographers snap away. In the background are six-foot blow-ups of the* Business Week *cover. The camera moves past* GREEN, CAPP *and several other men, past* SHERBERT, *to* ACE.

NICKY: (*Voice-over*) Now, all they needed was somebody they could trust to run the casino. And who better than Ace? I mean, he was already in Vegas a couple of years and he had the fuckin' place clocked.

*(Freeze frame on* ACE.*)*

EXT. TANGIERS SWIMMING POOL – DAY

*Camera looks straight down from the top of a hotel to a large pool area.*

NICKY: (*Voice-over*) But, typical Ace . . .


EXT. TANGIERS SWIMMING POOL/POOLSIDE – DAY

STONE, *in a bathing suit and robe, sits on a lounge chair with a telephone.* ACE, *in sports clothes, sits on another chair.*

NICKY: (*Voice-over*) . . . give him a shot at runnin' a casino and he tries to talk you out of it.

ACE: You know, I don't know if I could do this even if I wanted to. The Gaming Commission would never give me a license. I have at least two dozen gambling and bookmaking pinches on me.

STONE: You don't have to have a license to work in a casino. All you gotta do is apply for one. The state law says that you can work in a casino while they're processing your application. They got a ten-year backlog.

ACE: But what happens when they do find out?

STONE: Why would they want to find out? We're puttin' a
hundred million into this desert here. Why would they
want to lock us out? And besides, they'll never find out. All
you gotta do is keep changing your job title. Like, uh, from
Casino Executive to Food and Beverage Chairman. And
what happens is, they take your application, they put it at
the bottom of the pile. I know guys workin' there for thirty
years, don't have a license.

ACE: (*Exhales*) It's a tough proposition, Andy. You, you know,
if I did it, I'd have to run it my way.

STONE: You got it.

ACE: I'm serious. No interference.

STONE: Nobody's gonna interfere with your running the casino.
I guarantee it. (STONE *lights a cigarette.*)

INT. TANGIERS CRAPS PIT – NIGHT

ACE *blows on a die.*

NICKY: (*Voice-over*) And that's how they got Ace to take over.
(ACE's *hands place the die into a micrometer.*)
They wanted him because Ace ate, slept and breathed
gambling.

(*Camera swish tilts up to* ACE, *then swish pans to boxman, dealers and players watching him, trying to act calm.*)
They worked out a real cute job title too.
(*We see the die in the micrometer.*)
Tangiers Public Relations Director.
(*Satisfied the die is not loaded* ACE *sets it on the craps table, the camera cranes up to reveal the Tangiers Casino floor.*)
But the only thing he ever directed was the casino. He made his first bet when he was fifteen years old, and he always made money. But he didn't bet like you or me.
(*A* DEALER *is sliding chips, tossing them on to a craps table.*)
You know, havin' some fun with it, shit like that.

ACE: (*Approaching the* DEALER) Where the hell did you learn how to deal? (*He reaches down, stacking and arranging the chips.*)

NICKY: (*Voice-over*) He bet like a fuckin' brain surgeon.

ACE: (*To the chastised* DEALER) Place the checks properly. That's the way you do it.
DEALER: Yes, sir.

NICKY: (*Voice-over*) He had to know everything, this guy.
(*Direct overhead tracking shot as* ACE *walks between two rows of gaming tables.*)
He'd find out the kind of inside stuff nobody else knew, and that's what he'd put his money on.


INT. GYM/BOOKIE JOINT, BACK HOME, PRE-SEVENTIES – DAY

ACE *walks past two boxers sparring in a ring, through a doorway into a room where several gamblers are seated around a table.*

NICKY: (*Voice-over*) Even back home, years ago, when we were first hangin' out together . . .

TITLE IN: 'BACK HOME, YEARS AGO'

. . . he'd know if the quarterback was on coke.
(ACE *is looking at the odds board for college football games. The bookie,* LUCKY LARRY, *is waiting for* ACE *to hand in his picks.*)

ACE: I'll take Columbia for twenty.

NICKY: (*Voice-over*) If his girlfriend was knocked up.

LUCKY LARRY: Twenty dimes on Columbia . . .
(*As soon as* ACE *bets, a man erases a number from the chalkboard and replaces it with a '6', changing the odds. Two* GAMBLERS *saunter from the room.*)

NICKY: (*Voice-over*) He'd get the wind velocity so he could judge the field goals. He even figured out the different bounce you got off the different kinds of wood they used on college basketball courts, you know?

EXT. GYM/BOOKIE JOINT PUBLIC PHONES – DAY

*The two* GAMBLERS *we saw sauntering out of the bookie joint are racing to the nearest public phones. Another* GAMBLER *has already beat them to it.*

NICKY: (*Voice-over*) He'd be workin' on this shit day and night. There was nothin' about a game he was gonna bet that he didn't know.

GAMBLER #1: (*Into phone*) Ace got down at six.
GAMBLER #2: (*Into phone*) Charlie, hey. Rothstein got six.

INT. GYM/BOOKIE JOINT, SEVERAL DAYS LATER – DAY

*A bookie hands a stack of money to another bookie, who hands the money to* ACE. ACE *removes several bills from the top of his stack of winnings and holds them out to the* BOOKIES.

NICKY: (*Voice-over*) Season after season, the prick was the only guaranteed winner I ever knew. But he was so serious about it all that I don't think he ever enjoyed himself. But . . .
(*Ace exits.*)
. . . that's just the way he was.

INT. MOB SOCIAL CLUB BACK ROOM – NIGHT

*The room has an espresso machine and a saint's day calendar.*
*Assorted hoods are listening to* NICKY *at the bar. Camera dollies to*
REMO GAGGI, *at the rear table playing gin rummy with* OLD MAN
CAPO *and losing. Every time the* CAPO *picks up a card, he's able to*
*knock or get gin, sending* GAGGI *into a fit bemoaning his bad luck.*

NICKY: (*Voice-over*) But back then the bosses didn't give a fuck
    about whether he enjoyed himself or not. To them, he was
    a cash register. All they had to do was ring the bell and
    take the money. Especially Remo, who was a fuckin'
    degenerate gambler who always lost.

GAGGI: (*Slams down his cards and curses at his losing hands*) Ma
    che cazzo![1] All those fuckin' sweeps.

NICKY: (*Voice-over*) I mean, unless Ace made his bet.

GAGGI: That's enough now!
OLD MAN CAPO: I can't contest the cards.
GAGGI: *Va fa 'n culo!*[2] (*Summoning a young man.*) Johnny!

NICKY: (*Voice-over*) Ace made more money for them on a
    weekend than I could do heisting joints for a month.
    (ACE *enters and walks to* GAGGI's *table.*)
    Whatever Ace picked up on the street he told Remo.

NICKY: (*Walks over to* ACE *and whispers*) Hey, did you bring that
    thing?

NICKY: (*Voice-over*) You know, I mean fixed fights, doped
    horses, crooked fuckin' zebras . . . locked-in point spreads.
    He told fuckin' Remo everything. And to tell you the truth.
    I don't blame him.

    (GAGGI *stands up and shakes* ACE's *hand.*)
GAGGI: Ace.

NICKY: (*Voice-over*) Keepin' Remo happy with money was the
    greatest insurance policy in the world.

1 Italian-American slang for 'What a prick.'
2 Italian-American slang for 'Fuck off.'

(GAGGI *beams as* ACE *takes out an envelope filled with cash and hands it over to him.* GAGGI *sits back down and* ACE, *knowing his place, smiles and is about to leave.*)

GAGGI: Son-of-a-bitch. How the hell did you get Oklahoma–Michigan? Nobody ever had Oklahoma–Mi . . . How the hell'd you do it?

ACE: Well, that's why they paid so well.

GAGGI: You see? (*Chuckles.*) Never tells me nothin'. Ace, what do we got on for next week?

ACE: Well, it's a little too early. I'd say Thursday would be good. I'll know by then. Is that all right?

GAGGI: Okay. You come by the house?

ACE: I'll come by.

GAGGI: Seven o'clock?

ACE: Seven o'clock.

(GAGGI *gets up and kisses* ACE *as* NICKY *and* OLD MAN CAPO *look on.*)

GAGGI: Good job, my boy. Keep it up. Okay, Ace?

(ACE *nods in agreement and leaves the room.*)

(*To* NICKY) Hey, Nick. *Vien accá.*[1]

NICKY: (*To* ACE) I'll be right out.

GAGGI: *T'aggia parlá.*[2] Nicky . . . see that guy (*pointing to the off-screen* ACE)?

NICKY: Mm.

GAGGI: Keep a good eye on him. He's makin' a lot of money for us. And he's gonna continue makin' a lot of money for us, so keep a good eye on him.

NICKY: Mm.

GAGGI: Not like your fuckin' friends out there, that . . . without brains. Okay?

NICKY: All right.

GAGGI: Uh-huh. *Mi raccomando.*[3]

NICKY: Yeah.

GAGGI: Fine.

---

1 Italian-American slang for 'Come here.'
2 Italian-American slang for 'I've got to talk to you.'
3 Italian-American slang for 'I'm counting on you.'

NICKY: (*Reaching down to touch* GAGGI'S *money, joking with him*) Want me to take this for you? (*He walks out.*)

NICKY: (*Voice-over*) So, now, on top of everything else, I gotta make sure nobody fucks around with the Golden Jew.

INT. BACK HOME BAR — NIGHT

*We move past* JOE, *a guy at the bar entertaining a* BRUNETTE *and a* BLONDE, *to* NICKY *and* FRANK MARINO *at the other end. There are other bar patrons in the background.*

JOE: (*To the* BARTENDER) Chase, couple of shooters for the ladies.

BARTENDER: (*Off-screen*) All right.

ACE: (*Voice-over*) Yeah, we made a great pair. I made book and Nicky made sure we always collected. The old men loved us. And why not? They all made money with us.

NICKY: (*To* MARINO) They payin'?

ACE: (*Voice-over*) How did Nicky collect?

MARINO: They pay every week, like they're supposed to.

ACE: (*Voice-over*) Don't ask.

NICKY: Then where the fuck is the money? I don't see the money.
   (ACE *enters, and greets the two girls.*)

ACE: Hi, Melissa. Heidi.

BLONDE: Hi, Sam.

JOE: (*To the* GIRLS) Who's this guy?

MARINO: (*To* NICKY) Get the fuck out of here. It was nine. I laid nine.
   (ACE *approaches* NICKY *and* MARINO.)

NICKY: It was eight. Ace . . . tell him the line on the Bear's game.

ACE: Eight.

NICKY: If he don't know, nobody knows. Told you it was eight.

MARINO: Well, how come I laid nine?

NICKY: 'Cause you're a jag-off. I would have fuckin' made you lay ten . . .

22

(ACE *notices a pen lying on the bar. He taps* JOE *on the shoulder.*)

ACE: (*To* JOE) Excuse me.

JOE: What?

ACE: (*He holds up the pen*) Is this yours? Your pen?

JOE: Yeah, that's my pen. Why?

ACE: I ju– Well, it's a nice pen. I just didn't know whose it was. I thought it was yours. I didn't want it to get lost.

JOE: Well, thank you. Why don't you take that fuckin' pen and shove it up your ass, you fuckin' jag-off?
(NICKY *looks over.*)

ACE: Well, I was just offering you the –
(NICKY *moves towards* JOE.)

JOE: (*Turning his back to talk to the girls, referring to* ACE) This fuckin' asshole.
(NICKY *grabs the pen out of* ACE's *hand.*)

MAN #1: (*To* JOE) Look out –
(*Before* ACE *can react,* NICKY *grabs* JOE *and starts stabbing him in the neck with the pen.*)
– Joe! Look out, Joe! Look out!
(NICKY *grunts while* JOE *gasps and groans. The* BLONDE *screams while* NICKY's *hand continues to plunge the pen into*

JOE's *throat.* JOE *tumbles to the floor.* NICKY *pounces on him, still stabbing and now kicking.* JOE *whimpers.*)

NICKY: What's that? You hear? You hear a little girl, Frankie? You hear a little girl, Ace? Is that a little fuckin' girl?! What happened to the *fuckin'* tough guy? Told my friend stick it up his fuckin' ass?! Huh?! Huh?!

ACE: (*Over whimpers and pants*) Wait a sec, Nicky, Nicky, Nicky. Ta-take it easy.

(ACE *looks stunned.* NICKY's *still holding the bloody pen.*)

ACE: (*Voice-over*) While I was tryin' to figure out why the guy was sayin' what he was sayin', Nicky just hit him. No matter how big a guy might be, Nicky would take him on. You beat Nicky with fists, he comes back with a bat. You beat him with a knife, he comes back with a gun. And if you beat him with gun, you better kill him, because he'll keep comin' back and back until one of you is dead.

NICKY: (*Voice-over*) Listen . . .


INT. TANGIERS CASINO FLOOR, 1972 – NIGHT

*Camera swoops from a woman cheering as she wins at a slot-machine to a blackjack table, then to a roulette table and over to a craps table.*

*Montage of very short cuts of chips being picked up, dice thrown, money being poured from a bucket, stacks of money.*

NICKY: (*Voice-over*) . . . with me protecting Ace, he made a fortune for the bosses. I mean, that's what got him to Vegas. He was a money machine. A tremendous earner for these guys. As soon as he took over, he doubled the fuckin' drop. With Ace the casino never saw so much money. And the bosses, they couldn't be happier.


INT. TANGIERS CASINO FLOOR – NIGHT

*Camera moves in on* ACE *as he looks out over the casino. Dealers deftly stack chips, scoop up losses and pay off winners. Chips and money are everywhere.*

*In extreme close-up slow motion a die falls on to a table.*

INT. TANGIERS CASINO SLOT-MACHINE AREA – NIGHT

ACE *and* SHERBERT *are walking down a casino aisle by the slot-machines. Dealers immediately snap to attention at their approach.*

ACE: (*Voice-over*) In Vegas, I had to keep a few juiced-in local cowboys working. They were close to the, you know, good old boys.

ACE: (*To* SHERBERT) Pay him six hundred a week, tell him to walk around and look smart.

ACE: (*Voice-over*) I mean, without us, these guys, they'd still be shovellin' mule shit.

(ACE *points at paper cups, empty glasses and the debris of silver dollar wrappings on the floor.* DON WARD, *the Slots Manager in Western garb, immediately starts picking up the debris.* ACE *looks at* WARD *sternly.*)

ACE: Ward, you gotta keep a cleaner station. If you need 'Mr Clean', page him, all right?
(WARD *bends down and picks up some trash.*)

WARD: It won't happen again, Sam.

ACE: Mr Rothstein.

WARD: It won't happen again, Mr Rothstein.

ACE: (*To* SHERBERT.) Is this guy just another dumb fuckin' white man, or what? What's his story?

SHERBERT: We need this guy.

ACE: We can't get rid of him?

SHERBERT: He's juiced in. He's the County Commissioner's cousin.

ACE: I wouldn't give the bum a mop job.
(*They exit.*)


INT. TANGIERS BACCARAT TABLES – NIGHT

*A card shoe slides across the baccarat table. A state* SENATOR, *a little drunk, tips the dealer, kisses the blonde* HOOKER *with him, fills his pockets with his winnings and walks over to see* ACE.

ACE: (*Voice-over*) These yokels ran the state.

DEALER #1: Thank you very much, Senator.

ACE: (*Voice-over*) They passed the laws, they owned the courts.

SENATOR: Hi, Ace.
ACE: Hello, Senator.
  (*They shake hands.*)
SENATOR: (*To* ACE) Hey, I need a room. Need a room.
ACE: Good to see ya. (*To* SHERBERT.) William would you . . .
  (*The* SENATOR *shakes hands with* SHERBERT *as the* HOOKER *joins them.*)

ACE: (*Voice-over*) I had dozens of politicians and state officials comin' through that place every week.

SHERBERT: Nice to see you, Senator.
ACE: (*To* SHERBERT) Help the Senator, give him whatever he wants.
SHERBERT: Certainly. (*Leads the way.*) Senator.

ACE: (*Voice-over*) Why not make them happy?

SHERBERT: We have some nice penthouses you'll enjoy. Maybe the Presidential Suite.


INT. TANGIERS PRESIDENTIAL SUITE – DAY

*The* SENATOR *unzips the* HOOKER's *dress, kisses her and walks through the bedroom doorway, looking over his shoulder to her as she takes off her dress and walks out of his sight.*

ACE: (*Voice-over*) For politicians . . .


INT. TANGIERS BACCARAT TABLES – DAY

ACE *smoking a cigarette by the baccarat tables.*

ACE: (*Voice-over*) . . . like our state senator up there, everything was on the house.

**INT. TANGIERS PRESIDENTIAL SUITE – DAY**

*The* SENATOR *opens a bureau drawer and takes out a small velvet pouch and pours black $100 chips into his palm.*

ACE: (*Voice-over*) These guys won their comped life when they got elected. So, hey, why not take advantage of it? Still, the politicians came cheap. We could handle them.


**INT. TANGIERS, ICHIKAWA LUXURY SUITE – DAY**

K. K. ICHIKAWA, *a Japanese businessman, and a male associate pick up towels and soap from about the bedroom of their suite. A blonde woman checks herself in the mirror.*

ACE: (*Voice-over*) It's a whale like K. K. Ichikawa, who plays thirty thousand dollars a hand in baccarat. That's the one you really gotta watch.
(ICHIKAWA *and his associate walk into the suite's living-room and join a Japanese woman seated on a couch.*)
He plays fast and big and he has the cash and the credit to turn out your lights. About a year ago, he cleaned out a couple of casinos in the Cayman Islands.
(*They begin to stuff Tangiers soap and towels into their luggage.*)
Downstairs, he takes us for two million . . . and upstairs he takes free soap, shampoo and towels. Another billionaire cheapskate who loves his free rooms . . .


**EXT. TANGIERS JET, LAS VEGAS AIRPORT – DAY**

*The Tangiers jet with the Tangiers logo on its side as* ICHIKAWA *shakes* ACE'*s hands before boarding.* SHERBERT *follows him and his associates aboard.*

ACE: (*Voice-over*) . . . free private jets, and two million of our money.

ACE: Nice to see you again.

ACE: (*Voice-over*) But we got him back. I had our pilot tell him the plane was on the fritz.

DISSOLVE TO:

EXT. TANGIERS JET, STILL IN THE SAME SPOT – NIGHT

SHERBERT *apologizes to* ICHIKAWA *and his entourage as they all get off the jet.*
SHERBERT: Ken, I don't know what the hell went wrong. I'm awfully sorry.
ICHIKAWA: This is a big problem. Big problem.
SHERBERT: I can't understand it. These mechanical things, you know, they happen. Hey, be-better here than (*gesturing to the sky*) up there, you know what I mean?


INT. LAS VEGAS AIRPORT RESERVATIONS DESK – NIGHT

SHERBERT *arguing with* TICKET AGENT *as* ICHIKAWA *and entourage look glum.*

ACE: (*Voice-over*) Then he missed the commercial flights connecting with Japan.

AGENT: I'm so sorry. There's a convention in town, and all flights are booked.
SHERBERT: A convention? (*Turning to* ICHIKAWA.) I can't believe that there's a convention. It's never . . . ?
ICHIKAWA: What can I do?


EXT. TANGIERS CASINO – NIGHT

*A smiling* ACE *greets* ICHIKAWA *and his entourage as they drive up and get out of Tangiers limos.*

ACE: (*Voice-over*) We got him back . . . with a whole floor of rooms for himself.

ACE: I'm sorry you missed the plane.
ICHIKAWA: You want to get my money back, right? (*Chuckles.*)
ACE: No, no, no. No gambling. No.

INT. TANGIERS BACCARAT TABLES – NIGHT

ICHIKAWA, *with the Japanese woman, picks up some chips and places them on the table.* ACE *and* SHERBERT *watch from behind a barrier.*

ACE: (*Voice-over*) He bet one thousand a hand instead of his usual thirty thousand a hand.

(*A dealer's hands slide two cards on the table.*)

DEALER: The bank wins a natural eight over a five.
(*Another dealer's hands place two chips on the table.*
ICHIKAWA *looks on.*)

ACE: (*Voice-over*) But I knew, the trick with whales like Ichikawa was that they can't bet small for long. He didn't think of it as winning ten thousand, he thought of it as losing ninety thousand.
(ICHIKAWA *places a larger bet.*)
So, he upped his bets . . .
(*A dealer picks up some chips from a rack and places them on the table.* ICHIKAWA *is now seated with stacks of chips in front of him.*)
. . . until he dropped his winnings back and gave up a million of his own cash.

DISSOLVE TO:

(ICHIKAWA, *hours later, his chips depleted.* ACE *and* SHERBERT *still watch from behind the barrier as millions in chips are back in the dealer's racks.*)
In the casino, the cardinal rule is to keep them playing . . .
(*Move in on* ACE *as he smokes a cigarette.*)
. . . and keep them coming back. The longer they play, the more they lose. In the end, we get it all.

INT. TANGIERS CASINO – NIGHT

ACE, *with pit bosses next to him, looks out over the huge casino where hundreds of thousands of dollars are being poured into machines.*

ACE: (*Voice-over*) In Vegas, everybody's gotta watch everybody else.

(*Camera reveals the* DEALER *at a craps table.*)

DEALER: Six, an easy way. Six! All right, who's gonna give me . . . (*The* DEALER *places some chips on the table.*)

ACE: (*Voice-over*) Since the players are looking to beat the casino . . .

(*The camera is on the* DEALER.)

DEALER: . . . both dice must hit that back wall each and every roll. All right, make a six!

(*Camera pans to a* WOMAN *and a* MAN *at the table. The* WOMAN *tosses some dice.*)

ACE: (*Voice-over*) . . . the dealers are watching the players.

WOMAN: Gimme a six!

DEALER: Come on, baby, make a six!

(*A* BOX MAN, *seated mid-table is watching the* DEALER.)

ACE: (*Voice-over*) The box men are watching the dealers.

(*Camera pans to the* DEALER.)

DEALER: Humming, fielding, every roll.

(*Camera pans to a* FLOOR MAN, *standing directly behind the* BOX MAN.)

ACE: (*Voice-over*) The floor men are watching the box men.

(*Camera swish pans to reveal a* PIT BOSS *stepping in, scanning the floor.*)

The pit bosses are watching the floor men.

(*Swish pan to a* SHIFT BOSS *surveying the casino.*)

The shift bosses are watching the pit bosses.

(*Swish pan to* SHERBERT.)

The casino manager is watching the shift bosses.

(*Swish pan to* ACE.)

I'm watching the casino manager.

(*Camera swish pans and tilts up to a video camera mounted inside a glass dome hanging from the ceiling.*)

And the eye-in-the-sky is watching us all.

*(Swish pan to:)*

INT. TANGIERS-EYE-IN-THE SKY MONITOR ROOM — NIGHT

*Video monitors show a dealer fanning a row of bills. Swish pan to* ACE *and* SHERBERT *watching the monitor.* ACE *lights a cigarette.*

ACE: *(Voice-over)* Plus . . .
    *(Swish pan to surveillance catwalkers adjusting cameras and spying on players below with binoculars.)*
    . . . we had a dozen guys up there, most of them ex-cheats, who knew every trick in the house.

INT. TANGIERS EYE-IN-THE-SKY MONITOR ROOM — NIGHT

*On the video monitor we see a hot craps table with a crowd gathered around. Swish pan to* ACE *and* SHERBERT *looking at the screen. The monitor shows* GINGER MCKENNA, *with a* HIGH ROLLER, *about to roll some dice.*

INT. TANGIERS CRAPS TABLE — NIGHT

*Ginger squeals as she throws the dice across the table.*
HIGH ROLLER: Come on, come on.
    *(She rolls a winner.)*
GINGER: Yes!
HIGH ROLLER: Thank you. Very nice.
GINGER: *(Chuckles)* I told you I was hot tonight.

INT. TANGIERS EYE-IN-THE-SKY MONITOR ROOM — NIGHT

*Sound out: The monitor shows* GINGER *and the* HIGH ROLLER *cheering, she throws her arms around him. The crowd goes crazy.*

*Swish pan to* ACE *looking on intently.*

*On screen,* GINGER's *hand sneaks a chip from the rack and subtly moves it towards her purse.*

INT. TANGIERS CRAPS TABLE – NIGHT

*Sound in:* GINGER *slips the chip quietly into her bag.*

HIGH ROLLER: (*Off-screen*) Let's go. This is for Ginger. Come on. This is for Ginger.

(*The* HIGH ROLLER *notices* GINGER's *hand on her purse. She pretends to have taken out her lipstick.*)

GAMBLER #1: Let me have a hundred on the hard ten. Thank you.

GAMBLER #2: Hard ten. One hundred.


INT. TANGIERS EYE-IN-THE-SKY MONITOR ROOM – NIGHT

ACE *continues to look at the monitor.* SHERBERT *and a security man seated at a video console also look on.*


INT. TANGIERS CRAPS TABLE – NIGHT

*A craps stick pushes some dice towards* GINGER. *She rolls again, only this time she craps out. Gamblers groan, then applaud her. She's made so much money for the table that the winners toss chips in her direction.*

HIGH ROLLER: I'm sorry.

GINGER: Oh, I'm sorry. I'm sorry. (*To the table.*) Thank you very much. Thank you very much.

(ACE *and two casino execs are now on the floor watching her.*)

GINGER: Thank you, sir, I appreciate that. Everybody, thanks. (*Gives some chips as tips to the dealer and box man.*) Thanks. Take care, Steve. Take chances and drive fast.

HIGH ROLLER: Ginger, honey.

DEALER: Thank you very much, now.

HIGH ROLLER: Ginger, honey, this is for you, love. Thanks for your time.

(*She turns to the* HIGH ROLLER, *who is handing her a thin stack of chips worth about $2,000.*)

GINGER: (*Chuckles*) Come on.

HIGH ROLLER: What's the matter?

GINGER: What do you mean, 'What's the matter?' I made a lot of money for you. I want my cut.

HIGH ROLLER: What money? I've seen you stealing from me.

GINGER: What money? Look at this stack of chips. Don't give me that shit. I want my end.

HIGH ROLLER: Ginger, I've been watching you all night. You've been stealing from me.

GINGER: Don't give me that shit. I want my money.

HIGH ROLLER: That bag's full of fuckin' chips you –

GINGER: (*Interrupts*) What do you mean 'stole'? I didn't steal anything from you.

(ACE *watches the argument heat up.*)

HIGH ROLLER: Get lost, Ginger! Get lost!

GINGER: Get lost?

HIGH ROLLER: Yes.

GINGER: Get lost?

HIGH ROLLER: Yes.

(GINGER *knocks the chip rack out of his hands.*)

GINGER: Well, how 'bout that?

HIGH ROLLER: Come on! (*He bends down to pick them up.*)

(*Gamblers and dealers shout and yell. She picks up another rack of chips and tosses them into the air, then another, and another. Chips fly all over the casino. Everyone starts diving for chips. Dealers. Players. Security guards. Waitresses. Pit bosses. Bedlam.*

ACE *and the two execs with him are the only ones not diving for chips. He looks at* GINGER. *She looks at him.*

*Freeze frame on* GINGER.

*Slow motion:* GINGER *smiles at* ACE *and walks off.*)

ACE: (*Voice-over*) What a move. I fell in love right there.


INT. COCKTAIL LOUNGE – NIGHT

GINGER *and* ACE *are seated on a banquette. Close up of his hand attaching a diamond and ruby pin to her dress. Tilt up to* GINGER's *smiling face beaming at* ACE.

ACE: (*Voice-over*) But in Vegas, for a girl like Ginger, love costs money.

(*They kiss.*)

GINGER: I'm going to go powder my nose.
  (ACE *hands* GINGER *a single $50 bill. She smiles coyly. He
  hands her another fifty.*)

ACE: (*Voice-over*) Ginger's mission in life was money.

GINGER: I'll be right back.
  (*Off-screen, from following scene:*) See you, Ginger.


FLASHBACK – EXT. CASINO ENTRANCE – NIGHT

GINGER *waves goodbye to the* DOORMAN *and walks towards two*
VALET PARKERS *who greet her warmly. She gets a bottle of pills
from one of them and slips some cash into his hand in return.*
GINGER: Okay, thank you for asking.

ACE: (*Voice-over*) She was a queen around the casino. She
  brought in high rollers and helped them spread around a
  lot of money.

GINGER: (*To* VALET PARKER) Hello.
VALET PARKER: Hey, Ginger, how you doin'?
GINGER: Great. (*Handing the* VALET *some money.*) And I have
  something for you. You got me covered?
  (*The* VALET PARKER *places a vial of pills in her hand.*)
VALET PARKER: Yes. Something for you, there.
GINGER: And you do. Thank you very much.
VALET PARKER: Take care of yourself.


FLASHBACK – INT. HOTEL SUITE BATHROOM – NIGHT

GINGER *hands the pills to* HIGH ROLLER #2 *in his hotel bathroom,
where he is washing his face and trying to energize himself.*
GINGER: I got some lucky pills for you, honey.
HIGH ROLLER #2: Oh, yeah?

ACE: (*Voice-over*) Who didn't want Ginger? She was one of the
  best-known, best-liked and most respected hustlers in
  town. Smart hustlers like her could keep a guy awake for
  two or three days before sending him home broke to the
  little woman and his bank examiners.

INT. COCKTAIL LOUNGE – NIGHT

GINGER *comes back from the ladies' room. She kisses* ACE.
ACE: Any change?
GINGER: (*Chuckles*) I hit a few . . . uh, games on the way back.

ACE: (*Voice-over*) That was all bullshit. She just pocketed the cash.


FLASHBACK – INT. TANGIERS CASHIER'S CAGE – NIGHT

GINGER *converts her chips into a pile of $100 bills.*
GINGER: (*To* CASHIER) How you doin' tonight?
CASHIER: Good. How are you?
GINGER: (*Sighing*) Oh, beat.

ACE: (*Voice-over*) Ginger had the hustler's code.

CASHIER: Okay.
GINGER: Take one for you.
CASHIER: (*While she counts out the cash*) Thank you.

ACE: (*Voice-over*) She knew how to take care of people. And
that's what Vegas was all about.

CASHIER: (*As she pushes a stack of $100 bills across the counter*)
Sixty-eight hundred.
GINGER: Thanks. (*She picks up the cash.*)
CASHIER: You're welcome.

ACE: (*Voice-over*) It's Kickback City.

GINGER: You have a good night.
CASHIER: Thank you. You too.
(*Close-up of* GINGER *folding a $100 bill and placing it in her
palm. She slips the folded bill deftly into the palm of a floor
manager.*)

ACE: (*Voice-over*) She took care of the dealers . . .

GINGER: Hey, Mitch.

ACE: (*Voice-over*) . . . pit bosses, floor managers.

GINGER: Thank you.
ACE: But mostly . . .

EXT. TANGIERS ENTRANCE – NIGHT

GINGER, *on her way out of the casino, passes a folded $100 bill to a smiling older* SHIFT BOSS.

ACE: (*Voice-over*) . . . she took care of the valet parkers, the guys who could get you anything and take care of anything.

GINGER: Thanks a lot.
SHIFT BOSS: Thank you, Ginger.


EXT. TANGIERS ENTRANCE – NIGHT

GINGER *exits and gets into her car, slipping a* VALET PARKER *a $100 bill.*

ACE: (*Voice-over*) Ginger took care of the parkers because they took care of the security guards, who took care of the metro cops, who let her operate.

VALET PARKER #3: Thank you, Ginger.
GINGER: (*Getting into her car*) I need that stuff tonight.
VALET PARKER #3: No problem.
GINGER: You're a doll.

ACE: (*Voice-over*) The valet parking job was such a money-maker that they had to pay off the hotel manager just to get the concession.


FLASHBACK – INT. GINGER'S APARTMENT – DAY

GINGER *enters the room with $25,000 in her hands. She taps* LESTER DIAMOND'*s leg with it and he turns to her.*

ACE: (*Voice-over*) But one thing I could never understand, was that she could have everything under control, except for her old pimp boyfriend, Lester Diamond.

LESTER: Look, Gin, you know I got other people in this. I got partners. But I want you to understand that I am lookin' out for you in this thing. Okay? You're going to get yours back . . . and you're gonna get it back first. Okay?
GINGER: All right.

LESTER: Okay?

GINGER: Yeah.

LESTER: Where are you goin'? Where are you? You're in that place. Where are you?

GINGER: I'm here.

LESTER: No, you're not. Where are you? Where are you?

GINGER: I'm always here for you.

LESTER: You are.

GINGER: I am.

(*He hastily kisses* GINGER *and slips out the door.*)

ACE: (*Voice-over*) The Ginger I knew wouldn't even look at this creep.

GINGER: Good luck.

LESTER: Yeah.

ACE: (*Voice-over*) He was a moocher, a card cheat, a country – club golf hustler. A scumbag . . . chasing dentists for a few bucks.

GINGER: Careful.

(GINGER *looks out of the window and sees* LESTER *get into a convertible and drive off.*)

ACE: (*Voice-over*) I mean, the guy was always broke, he always
had a story. And somehow, she could never turn him
down. The way Ginger saw it, I guess, was that Lester was
just an unlucky guy. Somebody had to take care of him.

INT. BACK HOME AIRPORT/CUSTOMS – DAY

NICKY, *his wife* JENNIFER, *with a beehive hairdo, and their eight-
year-old son* LITTLE NICKY, *are detained while their luggage is
searched by a customs agent.*

TITLE IN: 'BACK HOME'

ACE: (*Voice-over*) But nobody had to take care of Nicky.

NICKY: (*To customs agent*) You find any cash in there, we'll
whack it up with you.

ACE: (*Voice-over*) I mean, he took care of himself only too well.
And that's why every badge back home wanted to nail him.

JENNIFER: (*To customs agent*) Excuse me, but I folded these
things beautifully and I would appreciate a little respect.
Jesus Christ!
NICKY: Don't look at me, pal. I gotta live with her.
(*We see* MARINO *waiting for* NICKY *outside the customs area.
Two* COPS *push past him.*)

ACE: (*Voice-over*) Even after a little vacation, they hassled him at
the airport.

COP #1: (*To* MARINO) Excuse me.

ACE: (*Voice-over*) I mean, Frank Marino was there to meet him,
but so were the cops. This time they wanted to pinch him
for some diamond burglary in Antwerp.

(*Camera dollies in on* JENNIFER's *beehive.*)

JENNIFER: Oh, yes. Will you help me fold these, please?

ACE: (*Voice-over*) They were ready to blame him for anything,
no matter where it happened.

40

FLASH FORWARD – INT. NICKY'S HOUSE/BACK HOME – DAY

NICKY, JENNIFER, LITTLE NICKY *and* MARINO *walk in.*

JENNIFER: (*To* LITTLE NICKY) You go and put your things away.

ACE: (*Voice-over*) And they were usually right.

> (NICKY, JENNIFER *and* MARINO *are gathered around the kitchen table.* JENNIFER *leans over and starts to shake her hair.*)

MARINO: Whoa, whoa, whoa.

NICKY: Hold it, hold it. Here.

> (NICKY *places a red towel down on the table.* JENNIFER *leans over again, tugs and shakes her hair until diamonds begin to fall out of her beehive.*)

ACE: (*Voice-over*) Because Nicky enjoyed being a gangster, and he didn't give a damn who knew it.

JENNIFER: Come on. There we go. Look at that. Beautiful.
(*Diamonds fall on the red towel in slow motion.*)

ACE: (*Voice-over*) I mean, that's what worried me, 'cause it turns out Nicky was about to be sent to Vegas.

JENNIFER: All right, we're clear.

NICKY: There's more!

JENNIFER: I think that's it.

NICKY: There's more! There's a couple stuck in there. I know there's more.

JENNIFER: God, I'm telling you, they're out!

NICKY: Come on, damn it. Don't get so defensive. It could be stuck in your hair, you know.
(NICKY *grasps* JENNIFER*'s hair.*)

JENNIFER: Look, there aren't . . .
(*A diamond falls out of her beehive.*)
There aren't, but –

NICKY: Oh, there aren't? (*Showing her the diamond.*) What's that? (*Slaps her.*) Huh? What's that?
(FRANK *chuckles.*)
There's no more. Thanks, hon. (*Kisses her.*)

INT. BACK HOME AIRPORT/CUSTOMS – DAY

*On* NICKY.

NICKY: (*Voice-over*) I couldn't wait to get my hands on Vegas. But the bosses didn't send me out there to have a good time.


INT. SAN MARINO ITALIAN GROCERY/BACK ROOM, KANSAS CITY – NIGHT

*Mob bosses* FORLANO, CAPELLI, GAGGI, BORELLI *and* PISCANO *seated around the back room table eating and talking as in the opening vignette.*

NICKY: (*Voice-over*) They sent me out there to make sure that nobody fucked with Ace and . . .


INT. ACE'S TANGIERS PENTHOUSE, LAS VEGAS – DAY

ACE *opens the door to* NICKY *and* JENNIFER.

NICKY: (*Voice-over*) . . . nobody interfered with the fuckin' skim.

ACE: (*Opening door*) Hey.
JENNIFER: Hey, how you doin'? (*Kisses* ACE.)
NICKY: Hey. Hey, Sammy, how are you?
    (JENNIFER *and* NICKY *take in* ACE's *spectacular Vegas-style penthouse.*)
JENNIFER: (*Whispering*) Wow.
NICKY: Boy, look at this place, huh?
JENNIFER: Incredible.
NICKY: All right.
ACE: Welcome to Vegas.
    (*Camera tilts up to reveal a sweeping view of the Las Vegas skyline.*)
NICKY: Okay, Sammy.
ACE: Somethin', huh?
NICKY: Yeah.
ACE: (*Calling her over*) Ginger.
    (GINGER *emerges from the bedroom.* NICKY *and* JENNIFER *are both stunned by her beauty.*)

NICKY: (*To* ACE) Holy shit, what've you been doin' out here?
ACE: Honey, come here.
   (*She walks to them.*)
   This is Jennifer and Nick. They're dear friends of mine.
JENNIFER: (*Shaking hands*) Good to meet you.
GINGER: Hi, Jennifer.
NICKY: Pleasure. (*Grasping* GINGER's *hand and kissing it.*) Very
   nice to meet you.
GINGER: Hi, how are you?
NICKY: Okay, Sammy.


INT. ACE'S CAR, LAS VEGAS STRIP – NIGHT

ACE *and* NICKY *are driving through town, the neon lights of Vegas
reflected in the windshield.*

ACE: (*Voice-over*) After we ate, we left Jennifer and Ginger alone
   and we took a ride to talk. And then . . . he hit me with it.

NICKY: What do you think about me movin' out here?
   (ACE *looks away.*)
   What's the matter? You got a problem with that?
ACE: No, of course not.
NICKY: (*Playfully*) You mean, I have your permission?
ACE: Sure, you have my permission. But I – I just gotta tell you
   it's no joke out here. It's no joke, you know? You gotta
   keep a low profile. It's not like back home. Right off the
   bat, they don't like guys like us. And this sheriff's a real
   cowboy. Even the coppers aren't afraid to bury people out
   in the desert here.
NICKY: I don't care. I want to get away from back home for a
   while. I'm tired of that shit back there. (*Referring to the
   Vegas lights.*) Look at this place. It's made of money. You
   know what the best part is? Nobody's gonna know what
   we're doin'! There's nobody here to see us! Everybody's
   back home.
ACE: Nick, I gotta tell you, I got pinched twice for no reason.
   You really gotta be careful. I'm running a licensed place.
   Everything's legit.
NICKY: Don't worry about it. I'm not gonna do anything. What

am I gonna do? I'm especially not gonna involve you in anything.
(ACE *gives* NICKY *a look.*)


EXT./INT. LAS VEGAS SPORTSBOOK – NIGHT

NICKY *and* MARINO *pull up in their car and get out.*

NICKY: (*Voice-over*) Ace saw Vegas one way.

NICKY: You call this guy and tell him I'm comin'?
MARINO: Of course.
(*They walk into the sportsbook, past numerous bar patrons and gamblers to* TONY, *the bookie at a betting counter.*)

NICKY: (*Voice-over*) But I saw it another. I saw it as untouched. I mean, they had bookies, pimps and drug dealers I could shake down. Who the fuck were they gonna run to? So, I started getting everybody in line. Best of all, for the first time in my life, I figured out a way not to lose.

ACE: (*Voice-over*) Yeah, he had a fool-proof scheme, all right. It wasn't very scientific but it worked. When he won, he collected. When he lost, he told the bookies to go fuck themselves. What were they gonna do? Muscle Nicky? (*Chuckles.*) Nicky was the muscle.

(NICKY *grabs* TONY *by the back of his neck.*)
NICKY: Tony.
TONY: Hey.
NICKY: How you doin'?
TONY: How you doin'?
NICKY: All right, yeah. You got that thing for me?
TONY: What thing? Oh, Nicky . . . I thought you was layin'.
NICKY: I was layin'? No, no, I'm taking it. I was takin' it.
TONY: You sure?
NICKY: I'm positive.
TONY: Well, I'm a little confused here.
NICKY: You're a little confused?
TONY: Yeah.
NICKY: (*Pointing to a window, above a counter with a tiny opening*

*to talk through*) Maybe if I stick your fuckin' face through this window over here like, you know, you'll – you'll get unconfused. Give me the fuckin' money!

(TONY *takes some money out of his coat pocket.*)

TONY: (*Groaning*) I'm sorry, Nicky. I didn't mean anything by it.

NICKY: Yeah, I know, that's why you had it ready. You thought I was fuckin' layin' it?!

(*He smacks the bookie on the head with the wad of money.*)

TONY: (*Gasps*) My fuckin' head.

NICKY: Your fuckin' head, huh? Don't fuck around, Tony.

MARINO: (*Pointing to* TONY) Smarten up.

NICKY: (*Walking out*) You jag-off.

CLASSROOM NUN: (*Off-screen, from following scene*) And now . . .


INT. CATHOLIC SCHOOL CLASSROOM – DAY

NICKY *and* JENNIFER *stand in the background with other parents listening to a* NUN *school teacher.* LITTLE NICKY *and other youngsters are seated at small children's desks.*

CLASSROOM NUN: . . . Nicholas Santoro will come up and tell us about our first president.

LITTLE NICKY: (*Stepping up in front of the class to begin a speech*) George Washington was born in a . . .

ACE: (*Voice-over*) But still, it was nice and quiet for a while. Ginger and I presented Nicky and Jennifer all over town, like regular Ozzie and Harriets.

LITTLE NICKY: . . . typical Virginia farmhouse.


EXT. LITTLE LEAGUE FIELD – DAY

NICKY *and* DETECTIVE BOB JOHNSON *are coaching their sons.* JOHNSON *pats* LITTLE NICKY *on the back and with encouraging words sends him running on to the field.*

DETECTIVE JOHNSON: (*To* LITTLE NICKY) Beautiful. You got a beautiful swing.

NICKY: (*Voice-over*) Ace got my son, little Nicky, involved with Little League, and it was great.

DETECTIVE JOHNSON: Now, I want you to get out there and get me singles and doubles, okay? 'Cause that's what's gonna win this game.

NICKY: (*Voice-over*) Turned out to be one of the other coaches was a fuckin' . . .

DETECTIVE JOHNSON: Now go out there and show your dad what you can do.

NICKY: (*Voice-over*) . . . metro intelligence cop. But it didn't matter. I mean, it was all about the kids, you know.

DETECTIVE JOHNSON: You know, he's gotta realize everything can't be a home run that he does.

NICKY: Yeah, well, that's exactly what I keep tellin' him, but that's the kind of kid he is ever since he's born.

DETECTIVE JOHNSON: It's instinctive, you know.

NICKY: He tries to do everything . . .
> (LITTLE NICKY *hits the ball*, NICKY *and* DETECTIVE JOHNSON *applaud.*)
> Ohh!

ACE: (*Voice-over*) And, Nicky being Nicky, he made his presence known.


INT. TANGIERS CASHIER'S CAGE CREDIT WINDOW – NIGHT

NICKY *saunters through the casino and up to* EDDY *and* JERRY, *two well-dressed hoods who are signing papers at the cashier's credit window near* ACE *and* SHERBERT.

ACE: (*Voice-over*) Especially at the casino, where he definitely did not work, people got the message.

NICKY: (*Voice-over*) Me? That's why the bosses sent me out here. They wanted me to make sure none of the other crews robbed the joint. Like these two fuckin' balloon-heads over here [EDDY *and* JERRY]. They were gonna try and bang us out of two hundred fuckin' grand? (*Chuckling.*) Yeah, right, I'm sure.

46

JERRY: (*Shakes* NICKY's *hand*) Hey, Nicky. How are you?

NICKY: Hey, Eddy.

EDDY: Hey, Nicky, how are you? What are you doin' here?

NICKY: I'm over here now.

JERRY/EDDY: (*In unison*) You're over here?

JERRY: You're over here?

NICKY: Yeah, I'm over here with him.

    (*Swish pan to* ACE *with* SHERBERT *off to the side.*)

EDDY: Oh.

JERRY: Oh.

EDDY: We're waiting on Carmine.

JERRY: Yeah, we're lookin' for Carmine.

NICKY: Carmine? He was here before. I saw him. He had a
    suitcase and everything, and then he left.

EDDY: Carmine left?

NICKY: Uh-huh.

JERRY: Carmine left?

EDDY: He's gone?

JERRY: He's not here?

EDDY: Carmine's gone.

NICKY: I think, you know, maybe he went across the street or
    somewhere else or somethin'. I don't know.

EDDY: Well, listen, uh . . . good luck with the joint, huh?
    (*Shakes hands with* NICKY.)

NICKY: Oh, thanks, Eddy.

JERRY: (*Shakes* NICKY's *hand*) Yeah, lots of luck. Lots of
    luck.

NICKY: Hey, great, Jerry.
    (*They walk away.*)
    Good luck to you too.

CREDIT CLERK: (*To* NICKY *from behind the cage*) Hey, they
    forgot to sign their papers.

NICKY: What?

CREDIT CLERK: They forgot to sign their papers.

NICKY: Yeah, they don't need those anymore.
    (*He looks over to* ACE *and* SHERBERT. NICKY *smiles.*)

ACE: (*Voice-over*) Out of respect, guys from other crews got
    away with a warning.

(ACE, *taking a drag off his cigarette, nods an 'okay'.*)
Everybody else: watch out.


INT. TANGIERS CASINO/BLACKJACK TABLES – DAY

*A blackjack* WINNER, *who looks like a school teacher, with over $100,000 in chips before him, has gathered a crowd.*

ACE: (*Voice-over*) Like these yokels here who never heard of Nicky or the bosses back home, 'cause they're the morons who give you the most trouble. Even after we'd catch 'em, they'd try sneakin' back with beards and wigs and fake noses.
(ACE *and* SHERBERT *walk up to watch the* WINNER *who is playing all six hands at the blackjack table.*)
You can spot these assholes by watching the way they bet. Like this guy. He's bettin' lavender chips at five hundred each with only one little problem. He's always guessed right. If he wasn't so fuckin' greedy, he'd have been tougher to spot. But in the end, they're all greedy.
(ACE *walks around the* WINNER'*s table, past the crowd, to the pit. Behind him are more blackjack tables, dealers and players.* ACE *bends down and ties his shoelace.*)
I saw that the dealer was weak, but he wasn't in on it.
(*The* DEALER'*s hands lift the corner of his hole card a half an inch to determine the casino's hand against the* WINNER. *The slightly exposed hole card is a six of clubs.*)
He just wasn't protecting his hand. He was lifting his hole card way to high.
(*On* ACE'*s face then to his POV of the card, past a* PIT BOSS, *panning to the* SIGNALLER *at the blackjack table to the right. The* SIGNALLER *is slumped down in his seat, tossing down some cards and sneaking looks at the* DEALER'*s hand at the* WINNER'*s table.*)
Now, here's this guy . . .
(*Overhead pan from the* SIGNALLER *slumped in his seat.*)
. . . reading the dealer's hole card . . .
(*Pan continues past* ACE *to reveal the* WINNER'*s table.*)
. . . and signalling his buddy [the WINNER] at this table.

(*Overhead dolly in on* SIGNALLER *who appears to be nervously tapping his thigh. We see through his trousers, that he is tapping a copper transmitter with a battery pack attached.*

*Back at the* WINNER'*s table we see inside his pant leg where a device strapped to his leg is receiving the impulse signal – buzz – buzz – buzz – from the* SIGNALLER.)
And that's just what these hustlers look for. They cruise from casino to casino, lookin' for weak dealers the way lions look for weak antelope.
(ACE *starts to get up.*)

ACE: (*Off-screen, from following scene*) Operator?

INT. TANGIERS BLACKJACK TABLES/TELEPHONE – DAY

ACE *is on the house phone right near the* SIGNALLER'*s table.*
ACE: This is Mr R. Get me Armstrong and Friday over at pit two right away. (*He hangs up, and fixes his tie in the mirrored panel above the phone.*)
(*Overhead view of the* SIGNALLER'*s table. Various security guards slowly begin to gather around it.*
ACE, *waiting, lights a cigarette.* ARMSTRONG *joins* ACE. *They look towards the* SIGNALLER'*s table.*)
(*To* ARMSTRONG) BJ nineteen, second base, the beard.[1]
(ACE *picks up the phone again.*) Operator . . . I need Mr Happy, loud.
(*On* ACE'*s signal,* WAITRESSES, *one carrying a cake with a sparkling candle, start singing 'Happy Birthday', attracting the crowd's attention.*)
WAITRESSES: (*In unison*) 'Happy Birthday to you. Happy Birthday to you. Happy Birthday, dear Jeff. Happy Birthday to you.'
(*Gamblers cheer and applaud.*

ACE *nods and* ARMSTRONG *lets a long metal object drop out from under his jacket sleeve and moves in close behind the* SIGNALLER, *as though looking at the game. He presses the object – a cattle prod – under the* SIGNALLER'*s arm near his*

1 Blackjack table number 19, second position, man with the beard.

49

*heart. The* SIGNALLER *instantly goes into convulsions, falling to the floor gasping and groaning. Several* SECURITY GUARDS *grab the* SIGNALLER *as he falls.* ARMSTRONG *walks away.*)

SECURITY GUARD #1: Man down!

(*The* WINNER *sees what has happened to his partner.*)

Notify medical! We got a cardiac arrest here!

SECURITY GUARD #2: He's fine, folks. Just give us some room, please!

(ACE *watches the scene. The guards lift the stunned* SIGNALLER *to his feet and help him away from the table. Play is immediately resumed.*)

Watch it now.

(*The* WINNER *hurriedly places his chips into racks.*)

SECURITY GUARD #1: (*Off-screen*) Stand back!

ACE: (*Voice-over*) They never know what hit them. And if and when . . .

(SECURITY GUARDS *drag the* SIGNALLER *out.*)

. . . they do find out that they just got zapped by a cattle prod . . .

(SHERBERT *follows the* WINNER *as he rushes away.*)

. . . they wish they really did have a heart attack.

(ACE *exits behind the* GUARDS *and the* SIGNALLER.)

INT. BASEMENT MAINTENANCE ROOM – NIGHT

*A grim, windowless utility room with tools on racks along the walls, some plain wooden chairs, and a workbench table.*

ACE: (*Voice-over*) Turns out this guy and his fuckin' pals, they were knockin' this place dead for years.

SECURITY GUARD #1: He's got a wire on him.
    (*The* SIGNALLER *is roughly shoved into the room. A* SECURITY GUARD *tears his trousers down revealing the signalling device strapped to his leg.*)
SIGNALLER: Hey, hey, what are you doin', man?
SECURITY GUARD #2: (*Exposing the device*) There it is! On the table!
SECURITY GUARD #1: Cheater's justice!
    (*The* SIGNALLER *is slammed down face first on the bench and the two* GUARDS *spread his arms out on the table.*)
SIGNALLER: (*In pain*) Oh, God! Oh!
    (*Another* GUARD *starts up a power saw and approaches the* SIGNALLER *who is now pinned to the table. He starts to scream.*)
    Hey, no! No! No!
    (ACE *walks toward the table, gesturing for the* GUARD *to turn off the saw.*)

ACE: (*Voice-over*) We had to make an example of these pricks that the party was over.

ACE: (*To relieved* SIGNALLER) I'm just curious. I saw you shuffling your checks with your right hand. Can you do that with both hands?
SIGNALLER: No.
ACE: Can't do it with both hands?
SIGNALLER: No, Sir.
ACE: Can you do it with your left hand?
SIGNALLER: Well, I . . . I never tried.
ACE: So, you're a righty?
SIGNALLER: Ye-yeah.

(ACE *nods to one of the* GUARDS. *Instantly a large rubber mallet smashes onto the man's right hand four times to the sound of screams.* ACE *watches.*)

ACE: Now, you're gonna have to learn with your left hand.

SIGNALLER: God! (*He moans and sits back.*)

WINNER: (*Off-screen, from following scene*) It's a hundred . . .


INT. CASINO CASHIER'S CAGE AREA – NIGHT

*The* WINNER *has been standing outside the cashier's cage waiting for his $110,000 in chips to be cashed.* SHERBERT *walks up behind him.*

WINNER: . . . a hundred ten.

CASHIER: Yes, it is.

WINNER: I think.

CASHIER: Yes.

WINNER: Okay.

SHERBERT: Hiya. That's a lot of money to be counting out in public.

WINNER: Yeah.

SHERBERT: (*To* CASHIER) Why don't I take him over to the office and verify it, huh?

CASHIER: Yes.

SHERBERT: A little privacy. And, by the way, send over a . . . nice bottle of champagne on ice, huh?

CASHIER: Sure will.

SHERBERT: Real special. Somethin' . . . (*To* WINNER.) By the way . . . I'm Billy Sherbert, your casino manager.
(*He shakes hands with the* WINNER.)

WINNER: Hi.

SHERBERT: Having a good time?
(SHERBERT *leads him away from the cage.*)

WINNER: Yes, uh . . .

SHERBERT: You'll want to count the money in privacy. You know, you don't need . . .

WINNER: Uh, I have a plane to catch to Cleveland . . . Can I get my winnings?

INT. BASEMENT MAINTENANCE ROOM – NIGHT

*The* WINNER *is pushed through the door by two* GUARDS *followed by* SHERBERT *and sees his pal moaning in pain and holding his broken hand.*

SIGNALLER: Look what they did to my hand, man!

ACE: (*Walks over to the* WINNER) All right, I'm gonna give you a choice. You can either have the money and the hammer or you can walk out of here. You can't have both. What do you want?

(SHERBERT *stands next to the* WINNER.)

WINNER: I just wanna get out of here.

ACE: And don't forget to tell your friends what happens if they fuck around here. You understand?

WINNER: I'm sorry. I made a bad mistake.

ACE: You're fuckin' right, you made a bad mistake. 'Cause if you come back here – we catch either one of you – we're gonna break your fuckin' heads and you won't walk out of here. You see that fuckin' saw? We're gonna use it. You don't fuck around in this place. You got it?

WINNER: Yeah.

ACE: Get out of here.

WINNER: Thank you.

(*The* GUARDS *usher the* WINNER *out of the room.*)

ACE: (*To the* GUARDS, *referring to the* SIGNALLER) Throw him out in the alley. And just tell the cops he got hit by a car.


INT. ACE'S TANGIERS PENTHOUSE

ACE *and* GINGER *are alone in the living room. The apartment looks out on the glittering neon signs of the Strip.*

ACE: (*Voice-over*) Within no time, everything was set in place. We got rid of the freelance scamsters. The per was way up. The gods were happy, or as happy as the gods can ever be. And I, I decided to complicate my life. For a guy who likes sure things, I was about to bet the rest of my life on a real longshot.

ACE: We're not gettin' any younger. Don't you think it's time?

Aren't you gettin' tired of all this shit? Bangin' around, hustlin' around?

GINGER: What, are you trying to handicap me?

ACE: I'm gonna do you one better. I'm trying to marry you. You want to marry me?

(GINGER *looks doubtful.*)

I'm serious. I mean, I – I want to settle down. I want a family.

GINGER: (*Sighs, laughing*) You got the wrong girl, Sam.

ACE: I know I'd be a good father. I know you'd be a good mother.

GINGER: You don't know me. What, you've known me, two, three months. What do you know?

ACE: I'm forty-three years old. I don't want to wait. I know you well enough to know that I really love you very much. And I can't think of anybody better to be with. And I don't feel like waiting anymore.

GINGER: You know a lot of happily married people, Sam? 'Cause I don't.

ACE: Yeah, I know all that.

GINGER: I care about you, a – But I just don't have those kind of feelings for you. I'm sorry. I'm not in love with you.

ACE: (*Brushing cigarette ash off his dressing gown*) I – I – I . . .

GINGER: Understand? (*Pause.*) I'm sorry.

ACE: No, I – I . . . mean . . . that can grow as I – as long as there's a mutual respect . . . that kind of thing can grow. I'm realistic. I can accept that. But, you know, what is . . . what is love anyway? It's a . . . it's a mutual respect. It's – it's a devotion. It's a . . . it's a caring from one person to another. And if we could set up some kind of foundation . . . based on that mutual respect . . . I feel that eventually you would care enough about me . . . that I could live with that.

GINGER: If it doesn't work out. You know, if it doesn't play out, then what happens to me?

ACE: You know I'm doin' well now. And I'm gonna do even better. And so, whatever happens, if it doesn't work out between us, I'm gonna make sure you're okay for the rest of your life. And if there are kids, especially, you know,

54

I'll take care of you better than you'd ever imagine.

GINGER: (*Interrupts*) What're you . . . what're you pitching me, here?

ACE: Just what I said. You'll be set up for the rest of your life. That I can promise you. (*Pause.*) Want to take a chance? (*She looks at him.* ACE *is holding her hand tightly.*)

INT. RIVIERA BALLROOM MARRIAGE – NIGHT

ACE *and* GINGER *are seated at a banquet table with various guests, drinking champagne.* AMY, *their six-month-old child is in a cradle.* NICKY *and* JENNIFER *are hovering around the baby with* LITTLE NICKY *and are blissfully happy. It is an elegant affair. City Officials, politicians and gaming officials are there, plus,* SHERBERT *and Ace's boss,* PHILIP GREEN. *A photographer takes pictures of the guests.*

ACE: (*Voice-over*) When I married Ginger I knew all the stories, but I didn't give a fuck. 'I'm Sam Rothstein,' I said. 'I can change her.'

NICKY: (*Voice-over*) It was typical Ace. He invited the biggest people in town and he knew they'd show. Because he knew they all wanted somethin' from him. With Ace, nobody ever got a free ride. Even Ginger. With her –
(*We see* AMY *in the cradle.*)
– he still covered his bets. They had to have the baby first, before they could get married. Even made Jennie and me watch Amy for a few days when they went on their honeymoon. But I didn't mind, we loved the kid.

(*In slow motion camera moves in on* ACE *and* GINGER, *standing next to a large wedding cake. They are kissing.* NICKY, SHERBERT *and other guests look on. Camera moves in closer as they kiss, then past them to the bride and groom figurines on the cake.*
   LESTER's *and* GINGER's *telephone conversation is heard in voice-over over this scene.*)

LESTER: (*Over telephone*) Can you feel my eyes on you? Can you feel me look into your heart? Can you feel me in the

55

pit of your stomach? Can you feel me in you? In your heart?

(*We see a wide view of the elaborate wedding, guests mill about the banquet hall.*)

Don't make me come there. Answer me.

GINGER: (*Over telephone, sobbing*) I love you.

INT. LESTER DIAMOND'S LOS ANGELES APARTMENT – NIGHT

LESTER DIAMOND *is talking on the phone softly, cutting up cocaine on a piece of glass.*

LESTER: (*Into telephone*) Bu-but, baby, do you know that I love you too?

GINGER: (*Over telephone*) No, Lester.

LESTER: (*Into telephone*) Do you know that?

GINGER: (*Over telephone*) Yeah. This is the best thing I can do for my life right now.

LESTER: (*Into telephone*) That's right.

INT. RIVIERA BALLROOM CORRIDOR – NIGHT

GINGER *is sitting alone on the phone. She's crying.*

LESTER: (*Over telephone*) So, it's gonna be okay, isn't it?

GINGER: (*Sobbing, into telephone*) Promise?

LESTER: (*Over telephone*) God . . . I wish you . . .

INT. LESTER DIAMOND'S LOS ANGELES APARTMENT – NIGHT

*There is a beautiful scantily dressed blonde girl in the apartment with him. She bends down to the table in front of him, snorts some cocaine, then walks away.*

LESTER: (*Into telephone*) . . . all the luck in the world.

GINGER: (*Over telephone*) You do?

LESTER: (*Into telephone*) Yeah, I do. I mean, it's – it's the – it's the best thing you can do right now. I mean this. And you'll have real security. Sweetheart . . . you're gonna be situated just right in Vegas.

### INT. RIVIERA BALLROOM CORRIDOR – NIGHT

ACE *enters from the ballroom and sees* GINGER *on the phone. He walks towards her, listening to her conversation.*

LESTER: (*Over telephone*) Come on, this is great for us. You know I'm gonna be here for you. I ain't going no place. Huh? I'm lookin' at you right now. I'm seein' you for the very first time, right this minute. I'm seein' you, and I can feel my heart click. I see you fourteen years old. I see you the first second I ever saw you. I see you, long-legged little colt –

(GINGER *notices* ACE *behind her.*)

– with stupid braces on your teeth.

GINGER: (*Into telephone, sniffing, trying to cut him off*) Okay, then.

LESTER: (*Over telephone*) Every time I ever see you, that's what I see.

GINGER: (*Into telephone*) Uh, talk to you later. Bye. (*She hangs up the phone quickly.*)

ACE: You all right?

GINGER: (*Drinking some champagne, wiping away tears*) Yeah.

ACE: Why're you crying?

GINGER: (*Laughs*) I'm not crying. (*Sniffs.*)

(ACE *walks up behind* GINGER.)

ACE: Maybe you shouldn't drink so much.

GINGER: I'm okay. I just – (*Sniffs.*) You just have to understand. I've been with Lester since I was a kid. I just wanted to say goodbye. I – I just . . . I don't . . . I think I have a right to do that. Okay?

ACE: It's all right. That part of your life is over with. Right?

GINGER: Yeah.

ACE: You're with me now.

GINGER: Yeah.

ACE: Right?

GINGER: Uh-huh.

ACE: You sure?

GINGER: Yeah. Yeah.

(*They are reflected in a mirror behind the telephone.*)

ACE: Want to go? Let's go back in.

GINGER: (*Sniffs*) Okay.
>    (ACE's *hands pick up a white rose and* GINGER's *gloves from the desk.*)


EXT. ACE'S HOUSE – DAY

ACE *and* GINGER *drive up to an expensive house which backs on to a country-club golf course.*


INT. ACE'S HOUSE – DAY

ACE *takes* GINGER *inside. It is fancy and lush.*
GINGER: Oh . . .
>    (*Through sliding glass doors, we see a patio and a pool area.*)
>    (*Sighing*) It's great.
>    (*The living-room has exposed white brick along the walls, bronze ostrich figurines, a white baby grand piano, and a zebra print rug surrounded by a few couches.*)
>    Oh, it's great.


INT. ACE'S BEDROOM CLOSET – DAY

ACE *takes* GINGER *past the bedroom to their huge room-sized closet. There are racks and racks of clothes.*
GINGER: (*Running into the closet*) Oh! It's all my stuff. Oh, my God.
>    (ACE *presents her with a long chinchilla coat.*)
>    You brought all my stuff. I can – (*She sees the coat.*)
ACE: Try it on. It's yours. (*He puts it on her.*)
GINGER: (*Whispering*) You're kidding? My God. What is it?
ACE: It's chinchilla.
GINGER: (*Looking at herself in the mirror*) Oh, it's so soft.
ACE: It's nice, isn't it?
GINGER: Oh . . .
>    (ACE *kisses her.*)
>    No one's ever been so nice to me.
>    (*They kiss and embrace.*)

INT. ACE'S HOUSE/BEDROOM – DAY

ACE's *hand opens a leather case full of gold Bvlgari jewelry.*
GINGER: (*Gasps*) Oh, my God.


INT. ACE'S HOUSE/BEDROOM – DAY

ACE *and* GINGER *lie on the bed, surrounded by jewelry.* GINGER *is swathed in the chinchilla coat. Ace watches as a transfixed* GINGER *tries on gold necklaces, rings, bracelets and earrings.*
GINGER: So, do you think it's too much if I wear all these in the same day?
ACE: You do whatever you want. Do I keep my promises, or do I keep my promises?
(ACE *kisses* GINGER.)
GINGER: You're so wonderful. The jewelry's not so bad, either.
ACE: The only thing is . . . you shouldn't keep this in the house. We gotta put it in a bank.
GINGER: (*Putting on a gold bracelet*) Come on. Can I keep this one in the house?
ACE: Now look (*gently holding her face, gathering her total attention*), pay attention to me. What I'm gonna tell you is very important.

GINGER: Okay.

ACE: All this stuff doesn't mean anything. Money, this, doesn't mean anything without trust. I have to be able to trust you with my life.


EXT. BURBANK PRIVATE AIRPORT – DAY

TITLE IN: 'LOS ANGELES'

ACE *and* GINGER *get off the Tangiers jet carrying two suitcases.* ACE *gives a chauffeur the luggage and follows* GINGER *into a brown Rolls Royce.*

ACE: (*Voice-over*) With over a million in cash and jewels tucked in a bank in Vegas only for Ginger, she was secure and happy.


INT. BEVERLY HILLS BANK – DAY

ACE *and* GINGER *walk into the bank lobby carrying the suitcases.*

ACE: (*Voice-over*) She loved that shit. But a guy in my line of work has to have a lot of pay-off cash around.


INT. BEVERLY HILLS BANK/VAULT – DAY

*There are several safe deposit boxes filled with cash.* ACE *and* GINGER *are closing a large box so crammed with cash that* ACE *has to lean on it for the clasp to lock.*

ACE: (*Voice-over*) Crooked cops and kidnappers, they don't take checks.

GINGER: Need a little help with that, Mr Collins?

ACE: (*Voice-over*) So, I put two million in cash in a Los Angeles bank under the name of Mr and Mrs Tom Collins. This was strictly my shakedown and kidnapping money.
(ACE *and* GINGER *struggle to push the crammed box into a slot in the wall.*)
And, since I'd either be in jail or locked in a closet when I needed the money the most . . .

(*The* BANK PRESIDENT *joins them, and he and* ACE
*simultaneously double-lock the outer safe box door with two
separate keys, after which,* ACE *gives* GINGER *his key.*)
. . . I gave Ginger the only key to the cash that could get
me back alive.


INT. BANK PRESIDENT'S OFFICE – DAY

GINGER *is on the other side of a glass wall, signing papers.*
BANKER: Now this is just a signature card.
ACE: So, once she signs those papers, she'll be the only person to
have total access to the box? No one else, including myself?
BANKER: That's right.
(*We see* GINGER *looking at* ACE.)
That's the way you wanted it, right?
(ACE *nods.*)
(*Quietly.*) Sam, let me ask you a question. You must really
trust your wife.
ACE: (*Quietly*) Yeah, sure I do. Why?
BANKER: No, tha-that's good. It's just unusual. To tell you the
truth, so many of my clients don't.
ACE: Well . . .
(ACE *looks over to* GINGER, *smiles and winks. She looks back
at him.*)


INT. TANGIERS LOUNGE – NIGHT

JERRY VALE *sings to a seated audience.* ACE *sits alone at a table.*

ACE: (*Voice-over*) With Ginger and the money in place, I felt
covered, and to play it safe I switched job titles again and
made myself, um, Food and Beverage Director. This way
nobody would bother me about a license. I mean, Vegas
was like a dream for me. Trouble was . . .
(NICKY *is seated at another table with* MARINO, *peeling off
money and giving it to* MIKE, *a crooked dealer.*)
. . . Nicky was dreamin' his own kind of Vegas.

NICKY: (*Voice-over*) To begin, I put money out on the street,

chargin' three points a week. You know – juice to the
fuckin' dealers.

MARINO: (*To* MIKE) Don't make us come lookin' for you.
MIKE: Oh, you won't have to look for me. I appreciate it.
Thanks, Nicky.
NICKY: All right, Mike.
(MIKE *gets up from the table.*)

NICKY: (*Voice-over*) They were degenerate gamblers, coke
freaks. In no time, I had half the dealers in the Tangiers in
my pocket. Then . . .


INT. TANGIERS POKER TABLE – NIGHT

NICKY *is at a table with his gang of card sharks:* SLIM, ROCKY,
MOOSH *and* COWBOY, *all secretly signalling each other, sandbagging
a mark.* MIKE, *the crooked dealer from the previous scene, deals*
NICKY *a winning hand.*

NICKY: (*Voice-over*) . . . the next thing I did, I started bustin'
out high-stakes poker players.

ACE: (*Voice-over*) It was so obvious. I mean, all of Nicky's half-
assed mechanics, they were real signal happy.

MOOSH: (*Scratching his arm*) I'm gonna open for five hundred.
ROCKY: Moosh, you open? (*Taps his fingers on some chips before
picking them up.*)

ACE: (*Voice-over*) Signalling back and forth.

CARD SHARK: I bet thirty-five hundred.
(NICKY *wiggles a toothpick back and forth in his mouth.*)
DOCTOR DAN: I've been losing for three days straight, non-stop.
(*Another shark pulls on his ear.*)
ROCKY: Oh, why're you crying, with three loaves of bread under
your arm?
(ACE *watches their signals with concern.*)

ACE: (*Voice-over*) Nicky thought nobody was watching him. But
he was wrong.
(*We see two undercover gaming agents, looking like tourists,*

*sneaking looks at* NICKY's *table.*)
And I didn't want any of those agents near my place.

NICKY: Four aces, Doc. (*His hands spread five cards on the table, showing four aces.*) What do you got?

DOCTOR DAN: (*Getting up in disgust*) Jesus Christ. I can't believe it.
(COWBOY, *the card shark with the cowboy hat, rakes in a large pot toward his side of the table.*)
If I didn't have bad luck, I wouldn't have any luck. I'm out of here, you understand?

ACE: (*Voice-over*) I mean, I wished to God Nicky and his whole crew would just get lost.
(*He walks towards* NICKY's *table.*)
What am I gonna do? Go back home and start a war?
(ACE *leans down to talk to* NICKY.)
I mean, Nicky's a made guy and I'm not. I can't do that.

ACE: (*Whispering in* NICKY's *ear*) Be careful. Gaming agents are all over the place.

NICKY: So, I'm lucky. I'm not allowed to get lucky in this place?

ACE: You been lucky all week. They're lookin' to nail ya.
    (ACE *walks away.* NICKY *looks over at the gaming agents.*)

NICKY: (*Voice-over*) Ace was so fuckin' worried about his
    casino, he forgot what we were doin' out here in the first
    place.


INT. TANGIERS CASINO – NIGHT

*Security people are pulling apart a husband and wife who are
fighting. Camera picks up* ACE *as he passes by them.*

NICKY: (*Voice-over*) A million times I wanted to yell in his
    fuckin' ear: 'This is Las Vegas! We're supposed to be out
    here robbin', you dumb fuckin' Heeb.'


INT. TANGIERS CASINO POKER TABLE – NIGHT

*Close-up of the* COWBOY's *white-socked feet with no shoes on a poker
table.*

ACE: (*To* SHERBERT, *referring to* COWBOY) I don't give a shit
    who he's connected to. Tell him to take his fuckin' feet
    off the table. What's he think this is, a goddamn sawdust
    joint?
    (SHERBERT *approaches* COWBOY.)

SHERBERT: Sir, would you mind taking your feet off the table
    and putting your shoes on, please?

COWBOY: (*Sighs*) Yeah, I would mind. I'm havin' a bad night.
    (COWBOY *remains the same with his feet on the table.*)

SHERBERT: (*Returning to* ACE) Fuckin' asshole won't budge.

ACE: Call security.
    (ACE *approaches* COWBOY.)
    How are you?

COWBOY: Good. How are you?

ACE: Good. You want to do me a favor? You want to take your
    feet off the table and put your shoes back on?

COWBOY: Fuck you.
    (ACE *walks to nearby* SECURITY GUARDS.)

ACE: (*To* GUARDS) I want you to exit this guy off the
    premises, and I want you to exit him off his feet and

use his head to open the fuckin' door.

(*Three* SECURITY GUARDS *approach* COWBOY.)

SECURITY GUARD #1: Sir, you're gonna have to leave. You mind accompanying us outside?

COWBOY: Bullshit, I ain't goin' anywhere with you!

SECURITY GUARD #1: Bullshit, you're out of here, cowboy! (SECURITY GUARD #1 *knocks his feet off the table, as* GUARDS #2 *and* #3 *lift him off his seat.*)

COWBOY: Fuck you! Fuck you!

SECURITY GUARD #1: Yeah?

COWBOY: You know who you're fuckin' with?! Huh? Do you?!

SECURITY GUARD #1: Now move along.

COWBOY: (*Screaming at* ACE, *who follows him*) You fuckin' faggot! Do you know who you're fuckin' with? (*The* GUARDS *carry him out and forcefully shove him towards a side exit.*) Leave me alone!

SECURITY GUARD #1: Here we go!

COWBOY: (*Grunting*) You've gotta be kidding me! (*Groans.*) (*The* GUARDS *lift him off his feet and, holding him like a battering ram, smash his head into the door.*)

ACE: (*Voice-over as* COWBOY *is thrown out the door*) Sure enough, an hour later, I get the call.


INT. VEGAS BAR – NIGHT

NICKY *is on a public wall-phone talking to* ACE. MARINO *is staring at the disheveled* COWBOY.

NICKY: (*Into telephone*) Ace, what happened over there? I mean, did you know that guy you threw out was with me?


INT. TANGIERS CASINO – NIGHT

ACE *is on a Tangiers house phone.* SHERBERT *looks on.*

ACE: (*Into telephone*) No, I didn't know that. But you know what he did?

NICKY: (*Over telephone*) No.

66

INT. VEGAS BAR – NIGHT

NICKY *gives* COWBOY *a look.*
ACE: (*Over telephone*) He insulted Billy. And then I walked over
    to him politely . . .


INT. TANGIERS CASINO – NIGHT

ACE: (*Into telephone*) . . . and he tells me to go fuck myself.
NICKY: (*Over telephone*) What?
ACE: (*Into telephone*) Then he called me a faggot.


INT. VEGAS BAR – NIGHT

ACE: (*Over telephone*) So what do you think I do? I threw that
    cocksucker out.
NICKY: (*Into telephone*) What? Ho–
    (*He puts down the phone; to* COWBOY:)
    Hey, come here.
    (COWBOY *walks up to him.*)
    You called my friend a faggot? You tell him to go fuck
    himself?
COWBOY: Nicky, I did –
NICKY: Is that what you did?
COWBOY: I did – I didn't –
NICKY: Tell him to go fuck himself? You fuckin' hick!
    Fuckin' . . .
    (NICKY *hits him on the head with the phone.* COWBOY *falls
    back, groaning.*)


INT. TANGIERS CASINO – NIGHT

ACE *listens to the noise of* NICKY *roughing up* COWBOY.
NICKY: (*Over telephone*) . . . you big fuckin' hick, you. Come
    here. Come here. Get him up. Come here.
    (ACE *looks at* SHERBERT.)
MARINO: (*Over telephone*) Get up.

INT. VEGAS BAR – NIGHT

NICKY: (*To* COWBOY) Come here, come here.
MARINO: Get up.
NICKY: You go over there right now and you apologize. You
better hope he lets you back in.


INT. TANGIERS CASINO – NIGHT

NICKY: (*Over telephone*) If you ever get out of line over there
again, I'll smash your fuckin' head so hard . . .


INT. VEGAS BAR – NIGHT

NICKY: (*To* COWBOY) . . . you won't be able to get that cowboy
hat on. You hear me? Fuckin' hick. (*Into telephone*)
Sammy, listen . . .


INT. TANGIERS CASINO – NIGHT

NICKY: (*Over telephone*) . . . this guy obviously doesn't know
who he was talkin' to, you understand? He doesn't . . .


INT. VEGAS BAR – NIGHT

NICKY: (*Into telephone*) . . . know that, uh, we're dear friends. I
mean, he's already very sorry. But, uh, if you could do me
a favor to let him back in, I swear to you he'll never get out
of line again. I promise you that.


INT. TANGIERS CASINO – NIGHT

ACE: (*Into telephone*) If he does it again, he's out for good. I
don't care what it is, Nick, I'm gonna ha– I'll – I'll never
let him in the place again.
NICKY: (*Over telephone*) I'm sorry about this. Really.

INT. VEGAS BAR – NIGHT

NICKY: (*Into telephone*) All right, Ace?
ACE: (*Over telephone*) Okay.
NICKY: (*Into telephone*) Thanks, pal.
(NICKY *hangs up the phone and turns to* COWBOY.)
You took your boots off? You put your feet on the table
. . . you shit-kicking, stinky, horse-manure-smellin'
motherfucker you! You fuck me up over there, I'll stick
you in a hole in the fuckin' desert! You understand?
(*Slapping him.*) Go over there and apologize. (*Kicking the
chastened* COWBOY *away.*) Go! Get the fuck out of –
COWBOY: Nicky, I'm sorry.


EXT. TANGIERS CASINO – DAY

*A tiger leaps towards the camera, which pans over to two showgirls
and then to* ACE's *hand holding the key to a Rolls Royce. He gives it
to* JONATHAN *and* DAVID *as reporters rush in to photograph the
moment.*

NICKY: (*Voice-over*) You know, Ace could be a very touchy guy,
especially when he got bigger and bigger in town. Like
when he hired that Jonathan and David and their tigers
away from the Palace by buildin' them a new stage and
then givin' them a silver Rolls Royce.


INT. BACKSTAGE TANGIERS THEATER – DAY

ACE *and* SHERBERT *watch as a* STAGE MANAGER *weighs in the
'Femme Fatale' Showgirls.*

NICKY: (*Voice-over*) But I'll tell you, he knew how to bring in
the crowds. He knew all the fuckin' angles. He brought
over the whole 'Femme Fatale' show from Paris. But he
forgot how lazy them European dancin' broads can get. I
mean, he had to weigh 'em in once a week to make sure
they didn't blow up like fuckin' balloons.

ACE: (*To* SHOWGIRL) You're still eight pounds over. (*To*
MANAGER.) What's the reason for this?

STAGE MANAGER: Mr Rothstein, sir, let me put her on
  suspension.
ACE: Never mind the 'sir'. Never mind the 'sir'.
STAGE MANAGER: Well, sir, I was just . . .
ACE: Why is she eight pounds over?
STAGE MANAGER: . . . trying to offer you the respect that
  your . . .
ACE: I . . .
STAGE MANAGER: . . . position . . .
ACE: 'Mr Rothstein' is good enough.
STAGE MANAGER: Mr Rothstein . . . well, sometimes, when you
  reach that pressure point, when you put that pressure point
  on them, you know, it shows . . .
ACE: She could at least lose a half a pound or a quarter.
  Listen . . .
STAGE MANAGER: . . . and she doesn't always –
ACE: . . . all you do is give me answers. Just – just give me the
  right answer.
STAGE MANAGER: But, sir. Well, I don't know why. I guess,
  maybe, because she's frightened that if she doesn't lose the
  weight she may even get fired.
ACE: That's right. She will get fired. In fact, I want you to send
  her back to Paris.
STAGE MANAGER: It's always been our policy –
ACE: No. Just stop everything.
  (SHERBERT *and* ACE *walk away across a huge stage.*)
SHERBERT: (*To* ACE) This woman's an institution.
ACE: I don't care what she is. She's an institution, that's the
  problem. She's lazy.


INT. TANGIERS CASINO SPORTSBOOK – NIGHT

ACE *standing in a large space surrounded by giant TV screens
showing sports events. Around him, long rows of bettors are seated at
betting stations, lined up at windows, or wandering around at the
bar. It's like a NASA control room on launch day.*

NICKY: (*Voice-over*) Hey, I gotta give the guy credit. He does
  the most obvious thing. This is the only town in the

country where a bookie joint is legit, so, why not take
advantage, right? So . . . he took bookie joints off the street
and then opened them up inside the casino. Well, within a
few years, by doin' all of this, he had every casino on the
Strip trying to copy off him.

ACE: (*Voice-over*) Between . . .


EXT. BACK ALLEY – NIGHT

NICKY, *with* MARINO, *punching and kicking a man next to the
open door of his luxury car.*

ACE: (*Voice-over*) . . . my innovations . . .
  (*The man falls to the ground.*)
  . . . and Nicky's dedication to his job . . .
  (NICKY *starts kicking him.*)
  . . . I soon had the best operation on the Strip.
  (NICKY *lifts an empty trash can and shatters the car's
  windshield.*)


INT. TANGIERS CASINO FLOOR – NIGHT

ACE *and* NICKY *are standing on the casino floor near the slot-
machines. Gamblers are milling about behind them.*

ACE: You better watch yourself. There's a lot of heat on you
  already.
NICKY: Why, somebody's complaining?
ACE: I'm – I'm hearin' things from security. They're all ex-cops.
  The Sheriff's lookin' to bust your balls. They want to put
  you in the Black Book.
NICKY: That Black Book is a bunch of bullshit. They got two
  names in there for the whole country and one of them is
  still Al Capone.
ACE: Bullshit or no bullshit, they put you in that book, you're
  gonna be in a lot of trouble. You will not be able to walk
  into the casino. I'm telling you.
NICKY: What am I doin' out here? I'm tryin' to make a livin',
  that's all.
ACE: I'm just tellin' you. Don't say I didn't warn you.

NICKY: All right.

INT. VEGAS VALLEY COUNTRY CLUB, 1974 – NIGHT

*Tight on the filaments of a flash bulb as they ignite.*

*TV news crews and still photographers are taking pictures of* ACE
*and* GINGER *surrounded by clusters of celebrities and the Vegas
power elite, including* SHERBERT *and* GREEN, *at a black tie event.*

PHOTOGRAPHER #1: Mrs Rothstein, look straight ahead. Very
nice. Thank you.

PHOTOGRAPHER #2: Thank you.

PHOTOGRAPHER #1: Yes, nice smile.

PHOTOGRAPHER #3: Just look right at the camera. Hold that
pose.
(*We hear* GREEN *making a speech over flashing cameras and
freeze frames of himself,* SHERBERT, ACE *and* GINGER.)

GREEN: (*Off-screen*) Considering all of his hard work and
dedication and the new lifeblood he has instilled in Las
Vegas . . .
(*We now see* GREEN *at a mike speaking in front of the seated
club members.*)
Sam has established himself as an indispensable member of
the gaming community. As the head of the Tangiers
Gaming Corporation, it's my pleasure to welcome Sam
Rothstein to the Vegas Valley Country Club.
(*Members cheer and applaud as* GREEN *hands* ACE *a framed
citation. It reads: 'This Certificate of Appreciation. Sam
Rothstein. Charitable Foundations of Greater Las Vegas'. They
shake hands for the photographers.*)

ACE: (*Voice-over*) Back home, they would have put me in jail for
what I'm doing. But out here, they're givin' me awards.

ACE: (*Into the microphone*) It's with great pleasure that I accept
this certificate of appreciation from the . . .
(*Camera tilts up to a mounted plaque on the wall, reading:
'Charitable Foundations of Greater Las Vegas'.*)

INT. VEGAS VALLEY COUNTRY-CLUB BANQUET ROOM –
NIGHT

*A dazzling* GINGER *moves charmingly about the room chatting up top executives, lawyers, judges, bankers and their wives.* ACE, *standing with* GREEN *and an elderly man, watches her work the room.*

COUNTRY-CLUB WOMAN #1: Congratulations, sweetheart.
GINGER: Thank you.
COUNTRY-CLUB WOMAN #2: Sam raised more than we've ever raised before.
GINGER: He worked so hard.

ACE: (*Voice-over*) But my greatest pleasure was watchin' my wife, Ginger, work the room.

COUNTRY-CLUB MAN #1: Thank you for everything.

ACE: (*Voice-over*) They all loved her. How could you not love her?

GINGER: (*To* COUNTRY-CLUB WOMAN #3) Hi. Nice to see you.

ACE: (*Voice-over*) She could be the most charming woman you ever saw. People loved to be around her.

COUNTRY-CLUB WOMAN #3: Listen, you've got to bring Amy to Sasha's birthday party because he'd love to have her there.
GINGER: Thanks.
COUNTRY-CLUB WOMAN #3: We'll see you three o'clock Saturday.
GINGER: Thanks. Yes, all right.
COUNTRY-CLUB WOMAN #3: Great.

ACE: (*Voice-over*) She made everybody feel good.

(GINGER *joins* ACE. *He smiles proudly.*)


INT. VEGAS VALLEY COUNTRY-CLUB BANQUET ROOM – NIGHT

GINGER *and* ACE *are off alone by a dining-room table, talking intently. A young casino* EXECUTIVE *interrupts them.*
EXECUTIVE: Congratulations, Sam.

ACE: (*Shaking his hand*) Oh, thanks.
(*The flirting* EXECUTIVE *looks at* GINGER.)
EXECUTIVE: Hello, Mrs Rothstein.
GINGER: Hi.
EXECUTIVE: How are you?
GINGER: Oh.
(GINGER *gives the flirting* EXECUTIVE *her hand, he kisses it.*)
EXECUTIVE: You're one of the most gorgeous women I've ever seen. You're a lucky man Mr Rothstein.
(ACE *watches as* GINGER *flashes one of her dazzling smiles, but he's not sure whether she's flirting. He looks at the young man and back at his wife.*)
ACE: Thank you. Thanks for that compliment.

ACE: (*Voice-over*) He was a young kid from the casino . . . nice kid . . . bright boy. What balls on this fuckin' kid! The next day I fired him.

(*Freeze frame on* ACE *smiling at* GINGER.)


INT. VEGAS BANK VIEWING ROOM – DAY

GINGER, *with two-year-old* AMY *in a stroller, is seated on a bench going through large bank vault boxes containing her jewels.*
GINGER: (*To* AMY) Hey, do you want to see this one? Daddy gave me all this jewelry because he loves me so much. (*She places a gold bracelet on* AMY'*s hand.*) Put your arm in there.

ACE: (*Voice-over*) But as much as they loved her . . .

GINGER: (*To* AMY, *wearing the bracelet*) Oh, fabulous.

ACE: (*Voice-over*) . . . they didn't know what really moved her.

(*She holds up a necklace to the light.*)
GINGER: Look at this. Look at this.
(*Camera pulls away from the door leading to the viewing room revealing a bank manager seated at a desk. We hear* GINGER *and* AMY *behind the door.*)
(*Off-screen, from the viewing room*) Daddy gave me this pin when we were dating.

74

ACE: (*Voice-over*) And with Ginger happy, I was able to
  concentrate on what I knew best.

INT. TANGIERS CASINO, SLOT-MACHINES – NIGHT

ACE *is talking to* DON WARD.

WARD: Loose machines are right back over there.

ACE: What are they doin' way back there? Bring 'em up here
  where they belong. You can't even see 'em over there.

WARD: Okay. I'll –

ACE: What about the progressives with the high jackpots?
  Where are they? These machines are hidden.

WARD: Well . . .

ACE: These are our best machines. They bring all the action.
  No wonder the drop is off.

WARD: Yeah, okay.

ACE: The action is in the front, not in the back. Bring 'em up
  front.

WARD: All right, I will, I will.

ACE: Listen to me very carefully. There are three ways of doing
  things around here. The right way, the wrong way, and the
  way that I do it. You understand?

WARD: I do understand that. I'll get right on it. And thank
  you.

ACE: Don't thank me, just do it. You're the Slots Manager. I
  shouldn't have to tell you this.

WARD: Dang, you are right, Mr Rothstein, I am so sorry.

INT. CLASSY RESTAURANT – NIGHT

GINGER *follows a snooty* MAÎTRE D' *to* JENNIFER, *already seated
at a table.*

ACE: (*Voice-over*) So, I ended up workin' what? Eighteen-hour
  days? Ginger was the one who wound up enjoying the best
  of Vegas.

MAÎTRE D': (*To* JENNIFER) Come with me, please. I have a
  better table for you. Sorry.
  (*He shows the two of them to the best table in the place.*)

JENNIFER: (*Sitting down next to* GINGER) So, what'd you say to that fuckin' jerk anyway?

GINGER: (*Smiling*) I told him I was Mrs Sam Rothstein.

JENNIFER: (*Chuckles*) Well, you might as well get somethin' out of it.

(GINGER *lights a cigarette.*)


EXT. IDLE SPURS DESERT DINER – DAY

*Wide overhead of roadhouse café isolated in the middle of the desert with a sign out front that reads '60 miles to Vegas'.*

ACE: (*Voice-over*) Well, it wasn't long before what I was afraid was gonna happen, happened. Nicky managed to get himself banned from every casino in Las Vegas, and from then on, I couldn't be seen talkin' to him anywhere in Vegas, or even near it.

NICKY: (*From inside the diner*) What the fuck is that supposed to mean?


INT. IDLE SPURS DESERT DINER – DAY

ACE *and* NICKY *are at a table in the empty diner.*

NICKY: (*Reading from a document*) '. . . detrimental to gaming. And he will be ejected from any casino in Las Vegas . . . and the casinos can be fined as much as a hundred thousand every time he shows up.' (*He waves the document.*) Do you believe this shit?

ACE: (*Smoking a cigarette*) Yeah, I believe it. You got banned. (NICKY *hisses.*)

NICKY: (*Reading*) 'Who is of notorious and unsavory reputation . . .' (*He angrily wads the document and tosses it across the table.*) Motherfucker. Unsavory fuckin' . . . Is there any way around this?

ACE: Nope, there's no way.

NICKY: Let's say . . . for instance . . . I want to go in the restaurant which happens to be in the casino . . . to get one of those sandwiches I like?

ACE: Forget it. You can't even set foot in the parking lot. That's how serious it is.

NICKY: In other words, I'm fucked.

ACE: In so many words, yes.

ACE: (*Voice-over*) It just didn't sink into his head about the Black Book and what it meant. Not being able to go into a casino is just one thing, but being in this book etched your name into the brains of every cop and FBI agent in the state. I mean, you're listed in there with Al Capone. But Nicky didn't care.

NICKY: I gotta do somethin'. I gotta do somethin'. They ain't gettin' rid of me. They're not gettin' rid of me. I'm staying here. Fuck 'em. Fuck 'em.

EXT. GOLD RUSH JEWELER'S – DAY

*We move past the skull of a steer mounted on an exterior wall and a wooden cigar store Indian statue, to reveal* DOMINICK SANTORO *(who looks a little like his brother* NICKY*) and* MARINO *who are waiting inside the Gold Rush. Camera comes to rest on extreme close-up of* NICKY's *eyes as he stands on the outside porch.*

NICKY: (*Voice-over*) So, once they pulled that shit, I started doin' my own things in Vegas nobody ever thought of doin'. To keep an eye on things, I brought in my kid brother Dominick . . . and some desperados from back home and started knockin' over high rollers, casino bosses, bookmakers, anybody, right here in town. I had a good fuckin' crew goin' for me, I'll tell you that.

(SAL FUSCO, JACK HARDY *and* BERNIE BLUE *are getting out of a car and walking into the jewelry store which is designed to replicate an old-fashioned Western town with peaked roofs, wooden planked sidewalks and hitching posts. The camera tracks by each man as they're introduced.*)

I had Sal Fusco, a great second-story guy. Jack Hardy, he worked for a safe company after he did a six-year bit. And then there was Bernie Blue. This guy could bypass any alarm for me. And I opened up my own jewelry store, too: 'The Gold Rush'.

INT. BEDROOM OF LUXURY HOME – NIGHT

NICKY *places some jewelry from a vanity table into a sack and turns over some family photos.* MARINO *and* HARDY *are struggling with a safe.*

NICKY: (*Voice-over*) Sometimes I used to go along on a heist just for the fun of it. But I didn't like the people I was rippin' off lookin' at me, so I used to turn their fuckin' pictures around.

NICKY: (*To* MARINO *and* HARDY) What's takin' so long over there?

MARINO: This peter's a motherfucker.

HARDY: (*Grunting*) It's workin'. Just keep workin' it. It's comin'.

NICKY: Gotta learn how to open these fuckin' things so you won't have to take 'em.

INT. GOLD RUSH BACK ROOM – DAY

NICKY *is looking at diamonds with* MARINO, HARDY *and* BLUE.
NICKY: Frankie, some of these stones got a lot of niggers in
    'em.
    (*Zoom in tight on a diamond.*)
    Tell that fuckin' Pepe if he's switching stones on us, he'd
    better take a fuckin' camel –
    (*Phone rings.*)
    – back to (*picking up phone*) Nigeria. (*Into telephone*) Yeah.
HOTEL RECEPTIONIST: (*Over telephone*) Listen . . .


INT. TANGIERS RECEPTIONIST'S DESK – DAY

HOTEL RECEPTIONIST: (*Talking quietly into telephone*) . . .
    they're in Penthouse K.


INT. GOLD RUSH BACK ROOM – DAY

NICKY: (*Into telephone*) They check in alone?


INT. TANGIERS RECEPTIONIST'S DESK – DAY

HOTEL RECEPTIONIST: (*Into telephone*) They checked in alone.


INT. GOLD RUSH BACK ROOM – DAY

NICKY: (*Into telephone*) Are they out now?


INT. TANGIERS RECEPTIONIST'S DESK – DAY

HOTEL RECEPTIONIST: (*Into telephone*) Yes, don't worry.
NICKY: (*Over telephone*) All right.


INT. GOLD RUSH BACK ROOM – DAY

NICKY: (*Into telephone*) Thanks. (*He hangs up.*)

ACE: (*Voice-over*) He had tipsters . . .

INT. CASINO HOTEL BELL STATION – DAY

*We see some luggage on the floor. A* BELLMAN *is on the phone with* MARINO.

ACE: (*Voice-over*) . . . all over town. Bellmen.

BELLMAN: (*Into telephone*) This one looks good. But you got to hurry.
MARINO: (*Over telephone*) Yeah . . .


INT. GOLD RUSH – DAY

MARINO: (*Into telephone*) . . . yeah, okay. (*He hangs up.*)


EXT. CASINO – DAY

*A* VALET PARKER *standing outside a casino.*

ACE: (*Voice-over*) Valet parkers.

VALET PARKER: (*Into telephone*) They're just checking in now.


INT. GOLD RUSH BACK ROOM – DAY

FUSCO: (*Into telephone, seated on a couch*) Okay, I'll tell him.


INT. CASINO FLOOR – DAY

*A* PIT BOSS *is on the phone.*

ACE: (*Voice-over*) Pit bosses.

PIT BOSS: (*Into telephone*) Yeah, room twelve-thirty, at the Sirocco.


INT. GOLD RUSH BACK ROOM – DAY

MARINO: (*Into telephone*) Twelve-thirty, right.

INT. OFFICE – DAY

*A* SECRETARY *seated at a desk.*

ACE: (*Voice-over*) Secretaries.

SECRETARY: (*Into telephone*) It's all in mint condition coins.


INT. GOLD RUSH BACK ROOM – DAY

HARDY: (*Into telephone*) Mint condition? All right.

ACE: (*Voice-over*) And they all . . .


EXT. WAREHOUSE/JEWELRY STORE – NIGHT

HARDY *and a hood are in a van parked in front of a warehouse next door to a jewelry store.*

ACE: (*Voice-over*) . . . got a piece of the score.

HARDY: (*From inside the van, into a walkie-talkie*) Car's comin'.
    (*We move past the van to a larger truck parked in an alley.
    Unseen, the truck has an open side door abutting the jewelry
    store's wall.* SAL FUSCO *and* BERNIE BLUE *are inside the
    truck drilling into the wall using a heavy-duty battery-
    powered drill. The drill is muffled with sheets of insulation
    material.*)

ACE: (*Voice-over*) They were very careful. And they always
    bypassed the alarms, or else . . . if not, they'd drill enough
    holes to knock through the walls with a sledgehammer.

    (BLUE *widens the hole with a hammer muffled with
    insulation.*)


EXT. JEWELRY STORE WALL – DAY

*A flashbulb explodes.*

*Cops and detectives are photographing and inspecting holes drilled in
the wall of the shop, through which the thieves have come and gone.
The camera moves in through the hole.*

ACE: (*Voice-over*) Nobody out there was expecting a guy like him.

INT. JEWELRY STORE – DAY

*The stunned* STORE OWNER *looks at the rubble and the empty jewelry boxes. Detectives collect evidence.*

ACE: (*Voice-over*) For Nicky, Las Vegas was the fuckin' Wild West.

STORE OWNER: (*Leading a detective to his showroom*) I just got a shipment of diamonds from Israel . . .

NICKY: (*Voice-over*) But what the fuck they expect from me? I had to earn, didn't I?

INT. PALM SPRINGS JEWELRY STORE – DAY

MARINO *stands above two* IRANIANS *who are looking at the stolen gems.*
IRANIAN #1: You know, this diamond has flaws in it.
MARINO: No, no, there's no flaws in it.
IRANIAN #2: Don't tell me. I'm doing this for twenty-five years.
MARINO: You better clean your fuckin' loupe. 'Cause there's no flaws in these diamonds.
    (*The two* IRANIANS *speak to each other in Farsi.*)

NICKY: (*Voice-over*) Whenever we got local merch, we'd usually send it to Palm Springs or Arizona . . . LA. I had a couple of sand niggers out there. You know, Arabs.

MARINO: What, are you gonna have a fuckin' meeting here, or are you gonna buy some diamonds?
IRANIAN #2: (*Chuckling*) No, no. I know his language. I'm talking with him.
MARINO: Forty thousand dollars, you can buy the whole package.
IRANIAN #1: Twenty thousand, and that's my final offer and . . .
MARINO: (*To* IRANIAN #2) All of a sudden he talks English,

82

now. (*To* IRANIAN #1.) Let's talk turkey here, how 'bout twenty-five thousand?

(IRANIAN #1 *laughs*.)

INT. NICKY'S HOUSE — NIGHT

NICKY *and* MARINO *sneak into the house past* JENNIFER *who is asleep on the sofa in front of a TV set.* NICKY *takes out a key and opens the metal door into his bedroom.*

NICKY: (*Voice-over*) I actually turned my bedroom into a bank vault where I kept the choice stuff.

MARINO: (*Referring to* JENNIFER *as they pass the kitchen*) She asleep?
NICKY: Every night, on the couch.

NICKY: (*Voice-over*) I couldn't leave it at the Gold Rush in case we got raided by the cops . . . or if my crew got cute. (*Opening the metal door to his bedroom.*) I had the only key.

INT. NICKY'S BEDROOM/CLOSET — NIGHT

*Camera pans across bedroom to closet door.*

NICKY: (*Voice-over*) Jennifer didn't give a fuck. She used to fall asleep on the couch watchin' television every night. This stuff was all mine. I didn't send any of this back home. (NICKY *opens the closet door. He and* MARINO *walk in and bend down to lift up a small square of carpet to reveal a floor safe.*)
Actually, I couldn't because I wasn't even supposed to be doin' it. The bosses were makin' so much fuckin' money with the casinos (*unlocking the safe*) that they didn't want anybody makin' any waves for them.

(*In the floor safe, there are several handguns and silencers.* FRANK *hands* NICKY *a roll of money.*)
NICKY: Give all the guys in your crew a piece of that?
MARINO: I took care of everybody.
NICKY: Yeah? (*He searches* MARINO'S *jacket.*)

NICKY: (*Voice-over*) That's why there was no real organized street stuff in Vegas before I came here.

(NICKY *throws the cash in the safe and closes the lid.*)

INT. NICKY'S HOUSE – DAY

NICKY *is being shown papers by* CHARLIE CLARK, *a heavy-set banker with a moustache. They're both seated at a table in the living-room.*
CHARLIE CLARK: Yeah, that works out.

NICKY: (*Voice-over*) But how much cash could I bury in my closet, right?

CHARLIE CLARK: You need to understand, and I – I'm sure you do . . . that in a venture of this kind, you have to be prepared to take some kind of loss.
NICKY: Oh, listen, I understand that there's always a risk . . . you know, I might have to take a loss somewhere.

NICKY: (*Voice-over*) So I put some of the money into legitimate deals with Charlie Clark. He was Ace's banker.

NICKY: I mean, you will try to push it through, won't you, Mr Clark?
CHARLIE CLARK: Yes.
NICKY: Well, you gotta understand, I'm giving you fifty thousand cash.
(CHARLIE CLARK *chuckles.*)

NICKY: (*Voice-over*) Then I put some more of the money . . .

INT. LEANING TOWER RESTAURANT, KITCHEN – NIGHT

*A prosciutto sandwich is being prepared on a kitchen counter.*

NICKY: (*Voice-over*) . . . in some legitimate places, like my restaurant.

DOMINICK: (*To* COOK *preparing sandwich*) Is that the last one?
COOK: Yeah.
(*He hands the sandwich to* DOMINICK *who spits in it.*)

NICKY: (*Voice-over*) I had my kid brother, Dominick, run it for me.

DOMINICK: (*Spits*) Fuckers!
(DOMINICK *wraps it in plastic and puts it into a brown paper bag.*)


INT. LEANING TOWER RESTAURANT – NIGHT

DOMINICK *sets the bag with the wrapped sandwich in it on top of pizza boxes being held by two uniformed Vegas* COPS.

DOMINICK: Here you go, guys.

COP #1: All right. Thanks, a lot.

DOMINICK: Yeah . . . yeah, enjoy.

COP #2: Yeah.
(*He shakes* COP #2's *hand before heading back into the restaurant.*)

DOMINICK: Have a good time. (*Muttering to himself.*) Choke on it, ya motherfucker!

MAN #1: (*Passing* DOMINICK *on his way out*) Hey, Dom.

DOMINICK: Hey, how you doin'?
(DOMINICK *walks over to some patrons in the bar area.* NICKY *enters, kissing his brother.*)

ACE: (*Voice-over*) Yeah, Nicky loved restaurants. He was a real restaurant buff. And over the years, he always made money with them.

NICKY: (*Looking at one of the patrons*) Hey, Rich.
(*The camera follows* NICKY *around the restaurant past Las Vegas types – dealers, lounge acts, showgirls, TV and movie celebrities, waitresses and barmen – who use the jammed place as their hangout.*)

ACE: (*Voice-over*) In Vegas, he had The Leaning Tower. It was a very popular spot. He had politicians, showgirls and movies stars hangin' out all over the place.

(NICKY *walks up to* STEVE ALLEN *and* JAYNE MEADOWS *seated at a table, he whistles their theme tune as he approaches from behind.*)

85

NICKY: Listen, that show over at the Flamingo gets better and better.

STEVE ALLEN: By the way, Sammy said whenever you have a minute, give him a call.

NICKY: Made a messenger out of you too, huh?

STEVE ALLEN: (*Laughs*) I'll do anything for a buck.

NICKY: He does it. He does it to everybody. Enjoy your dinner.

JAYNE MEADOWS: (*Chuckles*) Thanks.

STEVE ALLEN: Okay, thanks.

ACE: (*Voice-over*) But I gotta tell you, the thing Nicky liked the most was the showgirls, naturally. I mean, to them, Nicky was the movie star.

(NICKY *walks across the room to* MARINO *and two showgirls,* SHELLY *and* STACY.)

NICKY: (*To* MARINO) You walk past me?

MARINO: Hey. This is Shelly.

NICKY: Hey, Shelly. (*Kisses her hand.*)

SHELLY: Hi.

NICKY: How are you? Nice to meet you.

MARINO: (*Pointing to* STACY) And this is Stacy.

NICKY: Stacy. (*Kisses her hand.*)

MARINO: (*To the* SHOWGIRLS) This is Nick.

NICKY: Pleasure.

STACY: Hi, Nick.

MARINO: We're gonna have dinner. Come on.

NICKY: All right, uh, (*To* SHELLY) let's just check the kitchen first. Excuse us one second. Come on, I'll show you.
(*He takes* SHELLY's *hand and leads her out.*)
(*Voice-over from following scene*) 'Cause I fly stuff in fresh every day.


EXT. LEANING TOWER RESTAURANT, PARKING LOT – NIGHT

NICKY *and* SHELLY *walk across the parking lot and get into his two-tone, red and white car.*

NICKY: I get bread from back home. I get fish from California. And you can always tell a great kitchen like ours because of the milk-fed veal. That's the secret.

(*Opening the car door from the passenger's side, she gets in.*)
See, milk-fed veal is pure white. Out here, they got that
pink veal. Slide over, honey.
(*She slides over, he gets into the passenger's seat and closes the
door.*)
Now, pink veal, you can pound that shit for two days and
it'll never ever get tender, you know what I mean?
(SHELLY's *head disappears into* NICKY's *lap.*)


INT. LEANING TOWER RESTAURANT – NIGHT

FRANK *and* DOMINICK *are at the bar watching as* NICKY *chastises*
AL, *a gambler. The restaurant is empty except for a waiter milling
around in the background, setting a few tables.*
AL: When I left here with the money . . .
NICKY: Mm.
AL: . . . I got muscled on the street.
NICKY: Mm.
AL: A couple of guys, I owe them. So, that's what I did. I gave
    'em the money. That's what I did.
NICKY: Yeah?
AL: Yeah.
NICKY: You call yourself a man? You know you're a lyin', low-
    life, motherfuckin' gambling degenerate prick? You know
    that's what you are? Two small kids at home. I gave you
    money to pay the fuckin' rent and buy groceries, put the
    heat on. You know your wife called Frankie and told him
    the fuckin' heat's off?
    (AL *glances over to* MARINO.)
    Huh? And you didn't gamble that fuckin' money? You're
    gonna stand here and tell me that?
    (*He shakes his head 'no'.*)
    No, no? You didn't?
AL: I didn't give 'em the m–
NICKY: Don't fuck with me, Al! Don't make a fuck out of me!
    You want to embarrass me and make a fool out of me?!
    You didn't gamble?! Tell me you gambled the fuckin'
    money, I'll give you the fuckin' money to put the fuckin'
    heat on! Did you gamble?! Huh?!

(*The chastised gambler nods 'yes', bowing his head in shame.*)
Fuckin' degenerate, you.
(NICKY *takes some money from his coat pocket and starts counting out some bills.*)
Fuckin' kids at home! Here. (*Giving him the money.*) Get the fuck out of here.

AL: Thanks, Nick.

NICKY: Yeah, thanks.

(AL *walks out.*)
Let me find out you fucked up, I'll leave you wherever I find you.


INT. NICKY'S HOUSE, KITCHEN – DAY

NICKY, *worn out from the night before, is making pancakes for* LITTLE NICKY.

NICKY: (*To* LITTLE NICKY) How many of these you gonna eat, huh?

LITTLE NICKY: Two.

NICKY: Two?

ACE: (*Voice-over*) But around six-thirty in the morning when he finished his day –
(NICKY *hugs and kisses his son.*)
– no matter where he was or what he was doing, he always went home to make breakfast for his son, Nicky-Boy.

NICKY: (*Pouring some syrup on his son's pancakes*) Here, let's put a little of this on for you. I know you like this. A little butter, right, not a lot?

LITTLE NICKY: Mm-hm.

NICKY: You know why, right?

LITTLE NICKY: Yeah.

NICKY: Why?

LITTLE NICKY: 'Cause it clogs up your heart.

NICKY: What a smart kid you are! (*Kisses him.*) Okay, eat.


INT. ALL-AMERICAN GAS STATION, BACK HOME – DAY

MARINO *walks through an office past a few hoods.*

NICKY: (*Voice-over*) Every couple of weeks I used to send Marino back to the bosses with a piece of what I made.

TITLE IN: 'BACK HOME'

(MARINO *walks out of the office and through the garage.*)

NICKY: (*Voice-over*) Not a big piece, but fuck them, what did they know? They were fifteen hundred miles away . . .

EXT. ALL-AMERICAN GAS STATION, BACK HOME – DAY

*Wide shot of gas station. There is snow on the ground. The cloudy, Midwestern skyline of warehouses and skyscrapers can be seen behind the gas station sign: 'All-American Gas'.*

NICKY: (*Voice-over*) . . . and I don't know anybody who can see that far. Their drop was a truck stop/garage where . . .

INT. ALL-AMERICAN GAS STATION, GAGGI'S BACK OFFICE – DAY

REMO GAGGI *is seated in a chair as* MARINO *walks in.* CURLY, *one of Gaggi's men, and two of the bosses are there.*

NICKY: (*Voice-over*) . . . Remo and the guys used to hang out and count their millions.

MARINO: Remo. (*He bends down and kisses him.*)
GAGGI: Hey, Frankie.
MARINO: How are you?
GAGGI: Fine, fine.

NICKY: (*Voice-over*) I mean, the cops knew, but they didn't give a fuck. I mean, you know, they all worked it out together.

MARINO: Nicky sends his warmest regards.
(MARINO *unzips a small sack and hands* GAGGI *a thick stack of cash.* GAGGI *inspects it before handing it over to one of his men.*)
GAGGI: Uh-huh. Good.

NICKY: (*Voice-over*) But I knew how to keep the bosses happy.

Whenever they gave me little jobs to do, you know, to send a message, I would carry things out . . .

GAGGI: And how are things going down there?
MARINO: Fine. Everything's goin' good.

NICKY: (*Voice-over*) . . . to a tee. Like the time Tony Dogs . . .

INT. OUTSKIRTS OF VEGAS BAR – NIGHT

*Flash cut of* TONY DOGS *and two men shooting up a bar with automatics hitting the owner, bartenders and a waitress.*

NICKY: (*Voice-over*) . . . who was supposed to be the new
    maniac tough guy in town, shot up one of Remo's bars.
    Here's a fuckin' guy, kills two of Remo's guys and a poor
    fuckin' waitress, who was just workin' on her night off, of
    all things.
    (*Slow motion on* TONY DOGS.)
    I mean, this guy's just beggin' to be made an example of.

    (*The men and the waitress lie dead on the floor. The bar is left
    in shambles.*)
GAGGI: (*Voice-over, from his office*) Frankie . . .

INT. ALL-AMERICAN GAS STATION, GAGGI'S BACK OFFICE –
NIGHT

*An enraged* GAGGI *gives* MARINO *orders.*
GAGGI: . . . I want all the names of all the other people he had
    with him. And I don't care what you have to do to him to
    get 'em. You understand?
MARINO: I'll take care of it, Remo.
GAGGI: *E mo va!*[1]

INT. SLOT-MACHINE SHOP, LAS VEGAS – NIGHT

MARINO *and* BLUE *are dragging* TONY DOGS, *who is beaten to a
pulp, across the floor toward a workshop table.* NICKY *follows them.*

1 Italian-American slang for 'Now, go!'

NICKY: (*Voice-over*) To be truthful with you, I had to admire this fuckin' guy. He was one of the toughest Irishmen I ever met.

NICKY: This fuckin' guy, he got some stamina, don't he?

NICKY: (*Voice-over*) This son-of-a-bitch was tough.

NICKY: Personally, I don't give a fuck who was with him anyway. As long as he gives me a name I could give to them.

NICKY: (*Voice-over*) For two days and two fuckin' nights, we beat the shit out this guy. I mean, we even stuck ice-picks in his balls.

NICKY: You better hope he gives me a fuckin' name soon, or I'm gonna give him yours, Frank.
(MARINO *and* BLUE *lay* DOGS *on the table and put his head in a vise. They're exhausted from beating him.*)

MARINO: (*To* NICKY) Yeah, thanks a lot.

NICKY: (*Voice-over*) But he never talked.

NICKY: (*To* MARINO) I know you would have ratted by now.

NICKY: (*Voice-over*) In the end, I had to put his fuckin' head in a vise.

NICKY: Dogs. Dogs, can your hear me, Dogs?
(DOGS *gasps and mumbles.*)
Listen to me, Anthony. I got your head in a fuckin' vise. I'm gonna squash your fuckin' head like a grapefruit if you don't give me a name. Don't make me have to do this, please. Come on. Don't make me be a bad guy. Come on.

TONY DOGS: (*With what strength he has left*) Fuck you!

NICKY: (*To* MARINO *and* BLUE) This motherfucker, do you believe this? Two fuckin' days and nights! (*To* DOGS.) Fuck me?
(NICKY *begins to tighten the vise.*)
Fuck me, you motherfucker? (*Turning the vise.*) Fuck my mother? That's what you fuckin' tell me?

(NICKY *angrily keeps spinning the vise handle until suddenly one of* DOGS's *eyes bulges out of the socket.*)
Huh? You motherfucker, you, huh?
(MARINO *and* BLUE *are horrified by the sight. Everybody freezes.*)
Oh, God! Give me the fuckin' name!
TONY DOGS: Ch-Charlie M!
NICKY: Charlie M?
TONY DOGS: (*Blood streaming out of his mouth*) Charlie M.
NICKY: (*Screaming*) Charlie M? You make me pop your fuckin' eye out of your head to protect that piece of shit? Charlie M! You dumb motherfucker!
TONY DOGS: (*Pleading*) Kill me, you fuck, kill me.
NICKY: Kill you, (*unwinds the crank*) you motherfucker you! (*To* MARINO.) Frankie, do him a fuckin' favor.

ACE: (*Voice-over*) The word got around that finally . . .
(MARINO *places a knife against* DOGS's *neck.*)
. . . there was a real gangster in town. Nicky was the new boss of Las Vegas.

(*We hear* DOGS *gasp as the knife slices his throat.*)
NICKY: Charlie M!


INT. TANGIERS CASINO – DAY

*Extreme close-up of a slot-machine. Four reels with sevens across. Suddenly, the power goes out. Lights die down. Machine 'waaaooows' down to a dead stop. Security guards, on their hands and knees, are pulling the plugs on the three giant $15,000 progressive machines, as* ACE *talks to* DON WARD.
ACE: Four reels, sevens across, three fifteen-thousand-dollar jackpots? Do you have any idea what the odds are?
WARD: Shoot, it's gotta be in the millions, maybe more.
ACE: Three fuckin' jackpots in twenty minutes? Why didn't you pull the machines? Why didn't you call me?
WARD: Well, it happened so quick. Three guys won. I didn't have a chance to call you.
ACE: You didn't see the scam? You didn't see what was goin' on?

WARD: Well, there's no way to determine that, Sam.

ACE: Yes, there is. An infallible way! They won!

WARD: Well, it's a casino. People gotta win sometimes.

ACE: Hey . . . Ward, you're pissin' me off. Now, you're insulting my intelligence. What do you think, I'm a fuckin' idiot? You know goddamn well somebody had to get into those machines and set those fuckin' reels.

(SHERBERT *enters, stands next to* ACE.)

The probability on one four-reel machine is a million and a half to one. On three machines in a row, it's in the billions. It cannot happen . . . would not happen, you fuckin' mo-mo! What's the matter with you! Didn't you see you were bein' set up on the second win?

WARD: I really think you're –

ACE: (*Interrupts*) You – Wait! You didn't see that you were being set up on the second win?

WARD: I really think you're overreacting in this whole –

ACE: (*Interrupts*) Listen, you fuckin' yokel, I've had it with you. I've been carryin' your ass in this place ever since I got here. Get your ass and get your things and get out of here.

WARD: You're firin' me?

ACE: I'm firin' you? No, I'm not firin' (*mocking* WARD), I'm
    firin' you, you – (*Gives* SHERBERT *a look.*)
WARD: You might regret this, Mr Rothstein.
ACE: I'll regret it even more if I keep you on.
WARD: This is not the way to treat people.
ACE: Listen, if you didn't know you're bein' scammed, you're
    too fuckin' dumb to keep this job. If you did know, you
    were in on it. Either way, you're out! Get out! Go on. (*To*
    SHERBERT.) Let's go.
    (ACE *and* SHERBERT *walk off,* WARD *turns to leave.*)


INT. TANGIERS CASINO, AKU-AKU LOUNGE – DAY, AN HOUR
LATER

ACE *and* GREEN *are seated having coffee and muffins in the
Hawaiian lounge by the casino floor.*
ACE: I mean, the guy is history as far as I'm concerned. History.
GREEN: But you can't just fire him. Webb's his brother-in-law.
    He's County Commissioner.
ACE: So what? Everybody out here with cowboy boots is a
    fuckin' county commissioner or related to a county
    commissioner. I'm fuckin' sick of it.
GREEN: This is his state. His uncle's Chief Judge. His brother-
    in-law runs the County Commission. I don't know how
    many other relatives he's got in town. There's gotta be a
    way to work him back in.
ACE: Phil, I can understand. You're in the finances, you're
    upstairs, but you are not on the floor. I got thousands of
    players. I got five hundred dealers. They're all lookin' to
    rob me blind, twenty-four hours a day. I have to let them
    know I'm watching all the details, all the time; that there is
    not one single thing I will not catch as I am over here.
    (*Breaks open his blueberry muffin, puts it down and points to
    Green's.*) Look at yours.
GREEN: What?
ACE: Look at that. Look at this. There's nothin' . . . look how
    many blueberries your muffin has and how many mine has.
    Yours is falling apart. I have nothing.
GREEN: What are you talking about?

94

ACE: It's like everything else in this place. You don't do it yourself, it never gets done.

(GREEN *follows* ACE *to the kitchen.*)

GREEN: Where you goin'?

INT. TANGIERS KITCHEN — DAY

ACE, GREEN *and the* BAKER *are gathered around the* BAKER's *counter surrounded by muffin tins and batter.*

ACE: (*Handing the* BAKER *the two muffins*) From now on I want you to put an equal amount of blueberries in each muffin. An equal amount of blueberries in each muffin.

BAKER: You know how long that's going to take?

ACE: I don't care how long it takes. Put an equal amount in each muffin.

(ACE *leaves,* GREEN *looks on in amazement as the* BAKER *holds the muffins.* GREEN *follows* ACE *out.*)

INT. ACE'S HOUSE, KITCHEN — DAY

ACE, *seated at the kitchen table, is feeding* AMY *in a high chair. The nanny is in the background.*

ACE: Come on, honey, just a little. That a girl, that a girl. Oh, boy, look.

(GINGER *enters and goes to the sink.*)

(*To* AMY, *who is sobbing and mumbling*) Okay, want to go with Mommy?

GINGER: (*Picking her up*) Hey there. Want to come to Mommy? It's all right, sweetheart. (*To* ACE) I need to talk to you. I need some money.

ACE: What do you need?

GINGER: (*Giving* AMY *to the* NANNY) You got her? Okay. (*To* ACE.) Well, I need a lot. I need more than usual.

ACE: Well, why don't you take it out of your account? There's a lot there.

GINGER: Well, I would, you know, Sam. It's just that . . . well, I need more than that. I need twenty-five thousand.

(*She sits down at the table next to him.*)

ACE: Twenty-five thousand? For yourself?

95

GINGER: (*Picking up an empty carton of milk*) Yeah.

ACE: Why do you need that much?

GINGER: Well, what's the difference? I just need it.

ACE: Well, I mean . . . you know, I gotta ask you. That's a lot of money. You're not asking for a box of popcorn, you know. I mean . . .

GINGER: I'm aware of that. We don't have to turn this into a big deal. (*Getting up to the refrigerator.*) Okay? We don't have to have a fight. It was important to me. But forget it. Just something I wanted to do for myself.

ACE: Who's fighting? I mean, I'm, you know, tell me what it's for.

(GINGER, *annoyed, closes the refrigerator door.*)

Why can't you tell me what it's for?

(*She stirs her coffee.*)

Huh? (*Pause.*) Well, you know what? Now, I want you to tell me. I mean, my wife comes to me and asks me for twenty-five thousand. I mean, what do you want? Do you want a coat?

GINGER: No.

ACE: Well, if you want a coat, you got it. You know that. It's not the money, it's just why do you want it? That's all I'm askin'. Am I not entitled to ask that?

GINGER: Look – Sam, I've been independent my whole life. I never had to ask anybody for anything. Now you're making me beg you for this.

ACE: What are you talkin' a– ?

GINGER: (*Interrupting*) Okay? And you're embarrassing me. Why do you want to make me feel so bad?

ACE: You're askin' me for twenty-five thousand. I'm not out to make you feel bad. I want to just be able to trust you. You know, it's about trust. I have to be able to trust you with my life. Do you understand? Can I trust you? (*She doesn't answer.*) Can I trust you? . . . Can I trust you? . . . Answer me. Can I trust you?

GINGER: (*Quietly*) You can trust me.

ACE: Good, so then you could tell me what the money is for.

(GINGER *gives him a look and leaves.*)

INT. VEGAS BANK VAULT – DAY

GINGER *takes about two inches of $100 bills out of a safe deposit box and slips it in an envelope.*

EXT. VEGAS BANK/PUBLIC PHONE – DAY

NICKY *is on a phone watching* GINGER *leave the bank.*
NICKY: (*Into telephone*) Yeah, she's leavin' the bank now. All right, I'm gonna follow her. (*He hangs up.*)

INT. SALVADORAN DINER BOOTH – DAY

GINGER *is in a booth with* LESTER DIAMOND, *handing him the envelope filled with money.*
LESTER: What does that mean? No, I know that look. What does that mean?
GINGER: It means I got the money.
LESTER: You got money. That's a – That's a good look.
(*Swish pan to* ACE *entering, followed by a* HOOD. *He sits down at the booth with* LESTER *and* GINGER.)
ACE: How you doin', Les? It's Lester, right? Sam.
(*Extends his hand to* LESTER, *who shakes it.*)
From my recollection, aren't you the card shark . . . the golf hustler . . . the pimp from Beverly Hills?
(LESTER *gives* GINGER *a 'how did you fuck this up?' look.*)
If I'm wrong, please correct me, 'cause I never knew you to be a heist man.
(LESTER *sighs.*)
But if you are, you know what . . . here, take mine too.
(ACE *takes some money out of his coat and puts the thick wad of bills on the table.*)
Go ahead, take it. 'Cause you already have hers.
(LESTER *turns and sees two* HOODS *standing by the front and back doors of the diner.*)
She's my wife. (*To* LESTER.) Look at me. You did know that, didn't you? You knew that she's my wife? Huh? Hey, look at me.
LESTER: Yeah, yeah. I know that.

ACE: You do? Yeah? Well, if you ever come back again . . . ever
. . . to take her money . . . next time bring a pistol. That
way you got a chance. Be a man, don't be a fuckin' pimp.
Now, you want to do me a favor? Get out of here. I want to
be alone with my wife. Get the fuck up and get out of here.
(*After stammering for a moment,* LESTER *gets up and begins to
move towards the back door.*)

LESTER: (*Quietly*) Okay.

ACE: You fuckin' piece of shit.

LESTER: Hey, that's just fuckin' – That's bullshit. You know,
you know, what the fuck?
(*The thugs follow him out of the back door.* GINGER *freezes.*)

ACE: You remember when you called him that night? When you
said goodbye to him? He didn't say, 'Don't get married,
I'll be right down, we'll get married.' He didn't say that to
you, did he?

GINGER: (*Whispering*) No, he didn't.

ACE: (*Picks up the money*) Didn't. No, instead, what did he say?
'Fuck him. Take him for everything he's got.'
(ACE *takes* GINGER *by the arm to the rear of the diner where
they can see the parking area through a glass door.*)
Come here, I want to show you somethin'.

## EXT. REAR OF SALVADORAN DINER, PARKING LOT – DAY

*Three* HOODS *rush* LESTER *who is running towards his car.* GINGER *bursts through the door, trying to get to* LESTER. ACE *holds her back. They struggle.* LESTER *groans and gasps as the* HOODS *start to beat him up.*

HOOD #1: You fuckin' shit.

GINGER: No! No! No! Don't!

>    (ACE *restrains her.*
>
>       *The* HOODS *punch* LESTER *in the face and stomach.*)
> Make them stop it! (*Sobbing.*) No! No! No! It's not his fault! It's my fault!
>    (NICKY *watches from a car in a parking lot across the street, out of* GINGER'S *sight.*
>
>       ACE *forces* GINGER *into the car as the* HOODS *finish the beating.*)

GINGER: (*Sobbing*) No! No!

>    (*The* HOODS *toss* LESTER *into his car.*)

LESTER: (*Falling into the front seat on his back*) Fuck!

>    (NICKY *watches as the* HOODS *walk away from* LESTER'S *car.*)

LESTER: Fuck you!

HOOD #2: You piece of shit.

>    (ACE *pulls out of the parking lot with a wailing* GINGER.
>    LESTER *groans, trying to sit up.*)

LESTER: (*As* ACE *and* GINGER *drive off down the street*) Couldn't do it yourself, you chickenshit cocksucker!


## INT. GOLD RUSH BACK ROOM – DAY

GINGER *and* NICKY *are in the back room.* NICKY *is sitting on a couch while* GINGER *stands by a mirror with a curling iron.*

GINGER: (*Throwing the iron on the counter*) He's such a prick. He had some guy from the hotel beat him up. He didn't want to do it himself. Oh, no, he didn't want to get his own hands dirty. (*She takes a pill with a drink.*) So, why'd he have to do that, huh? (*She walks towards* NICKY, *who is sitting on a couch across the room.*) Tell me.

NICKY: I know it wasn't a nice thing to do but –

GINGER: (*Interrupts*) Yeah, no shit. (*She sits down next to* NICKY.)

NICKY: Well, you gotta understand it. He doesn't know if this guy is shaking you down or taking advantage of you.

GINGER: No! No! I told him all about this guy before we ever got married. This is no fuckin' surprise.

NICKY: Oh, you did? I didn't know that.

GINGER: Yeah. He's just a friend of mine I was trying to help, so . . . so what?

NICKY: You know . . . the first time I ever saw you guys together . . . I never saw him so happy. I mean, I know he's a crazy Jew fuck and everything, but . . .
*(She smiles.)*
I never see – You know, I never seen him act like that with anybody else. I think he's crazy about you. I mean, he really loves you. He does.

GINGER: Oh, come on. I went into this with my eyes open, you know. I knew the bottom could drop out at any time. I'm a working girl, right? You don't think I'm gonna go into a situation like this if I don't think I'm gonna get covered on the back end.

NICKY: Sure.

GINGER: Am I right?

NICKY: I can see that. Sure.

GINGER: So, he put aside some jewelry for me. A lot of jewelry.

NICKY: You mean, like a lot of expensive jewelry? About how much?

GINGER: Mm, you want to steal it? *(Cracking a smile.)*

NICKY: No. I – I'm just curious, you know. I was wonderin' how much he would put into a thing like that. That's all.

GINGER: I'm told it's worth about a million dollars, maybe more. *(Sniffs.)*

NICKY: Well, there you go. But what does that tell ya? A million dollars in jewelry. Does that tell you the guy is crazy about you, or what?

GINGER: I should have never married him. He's a Gemini. A triple Gemini . . . Duality. *(Breaking down.)* Gemini's the snake. You know you can't trust the snake. *(Sniffs.)* I mean it.

NICKY: I know what you mean.
*(He moves closer to her.)*

Listen, Ginger . . . you know, this is probably not . . . I don't have the answers anyway . . . and this is probably not what you want to hear right now, because you're a little upset with Ace.

GINGER: I do.

NICKY: I understand that. But, you know, I think you should try to make the best of it now. Go slow, you know. See what happens.

GINGER: He could have killed him! Okay? He could have killed him. (*She gets up and walks to the counter by the mirror.*) He didn't have to hit him. It's not exactly like I'm sleepin' with the guy! And he makes me sneak around to see my own friends! What the fuck is that all about?

NICKY: Well, I guess it's 'cause he loves you so much. He's jealous and worried.

GINGER: (*Sighs, her voice starts to crack*) He gives a fuck what I do?

NICKY: (*Getting up*) Look, I'll try to find out what the hell's goin' on. When I see him I'll talk to him.

GINGER: Okay.

NICKY: All right?

GINGER: Yeah. (*Walking over to him, smiling.*) Thanks.
(*Towering over* NICKY, *holding a drink in one hand and his shoulder in the other, she leans down and kisses him.*)
Thanks for puttin' up with me.
(NICKY *takes the drink out of her hand.*)

NICKY: And take it easy with this shit, will you? I mean, this can only make matters worse.

GINGER: Oh, come on.

NICKY: You're a beautiful girl. You don't want to ruin your looks. I've seen a lot of girls get shot to hell from this stuff.

GINGER: (*Fidgeting with his jacket, then holding his face in her hands, smiling.*) You're so nice. (*She begins to cry.*)

NICKY: Come on, now, I don't want to see you unhappy.
(*She kisses him.*)

GINGER: (*Tenderly strokes his head*) Thanks.

NICKY: Yeah.
(*She embraces* NICKY, *wrapping her arms around him.*)

GINGER: (*Through tears*) Thank you.

NICKY: (*Feeling a little awkward with the hug*) It's all right.
    (*She kisses him again.* NICKY *doesn't move, holding back.*)


INT. ACE'S OFFICE – DAY

*Pull back from a sign, with a tiny 'yes' on top of a gigantic 'no',
leaning on a window overlooking the sportsbook. We see* ACE, *behind
his desk, taking a swig of Mylanta. His* SECRETARY *telephones.*


INT. ACE'S OUTER OFFICE, SECRETARY'S DESK – DAY

*We see past* PAT WEBB's *cowboy hat down onto Ace's* SECRETARY
*on the phone.*
SECRETARY: (*Into telephone*) Mr Rothstein? County
    Commissioner Pat Webb is here to see you.
ACE: (*Over telephone*) Okay . . .


INT. ACE'S OFFICE – DAY

ACE: (*Into telephone*) . . . give me a minute.
SECRETARY: (*Over telephone*) Okay.
    (ACE *hangs up the phone.*)


INT. ACE'S OUTER OFFICE, SECRETARY'S DESK – DAY

SECRETARY: (*To* WEBB) It'll be just a minute.


INT. ACE'S OFFICE – DAY

ACE *gets up from his desk and we see he is in his boxer shorts. He
opens the closet and carefully puts on the trousers hanging inside.*


INT. ACE'S OUTER OFFICE, SECRETARY'S DESK – DAY

*A very patient* WEBB *is leaning against some double doors across
from Ace's* SECRETARY.
SECRETARY: Mr Webb . . . can I get you anything?
WEBB: Oh, no. (*Cordially tipping his hat.*) No, thank you, little
    lady.

INT. ACE'S OFFICE – DAY

ACE: (*Into telephone*) Okay, send him in and call me four
   minutes after.
   (WEBB *walks in. He is big, tough and western, wearing a
   Stetson, tooled boots, jeans, an elbow-patched jacket and a
   turquoise bear claw string-tie. His headband contains a
   rattlesnake head. Ace's* SECRETARY *shuts the door on her way
   out.*)
WEBB: Mr Rothstein . . . (*With hand outstretched to* ACE.) I'm
   Pat Webb.
ACE: How do you do?
   (*They shake hands.*)
WEBB: Hey, it is my pleasure.
ACE: Yeah, I heard a lot about you.
WEBB: Oh, thank you, sir. (*Looking out Ace's office picture
   window overlooking the sportsbook.*) Hey, house is doin' well.
   (*Chuckling.*) Hey, all that money is rollin' in. I appreciate
   you takin' the time to see a poor ol' civil servant.
ACE: No, that's quite all right.
   (*Tilt up from* WEBB's *snakeskin cowboy boots and* ACE's *blue
   shoes as they continue talking.*)
   . . .Why don't you have a seat?
WEBB: Hm? Oh. Thank you, sir. (WEBB *sits down in a chair in
   front of* ACE's *desk.*)
   Uh, I come here personally to kind of smooth over a fracas
   about a certain matter. See, uh, maybe you didn't know it,
   but, uh, Don Ward is a very well-liked man in this town.
   He's got lots of friends here. Now, his family and their
   money go back many, many years. Now, friends vote . . .
   family and money votes. That's important to me . . . and
   you. And if you'll think about our little problem along
   them lines . . . and you forgive me for sayin' it, maybe he
   did not deserve to be fired.
ACE: I'm sorry, but he knew about our gettin' hit on three big
   machines in a row and he did nothing about it. That
   means either he was in on it or, forgive me for saying this,
   he was too dumb to see what was going on. Either way, I
   cannot have a man like that workin' here.

WEBB: Before we point the dirty end of the stick at ol' Don, uh, we better be sure we can prove them charges.

ACE: Believe me, if I could prove it, he would be under arrest.

WEBB: Are, uh – (*Clears throat.*) – are we certain that you want the Gamin' Control Board eyeballin' your record and your gangster pals like Nicky Santoro?

ACE: I think you're way out of line talkin' to me like that. What you're sayin' is libelous, and you're in no position to challenge my expertise. I went way out of my way to be very helpful and courteous to that kid. He's weak, he's incompetent. He jeopardizes the whole place. There's not much more I can do for him.

WEBB: (*Chuckling*) You have got me there. Old Don is as useless as tits on a boar. (*Chuckles.*) But, he is my brother-in-law, and I would look on it as a personal favor if you'd think some more on hirin' him back.

ACE: I can't do that. And I appreciate the fact that he's your brother-in-law, and I do want to help you and I like to do favors, and I know who you are, but I cannot do that.

WEBB: Well, could there be any position . . . farther down the trough?

ACE: (*Pause*) I'm sorry, I can't do anything. He's too

incompetent. And the bottom line is, he cannot be trusted.
(*The telephone rings.* ACE *picks it up.*)
(*Into telephone*) Okay, thanks. (*To* WEBB.) Um . . . you
know, that's it. I'm sorry.

WEBB: Mr Rothstein. Your people never will understand the
way it works out here. You're all just our guests. But you
act like you're at home. Let me tell you somethin', partner
. . . you ain't home. But that's where we're gonna send
you if it harelips the Governor. (*Pause.*) Thank you for
your time.

ACE: No problem.
(*Getting up and shaking hands.*)
Sorry.

WEBB: (*Smiles slightly*) You bet.


INT. ACE'S HOUSE, BATHROOM/BEDROOM – DAY

ACE, *in pain from his ulcer, opens a bottle of pills in his bathroom
and sees that it is almost empty.*

ACE: What happened to my pills?
(*He leaves the bathroom and walks into the bedroom where*
GINGER *is stretched out on their imperial bed.*)

GINGER: Huh?

ACE: (*Waving the pill bottle*) Isn't it bad enough you're drinkin'
too much, you're takin' all my pills too?

GINGER: I didn't take your pills.

ACE: Look – for my ulcer, I take a half a one of these, a half a
one of these. And that's when I have extreme pain. I had a
three-month supply. What'd you do with 'em?

GINGER: (*Sobbing*) You didn't have to beat him up!

ACE: (*Walking back to the bathroom*) What?
(ACE *puts the bottle into the medicine cabinet.*)

GINGER: (*Sobbing*) I was just tryin' to help him. It's not like I'm
sleeping with the guy!

ACE: Yeah, how do I know?

GINGER: (*Sobbing*) You can't make me stop caring . . .

ACE: What? What?!

GINGER: I said, you can't make me stop caring about people.
(*She starts to cry.*)

107

ACE: (*Trying to calm her*) Listen. (*Stepping up to the bed.*) Ginger. I'm tryin' to make the best of everything here, you know? I mean, you're my wife, for chrissakes. Uh, I mean . . . people look up to you in this town. I don't know what to think –

GINGER: (*Interrupts*) You know what, Ace? I don't give a shit! I'm gettin' out of here. (*Crying.*) I am. (*She sits up woozy, and tries to pull on her trousers.*)

ACE: (*Walking around the bed to her*) It's okay. Look . . . (*holding her face, gently*) . . . you gotta get a hold of yourself.

GINGER: Okay.

ACE: If not for me, at least for Amy.

GINGER: (*Sobbing*) Okay, okay.

ACE: (*Gently*) You understand? Your drinking's gettin' way out of hand. I'm gonna get you into a program. They got plenty of good ones.

GINGER: I don't need one.

ACE: Yes, you do. It's very discreet. There's no names in the papers. You don't have to worry about any of that stuff.

GINGER: That's all you care about. (*Collapsing on the edge of the bed.*) You don't care about me at all.

ACE: (*Bending down to her*) Yes, I – yes, I do.

GINGER: No, you don't.

ACE: How could you say that? You're a beautiful woman. You're destroying yourself. You don't need that stuff. You don't need that fuckin' leech livin' off you. I know you better than you know yourself. You're a tiger, you're stronger than I am. And when you set your mind on doing something, you do it better than anybody. (*Strokes her hair. Then, quietly:*) You can do it. (*Kissing her.*) You can do it.

GINGER: (*Sobbing*) Oh, God. Oh, God. Okay. Okay . . . I'll try. I'll try.

(*She sits up and puts her arms around* ACE's *waist. He strokes her head.*)

I'll try. I will. Don't be mad at me, okay . . . I will.

### INT. TANGIERS HARD COUNT ROOM – DAY

*Move in on a door that reads: 'Notice – No Admittance – Caution – Hearing Protection Must Be Worn In This Area'.* NANCE *opens it with a key to reveal the hard count room. Coins tumble off a conveyor belt.*

NICKY: (*Voice-over, quietly*) No matter what the problems were outside the count room, it was all worth it. The cash kept rollin' in. And the . . .

### EXT. CASINO REAR LOADING PLATFORM – DAY

NANCE, *dumping two large suitcases in the trunk of a car.*

NICKY: (*Voice-over*) . . . suitcases kept comin' and goin'. And let me tell ya, the fuckin' bottom line here is . . . cash.

(*The trunk lid is shut.*)

### INT. TANGIERS SOFT COUNT ROOM – DAY

*The counters sort through a pile of cash on a table. The camera moves on one counter as he pockets some cash.*

NICKY: (*Voice-over*) The only problem was that, after a while, the bosses noticed that the suitcases were gettin' a little light.

(*Freeze frame on the counter pocketing a $100 bill.*)

INT. SAN MARINO ITALIAN GROCERY/BACK ROOM, KANSAS CITY – DAY

NANCE *is seated at a table eating with* FORLANO, CAPELLI, CAPP, BORELLI, PISCANO *and* GAGGI.

BORELLI: *Aspett'*.[1] Wait a minute. You mean to tell me that the money we're robbing is bein' robbed? That somebody's robbing from us? We go through all this fuckin' trouble, and somebody's robbin' us?

GAGGI: (*To* NANCE) Eh?

NANCE: Like I said, you know, i-it's part of the business. I-it's considered leakage.

CAPELLI: Leakage, my balls. I want the guy who's robbin' us.

INT. TANGIERS HARD COUNT ROOM – DAY

NANCE *enters through a door and walks past a man picking up a bucket of coins and dumping them into the trough. A clerk, seated at a coin weighing scale, places a ticket into a small tray.* NANCE *reads the printout of the machine.*

NICKY: (*Voice-over*) Even John Nance, that's the guy who ran the skim, he knew there wasn't much you could do about it. You gotta know that a guy who helps you steal, even if you take care of him real well, I mean, he's gonna steal a little bit extra for himself. Makes sense, don't it? Right? Well, you go try and make these hard-headed old greaseballs understand that.

1 Italian-American slang for 'Wait.'

INT. SAN MARINO ITALIAN GROCERY/BACK ROOM, KANSAS
CITY – DAY

BORELLI: What's the point of skimming if we're being
    skimmed? Defeats the whole purpose of what we're doin'
    out there.
GAGGI: (*To* NANCE) Huh?
NANCE: You know, they take this money because they're my
    guys. So you gotta give 'em some leeway.

NICKY: (*Voice-over*) But the bosses never believed in leeway, so
    listen to what they do: they . . .


INT. SAN MARINO ITALIAN GROCERY/BACK ROOM, KANSAS
CITY – DAY, LATER

BORELLI *is talking to* PISCANO, *his underboss.*

NICKY: (*Voice-over*) . . . put Artie Piscano, the underboss of
    KC, in charge of making sure nobody skimmed the skim.

BORELLI: What the hell you been doin' out there?
PISCANO: I was out there with my *cummà*.[1]
BORELLI: Your *cummà*? What are doin' with your *cummà*?
PISCANO: What else? I gave her a *schaff*.[2]

NICKY: (*Voice-over*) The only trouble was, Piscano was a
    disaster. This guy could fuck up a cup of coffee.

BORELLI: Artie, what the hell have you been doin' out there,
    Artie?
PISCANO: I'm out there more than I'm here.

NICKY: (*Voice-over*) And little did anybody know where this
    would all lead. If they did, they would have been better off
    makin' fuckin' novenas.

BORELLI: You gotta go back there and talk to that guy.
PISCANO: Come on, go back there? I never got paid my
    expenses for the last trip.

[1] Italian-American slang for 'girlfriend'.
[2] Italian-American slang for 'tap'.

BORELLI: What expenses?

PISCANO: Well, I'm goin' all over, layin' money out of my own pocket, and I never get anything back. What the hell's goin' on?

BORELLI: You gotta go back out there.

PISCANO: Well, then, from now on, I'm gonna start keepin' records.

BORELLI: Artie, no records, Artie. What are you gonna do with records? Pay taxes?

PISCANO: Well, I keep layin' out my own fuckin' dough for these trips and nothin' ever comes back. I mean, what the hell's goin' on? What are we doin' over here?

BORELLI: You're goin' out to Las Vegas, you're havin' a good time at my expense. What the fuck? I mean, after all, you're the one having a good time, not me.

ACE: (*Voice-over*) No matter how many novenas you could make, nothin' . . .


INT. TANGIERS, GREEN'S OFFICE – DAY

GREEN *is arguing with* ANNA SCOTT, *a fifty-year-old no-nonsense businesswoman.*

ACE: (*Voice-over*) . . . was gonna stop what came up next at the casino.

GREEN: I can't believe you're doing this.
SCOTT: We made a deal. You came to me, remember?
GREEN: Yes, I appreciated your advice . . .

ACE: (*Voice-over*) It turned out Phil Green, Mr Integrity, had a partner nobody knew about . . . and when she showed up and started demanding some money from the Tangiers . . .

SCOTT: Why are you doing this to me?
GREEN: Because you're wrong.
SCOTT: I'm not wrong.
GREEN: Yes, you are.
SCOTT: No, I am not wrong.

112

ACE: (*Voice-over*) . . . Green tried to stonewall her.

SCOTT: And you're not going to get away with this! I will see to it that you do not get away with this! (*She walks out.*)

ACE: (*Voice-over*) So . . .


INT. COURT-ROOM – DAY

*A* JUDGE *is seated at his bench.* SCOTT *and* GREEN, *surrounded by their lawyers, take their seats.* NANCE *watches from the back row.*

ACE: (*Voice-over*) . . . she sued him in court.

JUDGE: The court will now hear the matter of the plaintiff, Anna Scott, against Tangiers Corporation and its president, Philip Green.
LAWYER #1: Good morning, your Honor. John Momot on behalf of Mr Green.
LAWYER #2: Mitchell Logan on behalf of Anna Scott, your Honor.
JUDGE: Mr Logan, you may proceed.
LAWYER #2: Thank you, Judge.
　　(*As the* JUDGE *pounds his gavel, we see* ANNA SCOTT *and a grim* GREEN.)


INT. COURT-HOUSE CORRIDOR – DAY

ANNA SCOTT *holds an impromptu press conference.*
SCOTT: I believe he was absolutely fair and I'm delighted with the decision.
　　(NANCE *it talking at a pay phone,* SCOTT *and the reporters are in the background.*)
NANCE: (*Into telephone*) We got a problem.


INT. ALL-AMERICAN GAS STATION, GAGGI'S BACK OFFICE, BACK HOME – DAY

CURLY *hands* GAGGI *the phone. He listens.*
NANCE: (*Over telephone*) It didn't go too well.

INT. COURT-HOUSE CORRIDOR – DAY

NANCE: (*As* GREEN *and his lawyers walk past him, exiting the court-house*) Green has to open up the books . . . has to show how he got the financing. And, hey, that's – that's not good.

INT. ALL-AMERICAN GAS STATION, GAGGI'S BACK OFFICE, BACK HOME – DAY

GAGGI, *holding a cigarette, snaps his fingers in disgust, grunts, and slams down the phone. His men watch in silence.*
GAGGI: Shit.
(CURLY *takes the phone away.*)

NICKY: (*Voice-over*) She was doin ' pretty good with her lawsuit, but before she could start countin' her money, the boys back home decided to settle the case out of court instead.

INT. ANNA SCOTT'S HOME, KITCHEN, LAS VEGAS – DAY

SCOTT, *alone, is sitting at her kitchen table.*

NICKY: (*Voice-over*) So, they sent me.

(NICKY *swiftly enters the room, grabs* SCOTT *around the neck, and fires three shots into her head.*
*He leans* SCOTT *back against the chair, then gently, while stroking her hair, sets her head to the side. Blood flows from her mouth on to her pink robe.* NICKY *grabs his gun and leaves.*
*Reporters are heard shouting 'Mr Green'.*)

EXT. LAS VEGAS PRIVATE AIRPORT – MORNING

GREEN *gets off the Tangiers corporate jet and is assaulted by questions about the Scott murder.* GREEN *is stunned.*
REPORTER #1: Can you comment on the murder of Anna Scott?
GREEN: What are you talking about?
REPORTER #1: (*Off-screen*) She was found last night, shot in the head.

REPORTER #2: (*Off-screen*) Was this just a real-estate
    partnership?
REPORTER #3: (*Off-screen*) Her lawyer said you were partners.
GREEN: We were – We were involved in minor real estate deals
    many years ago. It was never a partnership.
    (*Reporters chase* GREEN *as he walks down the ramp and across
    the tarmac to his white limousine.*)
REPORTER #1: Police are calling this a mob-style killing.
REPORTER #2: Did you ever hear of the twenty-two-caliber
    killer?
GREEN: I'm a little in shock, quite frankly . . .

ACE: (*Voice-over*) Now, instead of the cops only lookin' at
    Nicky, they started looking at Green too. And he was
    supposed to be our squeaky . . .


INT. ACE'S OFFICE – DAY

ACE *is being interviewed by a female* Business Week REPORTER.
SHERBERT *and* RONNIE *are sitting on a couch, listening to the
interview. The* REPORTER *is seated across from* ACE, *at his desk.*

ACE: (*Voice-over*) . . . clean front man. So, I had to start giving
    interviews to make sure everybody knew the casino was on
    the up and up.

REPORTER: So, actually, how often do you really fill in for him?
    (ACE *looks at* SHERBERT.)
SHERBERT: (*to* REPORTER, *who looks his way.*) Green's here
    about two or three times a month, and he's busy –
    (REPORTER *glances back at* ACE.)
    – with other real-estate deals and – and things, you know.
REPORTER: (*To* ACE) So, in Green's absence, then, you're the
    boss.
ACE: I serve at the pleasure of the chairman of the board and
    . . . my, uh, responsibilities are to run the day-to-day
    operations.
REPORTER: So, day-to-day, then, you're the boss?
ACE: Well, in a sense, you could say that . . . I am the boss,
    when Mr Green is away. You could say that.

INT. GAMING CONTROL BOARD OFFICE – DAY

*A magazine headline reads 'Sam Rothstein: "I'm the Boss!"'.*

WEBB: (*Off-screen*) Hm. Have you read this?

> (*The magazine shows a photograph of* ACE. *A caption reads:* '*Rothstein asserts authority at Tangiers Casino'.*)

WEBB: (*Off-screen*) Hm? It's 'bout Mr Rothstein.

> (*We see* WEBB *holding up a copy of* Business Week *in the gaming board office of investigators* RONNIE DUPREY *and* MATT AUSTIN.)
>
> It says (*reading*): 'The Midwest bookmaker with mob ties says that he is the real boss of the new hundred-million-dollar Tangiers Casino empire.' (*To* DUPREY *and* AUSTIN) You believe that?

DUPREY: Did he really say that?

WEBB: Why, of course, he really said that. It's right here. Has that man even filed for his license yet?

AUSTIN: I don't know. We'll have to check the files.

WEBB: Well, without gettin' your shorts in a knot, would you do that? And kinda check closely, 'cause we may have to kick a kike's ass out of town. Thank you. (*He exits.*)


INT. ACE'S HOUSE – NIGHT

ACE *is watching the television news which features his photo and a police photo of* NICKY.

NEWSCASTER: (*On television*) A Gaming Control Board investigation of Tangiers executive Sam Rothstein's application for a (*photo of* ACE) gaming license is underway. Rothstein, who heads the Tangiers Casino operation and is a boyhood friend of Las Vegas mob boss Nicky Santoro (*photo of* NICKY), could lose his ability to work in the casino.

> (*The phone rings. It's* NICKY.)

ACE: (*Into telephone*) Hello.

NICKY: (*Over telephone*) Listen . . .

EXT. STRIP MALL PUBLIC PHONE BOOTH – NIGHT

*We see* NICKY *through the telephone booth glass.*
NICKY: (*Into telephone*) . . . I gotta meet Clean Face right away.
What about the Chez Paree?
SUPER SUBTITLE: 'I gotta meet Charlie the Banker right away
at your house, okay?'
ACE: (*Into telephone*) No, you, you can't. You gotta make a
reservation.

INT. ACE'S HOUSE – NIGHT

ACE: (*Into telephone*) It's all booked up.
SUPER SUBTITLE: 'I don't want a meeting at my house.'
NICKY: (*Over telephone*) No, no, it's okay.
ACE: (*Into telephone*) It's impossible. It's booked up, and you
gotta make a reservation. It's . . .

EXT. STRIP MALL PUBLIC PHONE BOOTH – NIGHT

ACE: (*Into telephone*) . . . very difficult to get in.
NICKY: (*Into telephone*) Well, it's okay. I'll use the service
entrance. I'll see you at nine.
SUPER SUBTITLE: 'I'll come in from the golf course side. See
you at six.'
ACE: (*Over telephone*) Uh . . .

INT. ACE'S HOUSE – NIGHT

ACE: (*Over telephone*) . . . all right. (*He hangs up and takes a drag
off his cigarette.*)
NEWSCASTER: (*On television, from following scene*) The battle
between . . .

INT. ACE'S HOUSE, UPSTAIRS DEN – DAY

ACE *and the banker,* CHARLIE CLARK, *are upstairs in the den,
which has a patio overlooking a swimming pool and golf course.*
CHARLIE *is seated on a couch watching TV.* GINGER *enters and*

*walks across the room, getting another drink from the bar.* ACE, *taking his ulcer medicine, watches her.*

NEWSCASTER: (*On television*) . . . state gaming officials and Tangiers Casino boss Sam 'Ace' Rothstein is heating up. Tonight, an up-to-the-minute look at Ace Rothstein's attempt to get state licensing despite law enforcement allegations of Rothstein's organized crime connections. Will Sam Rothstein's friendship with alleged organized crime figure Nicky Santoro keep Rothstein from running the Tangiers Casino? And can the integrity of state gaming laws be jeopardized by a boyhood friendship?

(ACE *walks over to* GINGER *at the bar.*)

ACE: (*Quietly*) Why don't you take it easy with that stuff? Huh? Come on. Let me help you. Come on. We're talkin' about some stuff.

NEWSCASTER: (*On television*) State officials say 'yes' when that relationship and those connections are with anyone as notorious as Nicky Santoro.

(ACE *takes* GINGER's *arm and leads her out of the room toward the stairs.*)

Tonight at six: 'Will a boyhood friendship unseat Rothstein as the Tangiers' Casino boss?' Exclusive on the KVVO Special News Report. (*Reading commercial.*) . . . Promise to keep my money fears away?

ACE: (*To* GINGER) Just go downstairs. Just . . . go downst– (*She struggles to break away from his firm grip, gives him a look and starts to walk down the stairs.*)

NEWSCASTER: (*On television, continuing commercial*) Promise to be financially secure? Money Time can help you keep those promises.

(ACE *looks down on* GINGER *as she slips on the stairs.*)

CHARLIE CLARK: You can't let this concern you, Ace. Don't worry about that stuff.

(*Outside the glass door* NICKY *arrives via the stairs from the golf course.*)

(*Off-screen*) It's just a political witch hunt.

(ACE *opens the sliding glass door and* NICKY *enters.*)

NICKY: Hey, Ace.

ACE: Hey.

(NICKY *walks over to* CHARLIE CLARK.)

Want something to drink? Charlie, you want a refill?

CHARLIE CLARK: Yeah, refill'd be great.

NICKY: (*Approaching* CHARLIE) No, I don't want one. (*Smiling, extends his hand.*) Hey, Mr Clark, how you doin'?

CHARLIE CLARK: (*Shaking hands*) Hi. Good.

NICKY: (*Sitting down with him on a couch*) I've been trying to reach you. You're tougher to get than the President.

CHARLIE CLARK: Well, I've been busy. (*Chuckles.*)

NICKY: Yeah, least you could do is return my phone calls, though.

CHARLIE CLARK: Listen . . . Nicky . . . we talked about this . . . and, uh, I explained to you that there was the possibility you might have to take some kind of loss.

NICKY: Yeah. (*Pause.*) I think I want my money back.

CHARLIE CLARK: (*Chuckling*) What're you gonna do? Strong-arm me?

NICKY: You know . . . I think that you've gotten the wrong impression about me. I think in all fairness, I should explain to you exactly what it is that I do. For instance, tomorrow morning I'll get up nice and early, take a walk down over to the bank and walk in and see you, and, uh . . . if you don't have my money for me, I'll crack your fuckin' head wide open in front of everybody in the bank. And just about the time that I'm comin' out of jail – hopefully – you'll be comin' out of your coma. And guess what? I'll split your fuckin' head open again. Because I'm fuckin' stupid. I don't give a fuck about jail. That's my business. That's what I do. And we know what you do, don't we, Charlie? You fuck people out of money and get away with it.

CHARLIE CLARK: (*As he puts a notepad in his briefcase*) You can't talk to me like –

NICKY: (*Grabbing* CHARLIE *by his jacket*) Hey, you fat Irish prick. You put my fuckin' money to sleep. You go get my money, or I'll put your fuckin' brain to sleep.

CHARLIE CLARK: (*To* ACE, *panting*) Sam?

NICKY: Never mind fuckin' Sam. This is personal. (*Walking with* CHARLIE *to the stairs.*) I'll be there in the morning. You can fuckin' try me, fatso.

(*A frightened* CHARLIE *hurries down the stairs.*)

You fuckin' try me.

(*He turns to* ACE *who's behind the bar.*)

You think he got the point?

ACE: (*Walking to* NICKY) What're you doin'? He's a square guy, for chrissakes. You can't treat him like that. He's gonna run to the FBI.

NICKY: Fuck the FBI! That prick's been dodging me for three weeks. And what is it with you? All of a sudden, you're tryin' to tell me what to do all the time.

ACE: I'm not tryin' to tell you what to do. But you were way out of line, Nick. What're you doin'? Where's your head?

NICKY: Where's my head? Where's your fuckin' balls? Huh? You know I'm tryin' to put somethin' really big together out here. You know what I'm talkin' about, huh? You know! If you're actin' like this now, how can I depend on you? There's a lot of things gonna change out here. And if you wanna be there with me, Sammy, you're gonna have to go my fuckin' way.

ACE: Listen, Nick, you gotta understand my situation. I'm responsible for thousands of people. I got a hundred million a year goin' through the place. It's all over, I'm gonna tell you, it's all over, if I don't get that license. And believe me, if it goes bad for me, it's gonna go bad for a lot of people, you understand?

NICKY: Yeah, forget about your fuckin' license. I plant my own flag out here, you ain't gonna need a fuckin' license. (*Pause.*) You know, I don't know what it is, Sammy, but the more I talk to you, the more I feel like you just don't wanna go along with me, is that it?

ACE: No, I don't wanna come –

NICKY: You should say so.

ACE: I don't wanna come along with you.

NICKY: Just say so.

ACE: I'll be honest with you.

NICKY: All right, fine.

ACE: I don't wanna be involved in anything you're talkin' about . . .

NICKY: Fine. (NICKY *walks to a table and flips through* Business Week *magazine.*)

ACE: . . . okay? I just wanna run a square joint. That's it. I just want my license. I want everything nice and quiet. That's it.

NICKY: (*Holding up the magazine*) You mean, quiet like this: 'I'm the boss.' That's quiet?

ACE: That's all taken out of context.

NICKY: Yeah, that's out of context. Okay.

ACE: I have no control over that. Ronnie and Billy were right there. They'll tell you exactly what happened.

NICKY: Well, back home they don't know about fuckin' control. That looks bad.

ACE: Looks bad? I'm gonna tell you what looks bad.

NICKY: Yeah?

ACE: Every time you're on television I get mentioned. That looks bad. *That* looks bad.

NICKY: What the fuck happened to you? Will you tell me?

ACE: What happened to me? What happened to you?

NICKY: Yeah.

ACE: You lost your control.

NICKY: I lost control?

ACE: Yes, you lost your control.

NICKY: Look at you. You're fuckin' walkin' around like John Barrymore.

ACE: All right.

NICKY: A fuckin' pink robe and a fuckin' . . .

ACE: All right.

NICKY: . . . uh, uh, cigarette holder. I'm – *I* lost control?!

ACE: Yeah.

NICKY: You know, I didn't want to bring this up, but you been treating a lot of people with a lot of disrespect. Even your own wife.

ACE: My wife?

NICKY: Yeah.

ACE: Now, what does she have to do with all this?

NICKY: Well, she came to see me. She was upset about a lot of things, especially that whole fuckin' Diamond – that Lester Diamond incident.

ACE: All of a sudden, you're the shoulder to cry on? Did you at least tell her about your little role in that whole situation?

NICKY: No, I didn't. What good would that do? That's not the fuckin' point.

ACE: Listen, I would –

NICKY: (*Interrupting*) The point is that she's upset. She's – and you got a fuckin' problem.

ACE: I – I would appreciate it if you'd stay out of my personal life, okay? You wouldn't like it if I did it to you.

NICKY: Hey, she came to talk . . .

ACE: Please . . .

NICKY: . . . to me.

ACE: . . . don't do it to me.

NICKY: She came to talk to me . . .

ACE: Okay?

NICKY: And I – what was I supposed to do, throw her out?

ACE: Ju-just stay away from her. It's none of your business, okay? There are certain things you don't do, and you know that.

NICKY: It's none of my business?

ACE: That's right, yeah.

NICKY: A week ago it was my business, now it's none of my business. In other words, when you need me to take care of somethin' for you, then you need me.

ACE: Yeah, that's right, the way you need me to vouch for you as a citizen and get you out of one of your jams. I'm gonna have to straighten out what you just did with this guy.
(NICKY *starts to walk out.*)
This guy is gonna run to the FBI.

NICKY: Your fuckin head is gettin' bigger than your casino. That's your problem, pal.

ACE: (*Voice-over*) I knew what he wanted, and I didn't want any part of it.

NICKY: (*Walking to the glass doors leaving* ACE *standing there*) Fuckin' walking around with a big head. You better check yourself . . .

ACE: (*Voice-over*) Nicky wanted to take over. He wanted to go after Gaggi, go after the skim, go after everything and everybody.

122

(NICKY *shuts the door behind him and walks down the stairs to the golf course.*)
Plus, he had stopped askin' permission from back home for every little thing.

EXT. VEGAS STREET – NIGHT

*Quick zoom out from a dead body with a gunshot wound in the chest. Cops and press are milling around.*

EXT. VEGAS HOUSE – DAY

*Camera spirals out from the bodies of a casino executive and his wife who have been gunned down on their front lawn.*

ACE: (*Voice-over*) A casino boss and his wife were killed. The bulls questioned Nicky.

EXT. PARKING LOT – NIGHT

*Police photographers taking pictures of a dealer, dead behind the wheel of his car, his eyes and mouth frozen wide open in a silent scream.*

ACE: (*Voice-over*) A dealer from the Sirocco . . . they questioned Nicky.

INT. UNDERGROUND GARAGE – DAY

*Two policemen open the trunk of a car and find a trussed-up dead body. They cover their noses because of the stench.*

ACE: (*Voice-over*) A bunch of stool pigeons wound up in the trunks of their cars . . . they questioned Nicky.

EXT. LAWYER'S HOUSE – NIGHT

*We see a brand-new car explode.*

ACE: (*Voice-over*) A lawyer . . . they questioned Nicky.

EXT. HOUSE DOORWAY – DAY

*A front door where a pile of newspapers have accumulated. Another newspaper is thrown at the door.*

ACE: (*Voice-over*) And when some guys who didn't pay their Shylocks began disappearing, Nicky's name was in every one of those newspapers.


EXT. STREET OUTSIDE COURT-HOUSE – DAY

NICKY *and* OSCAR GOODMAN, *his lawyer, leave the court-house, surrounded by reporters and photographers. They wait at the curb for the light and* NICKY, *smiling, politely cautions a photographer to be careful of the on-coming traffic.*

ACE: (*Voice-over*) Nicky was questioned in two dozen murders, but they always had to let him go. There were never any witnesses.

NICKY: (*Voice-over*) The coppers blamed me for everything that went wrong out here, and I mean every little fuckin' thing too.

NICKY: (*To photographer*) Watch yourself. You're gonna get runned over there.

NICKY: (*Voice-over*) If a guy fuckin' tripped over a fuckin' banana peel, they'd bring me in for it.

NICKY: (*To reporters*) Come on, huh. That's enough now. Be nice, huh? Be nice.


INT. ALL-AMERICAN GAS STATION, GAGGI'S BACK OFFICE, BACK HOME – DAY

MARINO *walks through a doorway to* GAGGI's *office.* CURLY *pats him on the back. He shakes* BEEPER's *hand, then* FORLANO's, *who is on the phone.*

NICKY: (*Voice-over*) And the bosses were no better. I mean, they complained day and night because things don't run smooth. Well, in my line of work, things don't run so

124

smooth, I'm sorry. I mean, I'm dealing with degenerate animals out here. But the bosses, what do they give a fuck? They're sittin' on their asses, drinkin' anisette. Meanwhile, I'm the guy in the trenches. Fuckin' bosses, they think it's a fuckin' free lunch out here.

(MARINO *hands a brown-paper bag filled with $100 bills to* GAGGI.)

GAGGI: (*Ignoring the money*) Frankie . . . they found a guy's head in the desert. Do you know about that?

MARINO: Yeah, I heard, yeah.

GAGGI: Yeah. Everybody's talkin' about it. They're makin' a big deal out of it.

MARINO: I know.

GAGGI: It's in all the papers.

MARINO: What're you gonna do?

GAGGI: And I mean . . . that's no good.

MARINO: I know.

GAGGI: You gotta tell him . . . to take care of things a little better.

MARINO: I'll tell him, Remo.

NICKY: (*Voice-over*) Fuckin' . . .


EXT. VEGAS STRIP BUS STOP BENCH – DAY

NICKY *is talking quietly to* MARINO. *They are surrounded by people waiting for the bus.*

NICKY: (*Voice-over*) . . . bosses. I mean, they're smokin' their Di Nobilis and they're eatin' *a trippa*[1] and fuckin' *suffritt'*, you know, fried pigs guts? While, if I wanna talk private, I gotta go to a fuckin' bus stop.

NICKY: (*To* MARINO) But, hey, what do they care, as long as I keep sendin' money back.

MARINO: Yeah, but they're complaining.

NICKY: Let 'em complain. I'm the one who's here.
(*The bus arrives, obscuring our view of them.*)

1 Italian-American slang for 'tripe'.

I do all the work. Somebody don't like it, fuck him.

MARINO: It's up to you.

NICKY: They want a fuckin' war, I'm ready.

(*When the bus departs it reveals* NICKY *and* MARINO *alone on the bench, talking.*)

I know one thing. All I gotta do is take care of four or five of those fuckin' guys, the rest will fall right into place. Believe me.


INT. GOLD RUSH – DAY

NICKY *is watching a police surveillance car with two agents through binoculars.*

NICKY: (*Voice-over*) Peekaboo, you fucks, you.

NICKY: I see you, you motherfuckers.

ACE: (*Voice-over*) The problem was, Nicky was not only bringin' heat on himself, but on me too. The FBI watched every move he made. But he didn't care. He just didn't care.
(*The camera moves past* NICKY *to reveal* MARINO, *seated in front of TV security monitors of the parking area in front and behind the Gold Rush.*)

NICKY: (*Voice-over*) If they're gonna watch me, fuck 'em, I'm gonna watch 'em right back. I spent a few dollars. Top dollar, who gives a shit?
(HARDY, *seated next to* MARINO, *is adjusting a knob on one of many police radio scanners. There are a couple of cameras on the table next to him.*

*A debugging expert is going over the walls with a metal detector.*)
I got the latest anti-buggin' equipment from the same places that sell to the fuckin' CIA. I had all the special police frequency radios, FBI descramblers, cameras that see in the dark, and because of that, the miserable sons-of-bitches that they are, they never once caught me doin' anything I couldn't handle.

(DOMINICK *and* FUSCO *are at a table arguing.*)

ACE: (*Voice-over*) I got my job . . .

EXT. GOLF COURSE – DAY

NICKY *swings a golf club.* MARINO, *and two men, are with him.*

ACE: (*Voice-over*) . . . on the line and this guy's out havin' the
time of his life. He has every cop in the state watchin' him,
and he's out playin' golf.

NICKY: Practice enough this week, you prick?

ACE: (*Voice-over*) And at the . . .


EXT. ACE'S PATIO – DAY

ACE *is with the Control Board investigators* AUSTIN *and*
DUPREY. *They are all pouring over legal files and record books out
on a table by the swimming pool.*

ACE: (*Voice-over*) . . . worst possible time for me.

AUSTIN: A record of the arrests . . .

ACE: (*Voice-over*) I had my license hearing coming up and I
didn't wanna leave anything to chance.

ACE: That was nineteen years ago, and they were simple
gambling pinches.

ACE: (*Voice-over*) I mean, if I can't work in Vegas, where am I
gonna go?

AUSTIN: You've been very open with us. I mean, uh, your
books and papers and . . . that – that's gonna mean
something when you go before the Commission.

ACE: Well, that's all I ask, gentlemen, a fair hearing.

DUPREY: Well, this kind of honesty will guarantee that fair
hearing.

ACE: Good.

AUSTIN: All right, well, we'll move on to –
(*Suddenly a sputtering airplane flies right over Ace's house.*)
(*Off-screen, as he looks at the plane*) I wanted to hear
something about . . . Kansas City.

EXT. GOLF COURSE — DAY

NICKY: (*Looking at the airplane*) What the fuck is this? Where's this fuckin' guy gonna land, on the fairway?


EXT. ACE'S PATIO — DAY

ACE *and the board investigators follow the plane as it lands on the fairway.* ACE *has taken off his sunglasses to get a better look. Two men in suits get out.*


EXT. GOLF COURSE — DAY

NICKY: (*To* MARINO) They're fuckin' agents, Frankie. Look at this.


EXT. ACE'S PATIO — DAY

*The* AGENTS *run across the golf course, past* ACE *and the investigators, who look on open-mouthed.*

ACE: (*Voice-over*) The Feds were watchin' Nicky play golf for so long, they ran out of gas. Just what I needed. Right in front of the Control Board.
(*The agents run behind the hedges by* ACE's *pool.* AUSTIN *and* DUPREY *stare at* ACE *as if he has something to do with it.*)


EXT. GOLF COURSE — DAY
NICKY: A hundred dollars, whoever hits the plane.
(NICKY, MARINO, *and the other men swing their clubs.*)


EXT. ACE'S PATIO — DAY

ACE: (*Voice-over, putting his sunglasses back on*) And, as if things weren't bad enough . . .


EXT. SAN MARINO ITALIAN GROCERY, KANSAS CITY — DAY

ACE: (*Voice-over*) . . . in comes Piscano, the Kansas City

underboss. He ran that little grocery store in Kansas City
where they brought the suitcases.

INT. SAN MARINO GROCERY, KANSAS CITY – DAY

PISCANO *and his* MOTHER *are at the counter of his elderly*
BROTHER-IN-LAW'*s store.*

PISCANO: They're fightin' over those suitcases again. You know
what that means, right? You know what that means, right?
That means I gotta take another trip out to Vegas, and it's
gonna cost me another couple of grand.

ACE: (*Voice-over*) He ran it with his brother-in-law, but mostly
what he did was complain, complain about his trips to
Vegas, to his brother-in-law and to his mother, all the time.

BROTHER-IN-LAW: (*Seated*) You gotta lay down the law.
Otherwise, they're gonna make a fool out of you.

PISCANO: They're not gonna make a fool out of me. I write it all
down in this book (*holding up a notepad*), every fuckin'
nickel that goes down. Right here, receipts . . .

PISCANO'S MOTHER: (*Chastising her son*) Hey! Oh!

PISCANO: Oh, sorry –

PISCANO'S MOTHER: What's the matter with you?

PISCANO: Receipts and bills and . . . everything's here.

PISCANO'S MOTHER: Since when do you talk like that?

PISCANO: I'm sorry.

PISCANO'S MOTHER: There's a lot of people here.

PISCANO: Nance gives me trouble and I'll tell him . . . screw
around with those suitcases and I'll take the eyes out of his
frickin' head.

PISCANO'S MOTHER: Again!

PISCANO: I didn't curse. I said 'frickin' head'.

PISCANO'S MOTHER: That's enough.

PISCANO: I'm sorry.

ACE: (*Voice-over*) And what happens next?
(*The camera tilts up to the ceiling air vent to a tiny microphone
and transmitter at its base.*)
You can't believe it. I mean, who the hell would believe

129

that the FBI had a wire in the place lookin' for some information about some old homicide about some guy who was whacked-out, God knows when, over God knows what?

PISCANO: Plus, what's to prevent him with the suitcases, that he can take what he wants? Fuckin' Nance, he brings us back two suitcases from the Tangiers, and what about three or four?

INT. POST OFFICE ACROSS THE STREET, KANSAS CITY – DAY

*A pen writes* 'NANCE' *on a piece of paper.*

INT. SAN MARINO ITALIAN GROCERY, KANSAS CITY – DAY

PISCANO: We got nobody in the room to watch. That's the law. You know, we can't even go into the count room to watch our money? Could you believe this cowboy bullshit?
(*His* MOTHER *shakes her head.*)
And sure he's got his people in there. But how do you know? They could all be in on it together, those miserable fucks.
(*His* MOTHER *reacts to his language.*)
I'll find out and, if it's Green himself, I'll bury that bastard.

INT. POST OFFICE ACROSS THE STREET, KANSAS CITY – DAY

*A pen writes the word* 'GREEN'.

PISCANO: (*Over transmitter*) I've never trusted him. And you know I got eyes . . .

INT. SAN MARINO ITALIAN GROCERY, KANSAS CITY – DAY

PISCANO: . . . behind my head. They trust that scumbag, I don't. Right now, the way I feel, I'll hit the two of them in the head with a fuckin' shovel.
PISCANO'S MOTHER: All right, take it easy now, take it easy.

PISCANO: Mom, I'm sorry, they're beatin' me left and right. (*Knocking down some bottles of olive oil.*) Ma, I'm sorry. I'm all upset.

PISCANO'S MOTHER: (*Tapping the counter*) I know, but that's enough.

PISCANO: You know – You know – You know what they're doin' to me?

PISCANO'S MOTHER: I know it, I know it.

PISCANO: I can't take this no more. Back and forth, back and forth.

PISCANO'S MOTHER: Take it easy, though.

PISCANO: All right, all right. But I – I –

PISCANO'S MOTHER: You'll get a heart attack like that.

PISCANO: You know, I – I'm too upset right now. And – An end has to be put to this.

ACE: (*Voice-over*) And the damn . . .
(*Camera pans off the listening device in the vent to a window and the post office across the street.*)
. . . thing is, they go and hear all this stuff about Las Vegas and the casinos and the suitcases, and that's it.

PISCANO: (*Off-screen*) If I have to start handlin' things the way I . . .

INT. POST OFFICE SMALL ROOM, KANSAS CITY – DAY

*Behind a window overlooking the grocery store are two FBI agents listening to Piscano's conversation.*

PISCANO: (*Over transmitter*) . . . did years ago, start kickin' ass, I – I'll do it, and I'll use the goddamn shovel! I mean, I . . .
(*We see an agent looking out of the window with a pair of binoculars.*)

PISCANO'S MOTHER: (*Over transmitter*) You are right.
(*The other agent, with headphones, is seated at a desk by a tape recorder, writing.*)

PISCANO: (*Over transmitter*) . . . everything's comin' out of my pocket. I gotta pay for all these trips back and forth, back and forth.

PISCANO'S MOTHER: (*Over transmitter*) You are right. What can I . . .


INT. WASHINGTON FBI OFFICE – DAY

PISCANO'S MOTHER: (*On tape recorder*) . . . tell you.

TITLE IN: 'WASHINGTON, D.C.'

(*The camera tilts down an American flag to reveal the tape now being transcribed by an FBI stenographer.*)

ACE: (*Voice-over*) Would you believe that such a thing could happen?

PISCANO: (*On tape recorder*) I'm in this to make money, not to lose money. And I – I –

ACE: (*Voice-over*) Every FBI man across the country had their ears open now.

PISCANO: (*On tape recorder*) Because . . .
(*The stenographer's pen writes:* 'BORELLI' *on a piece of paper.*)
. . . if you want somethin' . . .
(*Stenographer writes:* 'TANGIERS'.)
. . . done right, you gotta do it yourself.

PISCANO'S MOTHER: (*On tape recorder*) Then do it the way you want.
(*Pen writes:* 'VEGAS'.)
What can I tell you?

ACE: (*Voice-over*) I mean . . .
(*Pen writes:* 'SANTORO'.)
. . . Piscano, this guy basically . . .
(*The stenographer's pen taps twice on the word* 'SANTORO'.)
. . . sunk the whole world.

(*Focus on stenographer, listening.*)

PISCANO'S MOTHER: (*On tape recorder*) That's the way people are. There are some that are good and some that are bad.

INT. GAMING CONTROL BOARD HEARING ROOM, LAS VEGAS
1980 – DAY

ACE *is in court with* OSCAR GOODMAN, *his lawyer, facing the
Control Board's Chairman and six* COMMISSIONER MEMBERS.
*The Chairman is the* SENATOR *we saw earlier in the casino suite
taking chips out of the bureau drawer. The room is jam-packed:*
GREEN, GINGER, SHERBERT, *as well as* WEBB, *reporters and other
spectators.* ACE's *secretaries carry in legal papers. There are piles of
briefs and law books on* OSCAR's *and* ACE's *table.*)

OSCAR: Mr Chairman and members of the Commission. Mr
    Rothstein is pleased to be here today.

ACE: (*Voice-over*) And when the day finally came, I was ready. I
    felt so confident that all I had to do was present my case.

OSCAR: . . . evidence . . . and we have documents, one of which
    is a report by retired FBI agents, which completely
    absolves (*holding up a large file folder*) Mr Rothstein from
    any wrongdoing. I'd like this marked, please, Mr
    Chairman.

SENATOR: (*Into microphone*) Pardon me, counselor. Before you
    continue . . .

OSCAR: No, I want to have this marked, Mr –

SENATOR: (*Into microphone*) . . . this, uh, this Commission is
    prepared to act on a motion denying the Rothstein
    application.

OSCAR: Denying?

SENATOR: (*Into microphone*) Do I hear a motion seconded?

OSCAR: Mr Chairman –

CONTROL BOARD MEMBER #1: (*Into microphone*) Mr Chairman,
    I second the motion.

SENATOR: (*Into microphone*) Do I have a vote on the motion?

OSCAR: Mr Chairman –
    (*The* COMMISSIONERS *quickly repeat:*)

CONTROL BOARD MEMBER #2: (*Into microphone*) Aye.

CONTROL BOARD MEMBER #3: (*Into microphone*) Aye.

CONTROL BOARD MEMBER #4: (*Into microphone*) Aye.

SENATOR: (*Into microphone*) The ayes have it. This hearing is
    adjourned.

(*The* CHAIRMAN *bangs his gavel and prepares to leave. The*
COMMISSIONERS *hurriedly pack up their papers. An enraged*
ACE *rises and approaches the* SENATOR.
    *TV cameras roll.*)

ACE: (*Getting up*) You guys have to be kidding.
    (*The* SENATOR *picks up his briefcase.*)
    Adjourned! What do you mean, adjourned?

OSCAR: Mr Chairman, please.

ACE: Mr Chairman . . .
    (*The* SENATOR *picks up his folder.*)
    Senator, you promised me a hearing.
    (*We see* WEBB *seated in the first row, watching.*)
    You won't allow me a hearing? You didn't even look at the
    FBI reports.
    (*A reporter holds a microphone up to the* SENATOR.)
    When you were my guest, Mr Chairman, Senator, at the
    Tangiers Hotel, did you not promise me that I would have
    a fair hearing –
    (*The* SENATOR *bends down to a microphone.*)

SENATOR: (*Interrupting, into microphone*) I was never – I was
    never your guest at the Tangiers.

ACE: You were never my guest?!

SENATOR: (*Into microphone*) That's right.

ACE: I never comped you?! I don't comp you at least two or three times a month at the Tangiers?!

SENATOR: (*Into microphone*) Uh, I – I'd . . . I'd like to answer – answer that at this time.

ACE: Liar.

SENATOR: (*Into microphone*) Mr Rothstein is being very typical to this point. He's lying.

(WEBB *starts to leave.*)

The only time I was at the Tangiers was when I had dinner with Barney Greenstein.

ACE: Was I at that dinner? Just tell me –

SENATOR: You were wandering around.

ACE: Was I at the dinner?

SENATOR: You were wandering around.

ACE: Was I at that dinner?

SENATOR: You were wandering around.

ACE: Was I at that dinner?

SENATOR: You were in the m– You were in the building.

ACE: I was in the building!

(GREEN, *embarrassed by* ACE's *behaviour, starts to get up.*)

You know damn well I was at that dinner, and you swore to me that I would have a fair hearing at that dinner! Did you not?! Did you not?!

(*Pause,* ACE *looks at* OSCAR.)

Well, tell me I was at least at the dinner! A-allow me that much.

(*Pause.*) Give me that much at least!

SENATOR: (*Hesitates*) Yes, you were. (*The* SENATOR *starts to walk out.*)

ACE: Yeah, thanks for not callin' me a liar. You son-of-a-bitch. You son-of-a –

FEMALE NEWSCASTER: (*Voice-over*) Good evening, everyone, I'm Paige Novodor. (*On television.*) What should have been a routine licensing hearing turned into bedlam yesterday when the flamboyant Tangiers Casino executive, Sam . . .

(ACE *spots* COMMISSIONER CARTER *slipping out the door.*)

(*Voice-over, overlapping*) . . . 'Ace' Rothstein, accused the state's top gaming officials of corruption . . .

ACE: (*Overlapping*) What are you running for, Bob? What are you running for?

FEMALE NEWSCASTER: (*Voice-over, overlapping*) . . . and hypocrisy.

ACE: (*Into two reporters' microphones*) Don't you remember? You promised me a fair hearing when you were gettin' comped at my hotel and you were asking me for copies of your bills so –
(SHERBERT *and* GINGER *look on.*)
– you could put 'em on your expense account?

FEMALE NEWSCASTER: (*Voice-over*) In a (*on television*) wild and unprecedented outburst that followed his gaming license (*voice-over, overlapping*) denial, Rothstein followed several . . .

ACE: (*With several reporters, overlapping*) Bullshit! Bullshit!


INT. CONTROL BOARD LOBBY – DAY

*Putting on his sunglasses,* ACE *emerges from the courtroom with* SHERBERT, GINGER, OSCAR *and several reporters. He is surrounded by the press.*

FEMALE NEWSCASTER: (*Voice-over*) . . . stunned commissioners into the hallway, where he continued his harangue until his own lawyers and friends urged him to leave.

ACE: (*To* COMMISSIONERS *standing in the hallway, speaking into a TV news microphone*) We all have a past. You have a past, I have a past. And my past is no worse than yours. But you guys think you have the right to pass judgement on me.

FEMALE NEWSCASTER: (*Voice-over, overlapping*) Long suspected of running the Tangiers without . . .

ACE: (*Overlapping*) . . . twenty years in order to find nothin' on me –
(OSCAR *pulls him away,* ACE *looks back at the* COMMISSIONERS.)

– unsubstantiated truths on me. And if you look at your
own lives you'd all be in jail.
(OSCAR *ushers* ACE *out, past* WEBB *and Gaming Investigator*
AUSTIN.)

FEMALE NEWSCASTER: (*Voice-over, overlapping*) . . . a gaming
license, yesterday's hearing was to determine whether
someone with Rothstein's checkered personal history was
qualified to officially hold the top gaming post.


INT./EXT. GAGGI'S CAR, BACK HOME ALLEY – DAY

GAGGI *hands* STONE *an issue of the* Las Vegas Sun *showing a
photograph of* ACE *at the licensing hearing. Headline reads:
'Rothstein out of gaming: Control Board Rules against Rothstein
License Application'.*

ACE: (*Voice-over, from previous scene continued*) Fuckin'
hypocrites!

(STONE *stands beside* GAGGI's *car door.* GAGGI *is in the back
seat with his window down.*)
GAGGI: What the hell's he gonna do now?
STONE: I don't know. (*Sighs.*)
GAGGI: What's he doin'? He knows all those guys he yelled at
are friends of ours. What's the matter with him, making all
this mess?
STONE: Maybe he could run things with another job title.
Wouldn't be the best, but, uh, what are we gonna do?
GAGGI: However he runs things, it's gotta be quiet. Let him
hide upstairs in the office. Say he's the janitor, I don't give
a shit. But, please, whatever job he takes, make sure it's
something quiet.
(STONE *walks back to his car. Both cars pull out in opposite
directions.*)


INT. TANGIERS SPORTSBOOK/*ACES HIGH!* THE SAM ROTHSTEIN
SHOW – NIGHT

*A video monitor shows a title card, reading: 'From the Tangiers*

*Hotel'.* TRUDY, *Ace's showgirl sidekick, is heard over the opening credit sequence of the show.*

TRUDY: (*Off-screen*) Ladies and gentlemen, the Tangiers Hotel proudly presents the all-new Sam Rothstein Show, *Aces High*.

    TITLE CARD: 'ACES HIGH'

    (*The monitor shows a neon sign reading, 'Welcome to Fabulous Las Vegas, Nevada', then shows several gamblers at a craps table.*)

TRUDY: (*Off-screen*) Tonight, taped live from the all-new sportsbook, we present the première showing of *Aces High*. With the . . .

    (*The video monitor shows a neon sign: 'Stardust', then another: 'Tangiers'.*

    *We see* TRUDY *on a stage.*)

    (*Into microphone*) . . . Sasha Semenoff Orchestra . . .

    (*The camera pans to Sasha Semenoff conducting his band.*)

    . . . and the Sam Rothstein Dancers.

    (*The camera pans to a group of dancers on the other side of the stage.*

    *We see* ACE *greeting various guests in the audience as he moves towards the stage.*)

Mr Rothstein is a professional gambler and the best football handicapper . . .

    (*A video monitor shows a montage featuring showgirls, a chef carving beef and three women wearing bathing suits.*)

    . . . in America, a man who will take you inside the real Las Vegas as no one has ever done before. And now, ladies and gentlemen, the new . . .

    (ACE *joins* TRUDY *on the stage.*)

    . . . Entertainment Director of the Tangiers Hotel Casino: Mr Sam Rothstein.

    (ACE *approaches his desk as* TRUDY *sits on a long sofa. The audience applauds. The band plays and the dancers complete their number.*)

ACE: (*Seated at a desk à la Johnny Carson*) Welcome to the *Sam Rothstein Show*. We're very happy to have you here this evening. The young lady to my left is Trudy, who is a

lead new dancer in our fabulous show from Paris.
(*Audience applauds, she waves hello.*)
Our first guest this evening . . . is Frankie Avalon.
(FRANKIE AVALON *walks to the stage, embracing* TRUDY *and shaking* ACE's *hand. Audience applauds.*

    WEBB *stands in the rear of the sportsbook/theater with* AUSTIN *and* DUPREY, *watching* ACE.)
WEBB: Keep an eye on him. (*He exits.*)
FRANKIE AVALON: (*Off-screen*) . . . Well, I've got a large family.
ACE: (*Into microphone*) How many kids do you have?
FRANKIE AVALON: (*Into microphone*) Uh, I'm very proud to say that we have eight children.
ACE: (*Into microphone*) Eight children! (*He encourages the audience to applaud.*)
FRANKIE AVALON: (*Into microphone*) No, no, no, no, please, please, please, please, no, please.
ACE: (*Into microphone, to audience*) That's amazing.
FRANKIE AVALON: (*Into microphone*) There was nothing to it. (*Chuckles.*) It was my pleasure.


INT. TANGIERS, GREEN'S OFFICE – NIGHT

GREEN *and* ARTHUR CAPP *are solemnly watching another episode of Ace's TV show with an elderly juggler guest.*
GREEN: Ace, don't do it.
    (ACE *begins to juggle.*)
    Oh, no, no. No, no. Oh, Jesus . . . he's juggling!
    (*The audience cheers him on.*)
ACE: (*Off-screen, from next scene*) Let's not take County Commissioner Pat Webb too seriously.


INT. TANGIERS SPORTSBOOK/*ACES HIGH* – NIGHT

*We move past two television cameras to* ACE *behind his desk at another taping of his show.* TRUDY *is at his side.*
ACE: (*Into microphone*) I recently challenged him to a debate on this program and he declined. What are you worried about, Pat? You don't have to send me any questions. You can ask me anything you want.

STONE: (*Off-screen, from next scene*) What the hell is he doin' on television, anyway?

INT. ALL-AMERICAN GAS STATION, GAGGI'S BACK OFFICE, BACK HOME – DAY

Vegas Sun *newspaper front page photo of* ACE *on television. Headline reads:* 'Rothstein Sues Gaming Commission'.

STONE *is sitting across from* GAGGI *at his office.*
STONE: He's on all night, screamin' about how he's gonna take his damn lawsuit all the way to the Supreme Court. He really must be crazy. He's gonna go to Washington with this? (*Chuckles.*) He's out of his fuckin' mind.
ACE: (*Off-screen, from next scene*) It's a pity in this . . .

INT. TANGIERS SPORTSBOOK/*ACES HIGH* – NIGHT

ACE: (*Into microphone*) . . . state that we have such hypocrisy. Some people can do whatever they want. Other people have to pay through the nose.

INT. ALL-AMERICAN GAS STATION, GAGGI'S BACK OFFICE, BACK HOME – DAY

ACE: (*Off-screen, from previous scene*) But such is life.
GAGGI: Andy, go see him. Tell him maybe it's time he should quit.

EXT. MIGHTY MART CONVENIENCE STORE, REAR PARKING LOT, LAS VEGAS – NIGHT

SHERBERT *and* ACE *pull up beside another parked car.* ACE *gets out of his car in a robe and pajamas and gets into* STONE's *car.*

INT. STONE'S CAR – NIGHT

ACE: First of all, what they did was totally unconstitutional. We're already on the list to be heard before the Supreme

Court of the United States later this year.

STONE: These guys back home don't give a fuck about the Supreme Court and any of this bullshit! They want things to quiet down. They want you to walk away from –

ACE: Walk away? Andy, you can't be serious. How can I walk away? Don't you see what's goin' on here? Don't you see what's at stake?

STONE: The old man said, 'Maybe your friend should give in.' And when the old man says 'maybe', that's like a papal bull. Not only should you quit, you should run!

ACE: Know what my problem is? Every time they mention my name in the papers, these cocksuckers, they mention Nicky, too. How the fuck does that help? I mean, the heat he brought down is murder! We had a police department who was cooperative. He's pissed them off so much now that nobody can make a move anymore. I mean, what do you do about that?

STONE: What do you propose?

ACE: I don't know, he doesn't listen to me. Maybe he should . . . get lost for a while. Take a vacation. Would that be so bad?

STONE: They ain't sendin' Nicky nowhere.

ACE: All right, look, if he took a break, it would just give everybody some time to maneuver. That's all I'm saying. It's all that I'm saying.

STONE: I would forget about the maneuver. I would just get out.

ACE: (*Sighs*) I can't do that.

ACE: (*Voice-over*) Of course . . .


INT. NICKY'S HOUSE, KITCHEN – DAY

JENNIFER *is on the phone with* GINGER; NICKY *listens in.*

JENNIFER: (*Into telephone*) You know, I don't feel like playin' tennis.

ACE: (*Voice-over*) . . . as soon as Andy got back home, Nicky heard about our talk in the car.

JENNIFER: (*Into telephone*) Let's go to lunch. Do you want to go to the Riviera?

ACE: (*Voice-over*) Next morning bright and early, I get the call.

GINGER: (*Over telephone*) One o'clock?


INT. ACE'S HOUSE, LIVING-ROOM – DAY

ACE *listens in on* GINGER's *and* JENNIFER's *conversation.*
JENNIFER: (*Over telephone*) Great.
GINGER: (*Into telephone*) You know, I've got to do some shopping afterwards. Do you want to go?


INT. NICKY'S HOUSE, KITCHEN – DAY

JENNIFER: (*Into telephone*) Well, you know . . .

ACE: (*Voice-over*) But just getting a call from Nicky wasn't easy anymore. Even the codes didn't work. So, we figured out another act.


INT. FBI PHONE TAP ROOM – DAY

*A bored FBI man, seated at his desk with a tape recorder and headphones, looks at his wrist watch.*

ACE: (*Voice-over*) You see, if a phone's tapped, the Feds can only listen in . . .


INT. ACE'S HOUSE, LIVING-ROOM – DAY

ACE: (*Voice-over*) . . . on the stuff involving crimes. So on . . .


INT. NICKY'S HOUSE, KITCHEN – DAY

ACE: (*Voice-over*) . . . routine calls, they have to click off after a few minutes.

INT. FBI PHONE TAP ROOM – DAY

GINGER: (*Over telephone*) Yeah, and I get a sprained fuckin'
elbow.
(*The FBI man clicks off the tape recorder.*)

INT. NICKY'S HOUSE, KITCHEN – DAY

JENNIFER *quickly hands the phone to her husband.*

INT. ACE'S HOUSE, LIVING-ROOM – DAY

GINGER *hands the phone to* ACE.
ACE: (*Into telephone*) Yeah.

INT. NICKY'S HOUSE, KITCHEN – DAY

NICKY: (*Into telephone*) Meet me at three.

INT. ACE'S HOUSE, LIVING-ROOM – DAY

ACE: (*Into telephone*) What – what, Caesar's?
NICKY: (*Over telephone*) No, a . . .

INT. NICKY'S HOUSE, KITCHEN – DAY

NICKY(*Into telephone*) . . . hundred yards further down the road.

INT. ACE'S HOUSE, LIVING-ROOM – DAY

ACE: (*Into telephone*) Why?

INT. NICKY'S HOUSE, KITCHEN – DAY

NICKY: (*Into telephone*) Don't ask questions. Just be there.
(NICKY *gives the phone back to* JENNIFER.)

INT. ACE'S HOUSE, LIVING-ROOM – DAY

ACE *gives the phone to* GINGER.


INT. NICKY'S HOUSE, KITCHEN

NICKY: (*To himself*) Always asking questions. (*He exits.*)
JENNIFER: (*Into telephone*) Suzy Creamcheese has the exact . . .


INT. FBI PHONE TAP ROOM – DAY

*The bored FBI agent clicks on again and hears* GINGER *and*
JENNIFER'*s inane conversation.*
JENNIFER: (*Over telephone*) . . . same outfit.
GINGER: (*Chuckles, over telephone*) But I saw something . . .


INT. ACE'S HOUSE, LIVING-ROOM – DAY

GINGER: (*Into telephone*) . . . something very . . . cute.
    (ACE *sits down on the couch behind her and lights a cigarette.*)


INT. FBI STAKEOUT POST, MOTEL ACROSS FROM THE GOLD
RUSH – DAY

*Through a window of a motel room across the street from The Gold
Rush, an* FBI AGENT *watches* NICKY *and* MARINO *exit the jewelry
store, get into a parked car and drive away.*

*Iris out.*

FBI AGENT: (*Off-screen, into a radio*) Okay, he, uh, he's out. It's
    the ant, uh, Brown unit. And he's with, uh, bogie. I think
    it's Frankie.

ACE: (*Voice-over*) Nicky started out before me because it wasn't
    that easy . . .
    (*Swish pan to the* FBI AGENT *looking out the window talking
    into a radio.*)
    . . . for him to get around anymore.

FBI AGENT: (*Into radio*) Okay, pulled out . . .
    (*Swish pan to* NICKY *and* MARINO *driving down the street.*)

(*Off-screen, into radio*) . . . pretty fast. He's headed
upstream.

ACE: (*Voice-over*) Nicky couldn't even go for a ride without
changing . . .
(*Swish pan to FBI car trailing behind.*)
. . . cars at least six times before he could shake all his tails.

INT. UNDERGROUND PARKING GARAGE #1 – DAY

NICKY's *car with* MARINO *driving pulls in;* NICKY *jumps out and
gets in another car.*

ACE: (*Voice-over*) And because of all the planes, he had to use
underground garages.

(MARINO *drives off.*)

INT. UNDERGROUND PARKING GARAGE #2 – DAY

NICKY's *second car screeches in to another garage.*

INT. UNDERGROUND PARKING GARAGE #3 – DAY

NICKY *hurries across the lot to another car.*

INT. UNDERGROUND PARKING GARAGE #4 – DAY

NICKY *changes cars again.*

INT. UNDERGROUND PARKING GARAGE #5 – DAY

NICKY *running to yet another car. He drives off.*

EXT. DESERT SCENE – DAY

*A solitary* ACE *waiting in the vast desert, looking around.* ACE *looks
at sage brush and sand and a few rocks on the desert floor. This
could be a hole meant for him. He steps away from it.*

ACE: (*Voice-over*) Meeting in the middle of the desert always made me nervous. It's a scary place. I knew about the holes in the desert, of course, and everywhere I looked, there could have been a hole.

EXT. DESERT ROAD – DAY

*Aerial shot of* NICKY *driving.*

ACE: (*Voice-over*) Normally, my prospects of comin' back alive from a meeting with Nicky were ninety-nine out of a hundred. But this time, when I heard him say, 'A couple a hundred yards down the road', I gave myself fifty–fifty.

EXT. DESERT – DAY

ACE *still standing in the desert.* NICKY'*s car suddenly appears as a reflection in* ACE'*s sunglasses, shaking* ACE *out of his desert-induced reverie.* NICKY'*s car pulls up by* ACE. *He gets out and storms up to him.*

NICKY: Where the fuck you get off talkin' to people about me behind my back? Goin' over my head?

ACE: What people?

NICKY: What people! What'd you think, I wasn't gonna find out?

ACE: I don't even know what you're talkin' about, Nick.

NICKY: No? You said I'm bringin' heat on you?! I gotta listen to people because of your fuckin' shit?! You're ordering me out?! You better get your own fuckin' army, pal!

ACE: I didn't do anything. I mean, I didn't order you or anybody . . . I only told Andy Stone that you had a lot of heat on you, and that was a problem.

NICKY: You want me to get out of my own fuckin' town?!

ACE: Yeah, I said I – let the bullshit blow over for a while so I can run the casino. Anything goes wrong with the casino, it's my ass. It's not yours, it's my ass.

NICKY: Oh, I don't know whether you know this or not, but you only have your fuckin' casino because I made that possible!

ACE: I –

146

NICKY: (*Interrupting*) I'm what counts out here! Not your
fuckin' country clubs or your fuckin' TV shows! And what
the fuck are you doin' on TV anyhow?!

ACE: What are you –

NICKY: (*Interrupting*) You know I get calls from back home
every fuckin' day?! They think you went batshit!

ACE: I'm only on TV because I gotta be able to hang around the
casino. You understand that. You know that. Come on.

NICKY: Your fuckin' ass! You could have had the food and
beverage job without goin' on television! You wanted to go
on TV.

ACE: Yeah, I did want to go on TV. That way I have a forum. I
can fight back. I'm known. People see me. They know they
can't fuck around with me like they could if I was an
unknown. That's right.

NICKY: You're makin' a big fuckin' spectacle of yourself.

ACE: Me?! I wouldn't even be in this situation if it wasn't for
you. You brought down so much fuckin' heat on me. I
mean, every time I meet somebody here, the big question
is do I know you.

NICKY: Oh, sure. Now you want to blame your fuckin' license
on me, is that it?

ACE: No, it – it – Nicky, when you asked me if you could come out here, what did I tell you? I mean, you asked me, and I knew you were going to come out no matter what I said, but what did I tell you? Do you remember what I told . . .

NICKY: (*Interrupting*) Back –

ACE: . . . you? Do you remember what I told you?

NICKY: Back – Back up, back up a fuckin' minute here. One minute. I asked you?! When the fuck did I ever ask you if I could come out here?! Get this through your head, you –

ACE: (*Interrupting*) You never – ?

NICKY: Get this through your head, you Jew motherfucker, you. You only exist out here because of me! That's the only reason! Without me, you, personally, every fuckin' wiseguy skell[1] around'll take a piece of your fuckin' Jew ass! Then where you gonna go?! You're fuckin' warned! Don't ever go over my fuckin' head again! You motherfucker, you!
(NICKY *drives off, leaving an angry and frustrated* ACE *to ponder the desert and the holes.*)

INT. JUBILATION NIGHTCLUB – NIGHT

*Overhead of* ACE, OSCAR, SHERBERT, TRUDY *and showgirls walking down the zebra pattern carpet of the nightclub. They are escorted to their table.*

NICKY, MARINO *and* DOMINICK *are seated at another table in the rear of the club so no one can hear their conversation.*

MARINO: Well, we got company.
(ACE *avoids looking at* NICKY.)

NICKY: Do you see that? Dumb Jew motherfucker. Grew up together and he's actin' like he don't even know me. I know we're supposed to avoid each other, but, you know, there's ways to do things and there's ways not to.

DOMINICK: Yeah. Fuck him.
(SHERBERT *and the others make a toast.*)

SHERBERT: To Abraham Lincoln.

---

1 Skell: the lowest form of wiseguy – a drunken bum.

ACE: *L'chaim.*[1]
SHERBERT: Here we go. Good luck.
>    (NICKY *watches* ACE's *entourage.*)
DOMINICK: Forget about it, Nick. Don't let it bother you.
NICKY: Why, does it look like it's bothering me? What do I give a
>    fuck? Fuckin' Oscar too. All the fuckin' money I've given
>    that prick, he don't even look over here. What's his problem?
MARINO: Mm.
NICKY: Fuckin' Jews stick together, don't they?
MARINO: They're havin' a good time too.
NICKY: So are we.
>    (NICKY, MARINO *and* DOMINICK *are isolated and alone at*
>    *their table.*)

INT. ACE'S BEDROOM – NIGHT

ACE *sleeping. A hot line to the casino rings as a red light blinks.*
ACE: (*Into telephone*) Yeah?

INT. TANGIERS CASINO SPORTSBOOK – NIGHT

SHERBERT *is calling* ACE.
SHERBERT: (*Quietly into telephone*) Sam, we got a problem.

INT. ACE'S BEDROOM – NIGHT

ACE: (*Into telephone*) What is it?
SHERBERT: (*Over telephone*) The little guy. He's half in the bag,
>    and nobody told him he was eighty-sixed from the joint, so
>    we . . .

INT. TANGIERS CASINO SPORTSBOOK – NIGHT

SHERBERT: (*Into telephone*) . . . all turned our heads and made
>    out like we didn't know who he was. He's over at the
>    twenty-one table with his . . .

1 Yiddish for 'to life'.

INT. TANGIERS BLACKJACK TABLE – NIGHT

NICKY *is betting every spot on the blackjack table.* MARINO *is standing behind him. The* DEALER *is nervous.*

SHERBERT: (*Off-screen*) . . . nose wide open. He took the money out of his own kick. His nose is open for about ten thousand.
(SHERBERT *and the pit boss look on.*)
(*Off-screen*) Now, he's really pissed.


INT. ACE'S BEDROOM – NIGHT

ACE: (*Into telephone*) Oh, no. (*Sits up and throws off the bed covers.*)


INT. TANGIERS SPORTSBOOK – NIGHT

SHERBERT: (*Into telephone*) He wants a fifty-thousand marker.


INT. ACE'S BEDROOM – NIGHT

ACE: (*Into telephone*) No, just – just give him, give him ten. That's it. Ten. I'll be right down.

INT. TANGIERS BLACKJACK TABLE – NIGHT

SHERBERT: (*To* NICKY) He's gonna come up with ten
    thousand, just the way you wanted.

NICKY: Ten thou? No, no, no.

SHERBERT: . . . give you ten thousand –

NICKY: (*Grabbing* SHERBERT's *lapel*) Fifty! I said fifty!

SHERBERT: Look, take –

NICKY: (*Pushing him away and walking back to the blackjack
    table*) Fuckin' fifty thousand! Go get it. I don't give a fuck
    where you get it. (*To* FEMALE DEALER.) Fuckers! They
    take it, but they don't want to give it back.
    (NICKY *turns up another bad card and looks at the dealer. She
    smiles as she slides the house winnings over to her side of the
    table.*)
    How the fuck can you grin? How the fuck could you grin?
    (*The* FEMALE DEALER *looks to her* PIT BOSS *for help. He steps
    up to a* MALE DEALER *at a neighboring table.*)
    You know how much I'm stuck? You give a fuck?
    (*The* MALE DEALER *walks up to the* FEMALE DEALER *and
    taps her on the shoulder.*)
    Do ya?!
    (*She lays down some cards, claps her hands to show the Eye-in-*

*the-Sky that they are empty, and exits.*)

(*To departing* FEMALE DEALER) Yeah. Give yourself a hand right across your fuckin' mouth.

(*The* MALE DEALER *takes her place behind the table.*)

Look at this fuckin' beaut they put in now. Sherbert send you in here to rob me now? Been fuckin' knockin' everybody's dick in all night? Huh? You been beatin' all the customers tonight, motherfucker?

(*We see the* PIT BOSS *lock up the chip tray from the table the dealer has just left.* NICKY *has a diminished stack of chips and an upturned ten and a two.*)

Huh, jag-off? Hit me.

(*The card is a king or a 'paint', a picture card, meaning that* NICKY *has lost. Everyone freezes in fear.* NICKY *takes the paint and flicks it at the* DEALER'*s chest where it sticks to his shirt.*)

Take this stiff and pound it up your fuckin' ass! Hit me again.

(*The* DEALER *looks to the* PIT BOSS *who nods 'okay'. He turns over a card. It's another paint, a queen.* NICKY *flicks the card to the* DEALER'*s face.*)

Take this one and stick it up your sister's ass! Hit me again.

(*The* DEALER *looks to the* PIT BOSS *again.*)

That's it, keep lookin' at him, you fuckin' dummy. If you had any fuckin' heart at all, you'd be out fuckin' stealin' for a livin'. (*Tossing the card at the* DEALER.) Hit me again.

(*The* DEALER *looks at the* PIT BOSS.)

What the fuck you keep lookin' at him for, huh, you fuckin' pu–

(*The* DEALER *deals him another paint.*) Look at this, twenty fuckin' paints in a row. Hit me again!

(ACE *enters the casino with* SHERBERT.)

MARINO: (*To* NICKY) He's here.

NICKY: (*To the* DEALER) You should pay as fast as you collect, you know.

(NICKY *gets up to go over to* ACE, *glowering at* SHERBERT *as he walks past.*

   ACE *and* NICKY *are partially hidden behind a pillar by the slot-machines.*)

ACE: What are you doin'? You gotta get out of here!

NICKY: Hey, Sammy, tell this Jew motherfucker over here to pay that marker.

ACE: Nicky, Nicky, you're not listenin' to me. I'm here to help you. What's the matter with you? You're gonna bury us both.

NICKY: Just give me the money. Fuckin' give me the fuckin' money, Sammy.

ACE: I'm gonna okay you ten and get you even, and that's it. Then you got to get out of here before the cops and the newspapers are all over you.
*(To the PIT BOSS, holding up ten fingers.)*
Ten and that's it.
*(He makes a throat cutting gesture with his hand. ACE leaves. NICKY turns to walk back to the table. He sees SHERBERT standing right behind him.)*

NICKY: What are you starin' at, you bald-headed Jew prick?!
*(Before SHERBERT can answer, NICKY grabs the receiver off a wall phone and hits him across the face and back. SHERBERT falls to the floor. NICKY pulls the cradle off the pillar and tosses it down on his back. He and MARINO walk back to the table, SHERBERT winces on the floor in shock.)*
Sue me, you Jew fuck!

MARINO: Let's get out of here.

NICKY: What? Get out of here? I got a marker comin'.
*(He puts some chips down on the table.)*
*(To DEALER)* Deal.


INT. OSCAR, THE LAWYER'S OFFICE – DAY

ACE *and* GINGER *are seated across from* OSCAR, *their lawyer.*

OSCAR: I know, but everything's changed now. You're talking about a divorce. You're even asking for alimony payments and . . . child support . . . and now custody.

GINGER: I just want what any divorced woman would get.

ACE: I mean she's only sober about two hours a day. It's usually from eleven in the morning until one in the afternoon. And if I gave her her money and her jewels now, you know what she's gonna do? She's gonna piss it all away in about a year, and then where will she be? (*To* GINGER.) Where would you be then? Comin' right back to me, right back to me. (*To* OSCAR.) Or finding some other excuse to come, and I – I –

GINGER: (*To* ACE) We had a deal. Remember that? (*To* OSCAR.) He said if it didn't work out between us, that I could get my things and I could leave.

ACE: (*To* GINGER, *leaning closer to her*) Look in my eyes. Look in my eyes.

(GINGER *turns to him.*)

You know me. Do you see anything in these eyes that makes you think I would ever let someone in your condition take my child away from me? (*Pause.*) Do you? You know that won't happen.

ACE: (*Voice-over*) And after all this time . . . and as hard as I tried, as much as I wanted . . .


INT. *ACES HIGH* BACKSTAGE CORRIDOR/SHOWGIRLS' DRESSING-ROOM – DAY

ACE, *with Kleenex sticking out of his collar to protect his shirt from his television make-up, walks back to the dressing room with* TRUDY. *She pecks his cheek before exiting to her own room. A security guard opens the door for* ACE. *We follow him past numerous showgirls and costumes.*

ACE: (*Voice-over*) . . . I could never reach her. I could never make her love me. I always felt she should have gone for all that money . . . being somebody for the first time in her life, a home and a kid. But that's not what happened. It just didn't work out that way.

ACE: (*To the showgirls*) Everything all right?

ACE: (*Voice-over*) I mean, what could we do? After a while, we'd just take breathers from each other. You know, little separations. At that time, I remember Ginger took Amy and went to Beverly Hills. She was gonna spend a week or so shopping.

(ACE *picks up the phone at a make-up table.*)
OPERATOR: (*Over telephone*) Yes, Mr Rothstein.
ACE: (*Into telephone*) Operator, the Beverly Hotel in Beverly Hills, please.


EXT. LOS ANGELES. BEVERLY HOTEL – DAY

GINGER, *sporting a new short hairstyle, and* AMY *exit and walk towards camera.*
HOTEL OPERATOR: (*Off-screen*) Hello, Beverly Hotel.
ACE: (*Off-screen*) Mrs Sam Rothstein, please.
HOTEL OPERATOR: (*Off-screen*) I'm sorry. Mr and Mrs Rothstein have checked out already.
    (*Track back, as* GINGER *smiles, to reveal* LESTER DIAMOND.)
LESTER: Hey.
    (GINGER *kisses* LESTER.)


INT. SHOWGIRLS' DRESSING-ROOM – DAY

ACE: (*Into telephone*) M– Uh, Mr and Mrs Rothstein?


EXT. BEVERLY HOTEL – DAY

LESTER: (*To* AMY) Hey, little Dale Evans.
    (GINGER *laughs.*)
HOTEL OPERATOR: (*Off-screen*) Yes, they both checked out.


INT. SHOWGIRLS' DRESSING-ROOM – DAY

ACE: (*Into telephone*) Thank you. (*He hangs up.*)


INT. WAREHOUSE – NIGHT

ACE *steps up to a public phone as it rings.*
ACE: (*Into telephone*) Hello.
FORLANO: (*Over telephone*) Yeah.
ACE: (*Into telephone, sighs*) Uh, my wife is w-with an old friend of hers i-in LA.

INT. ALL-AMERICAN GAS STATION, GAGGI'S BACK OFFICE,
BACK HOME – DAY

FORLANO *is on the phone, taking notes with a pencil.* GAGGI *is sitting in the background.*
ACE: (*Over telephone*) Some low-life. A guy named Lester Diamond.


INT. WAREHOUSE – DAY

ACE: (*Into telephone*) My daughter's with 'em too and I think they're gonna try and kidnap her. Is there anybody you can send?


INT. ALL-AMERICAN GAS STATION, GAGGI'S BACK OFFICE,
BACK HOME – DAY

FORLANO: (*Into telephone*) We'll take care of it.
   (FORLANO *hangs up and walks over to* GAGGI. *We hear the doorbell from the following scene.*)


INT. ACE'S HOUSE – DAY

ACE *opens the door to two Tangiers* EXECUTIVES.
COUNT ROOM EXEC: (*To* ACE) We got a number and an address.


INT. ACE'S HOUSE, UPSTAIRS DEN – DAY

ACE *is standing behind his desk on the phone.*
ACE: (*Into telephone*) Hello.
LESTER: (*Over telephone*) Hello.
ACE: (*Into telephone*) Yeah, is this Lester? This is Sam . . .


INT. LESTER DIAMOND'S LOS ANGELES APARTMENT – DAY

ACE: . . . Rothstein. I want to talk to Ginger. Put her on the phone.
LESTER: (*Into telephone*) She's not here, Sam.
ACE: (*Over telephone*) Lester . . .

INT. ACE'S HOUSE, UPSTAIRS DEN – DAY

ACE: (*Into telephone*) . . . listen to me very carefully. I want to talk to Ginger. I want my kid back. I want her put on a plane immediately.

INT. LESTER DIAMOND'S LOS ANGELES APARTMENT – DAY

ACE: (*Over telephone*) I know she's there. Don't fuck around with me.
LESTER: (*Into telephone*) Uh, I'm not. Sam, I wouldn't . . .
    (*He snaps his fingers to get* GINGER's *attention.*)
    . . . wouldn't do it. Yeah, no, I, I . . .
    (*We see* GINGER *on* LESTER's *living-room couch, cutting lines of cocaine with a razor blade in front of* AMY.)
GINGER: (*Whispering to* AMY) You shouldn't do this.
    (LESTER *steps up to the living-room snapping his fingers to* GINGER. *She looks up.*)
ACE: (*Over telephone*) You understand? Put her on the fuckin' phone.
LESTER: (*Into telephone*) Sam, I – I don't know where she is, okay?

INT. ACE'S HOUSE, UPSTAIRS DEN – DAY

LESTER: (*Over telephone*) So, l-l-l-listen, I te- I te- I tell you – can I call you back in a few minutes?

INT. LESTER DIAMOND'S LOS ANGELES APARTMENT – DAY

ACE: (*Over telephone*) 702 472 1862.
LESTER: Mm-hm. (*Pretending to write it down.*) 1862. Okay, good. I'll call you right b–
ACE: (*Over telephone*) Right away.
LESTER: (*Into telephone*) I'll call you right back.

INT. ACE'S HOUSE, UPSTAIRS DEN – DAY

ACE: (*Over telephone*) Right back.

INT. LESTER DIAMOND'S LOS ANGELES APARTMENT – DAY

LESTER: (*Into telephone*) You got it. (*He hangs up; then, to himself as he walks through a doorway to the living-room*) Schmuck. (*To* GINGER.) All right. I just bought us a few minutes. Want to get back at this prick? (*He sticks his finger in the coke and rubs it on his gums.*) Hm? Okay, you got, what, two million dollars in that box?

(GINGER *snorts some cocaine.*)

Hey . . . you got a minute? Hey. He's got two million in the box, am I right? Okay, you let him keep your jewels. We take the cash and the only other thing he cares about. (*He points to* AMY.) Huh? Her majesty. We go to Europe. You dye your hair, get some pl–

AMY: (*Interrupts*) I don't want to go to Europe. I want to go to see *The Elephant Man.*

LESTER: We're not gonna go see any fuckin' elephants, okay?

GINGER: (*To* AMY) We'll go later.

LESTER: (*To* AMY) We're going to Europe. Let the adults talk. (*To* GINGER.) You dye your hair . . . you get plastic surgery, like we talked about. Right? You're the mother. How much do you think he's gonna pay to get this fuckin' kid back?

AMY: I don't want to go to Europe.

LESTER: (*To* AMY) Shut your mouth!

(GINGER *puts her hand over* AMY's *mouth.*)

You know where she gets this from!

AMY: You shut up.

LESTER: No, you – You want me to come over there? I'll smack your face.

(AMY *sticks her tongue out at* LESTER.)

Don't give me any of your shit! (*To* GINGER.) Okay, this has always been a dream, but we're going.

GINGER: Lester – he called you here.

LESTER: Right.

GINGER: Here.

LESTER: He was just on the phone.

GINGER: (*Sniffs*) He called you right here.

LESTER: I just talked to him.

GINGER: (*Sighs*) So, he knows where you are. That means he's sending some guys over here probably right now.

LESTER: Ginger . . . it means he's sitting by the phone like a dumb-bell, waiting for me to call him back. Now, I –

GINGER: (*Interrupting and getting up*) That's – Yeah, he's sitting by the phone like a dumb-bell, just waiting for you to call him back. That's what he's –

LESTER: (*Interrupting*) He's sittin' by the phone –

GINGER: (*Yelling*) What do you think we're gonna do? He's probably got guys outside the fuckin' house!

LESTER: It's this fuckin' bullshit of yours!

GINGER: (*Gathering* AMY, *hysterical*) Get your bag! Come on, get your bag! Get your things! Let's go!

LESTER: It's this bullshit. It's just bullshit right here. This is the fuckin' problem, you know.

GINGER: (*Hysterical*) Oh, what bullshit? What, do you want to fuckin' talk it over now?

LESTER: You're done yakkin', okay? You're done yakkin' now?

GINGER: (*Grabbing her purse and rushing* AMY *out*) Go! Go! Get in the car! Go!

LESTER: (*Mimicking* GINGER) 'Go! Go! Go!'

EXT. GOLD RUSH – DAY

NICKY *is leaning against a public phone.* MARINO *watches.*
NICKY: (*Into telephone*) You just relax. Nobody's killin'
anybody, do you hear?
GINGER: (*Over telephone*) No, I really do. I think he's gonna kill
me.
NICKY: (*Into telephone*) You just relax, and call me back here in
exactly an hour, on this phone, and I'll see what I can do.
GINGER: (*Over telephone*) Yeah, uh-huh . . . Okay.


EXT. LOS ANGELES STREET. PAY PHONE – DAY

AMY *is swinging her purse at* LESTER *in the background.*
GINGER: (*Into telephone*) So, I'm gonna call you back in an hour
. . . at this number, and you're gonna be there, right?
NICKY: (*Over telephone*) I'll be there.


EXT. GOLD RUSH – DAY

NICKY: (*Into telephone*) And listen, don't do anything else crazy,
okay? You all right? Okay.


EXT. LOS ANGELES STREET. PAY PHONE – DAY
GINGER: (*Into telephone*) Bye.
    (*She hangs up and walks over to* LESTER *and* AMY *who are
    fighting.*)
    Just knock it off! Would you two knock it off? Get in the
    car.
LESTER: She started it. She started the whole thing. I'm just
standin' here.
    (GINGER *opens the driver's side door.*)
    You're not gonna drive. Don't even think you're gonna
    drive.
GINGER: No, I'm gonna drive.
LESTER: (*Stopping* GINGER) No, I'm not gonna drive with some
crazy –
GINGER: (*Yelling*) You're driving me nuts! (*She walks around to
the passenger door.*)

LESTER: Get in the passenger's side! And I'm sendin' this kid to Bolivia in a fuckin' box.

EXT. ACE'S PATIO – DAY

*Through glass doors we see* ACE *seated in his living-room.* NICKY *slips into frame and taps on the window, gesturing that he wants to talk.* ACE *signals for him to go around to the garage.*

INT. ACE'S GARAGE – DAY

NICKY *walks past* GINGER'S *white Mercedes towards* ACE.
NICKY: Ginger –
   (*He's cut off by* ACE *who points to the passenger's side of his Cadillac.* NICKY *walks around and gets in.* ACE *starts the engine to make it harder for anyone to listen in on their conversation.*
      ACE *turns the volume down. He looks straight ahead, away from* NICKY.)
   (*After an awkward moment*) Ginger called me.
ACE: (*Polite, careful, smoking a cigarette*) Yeah.
NICKY: I just told you. She called me.
ACE: And what'd she want?
NICKY: She was afraid to call you.
ACE: Yeah, she's with that cocksucker again . . . and they got Amy.
NICKY: Well, that's why I'm here. She wants to come back, but she's afraid you're gonna whack her out.
ACE: Yeah, they're gonna kidnap my kid. What do you want?
NICKY: I know. Why didn't you come to me? I mean, this is family, it ain't business. Meanwhile, you make calls back home. Sammy, it makes us look bad out here, you know what I mean? Back and forth, this one and that one, and, in the meantime, she's gone anyway. Am I right?
ACE: (*Sighing*) I don't know. What am I gonna do with this woman? I don't know . . . (*Pause.*) She's drivin' me fuckin' crazy.
NICKY: I think if you, uh, okay it, you know, assure her that she's gonna be all right, she'll come back.
ACE: She's driving me fuckin' crazy.

161

NICKY: Well, once you get her here, you think about it, you know? But get the kid back here. She wants to come back. That's the, uh, that's the main thing here. You want your kid, don't you? Huh?

EXT. LOS ANGELES HIGHWAY. PHONE BOOTH – DAY

GINGER *is on the phone. In the background,* AMY *is acting up in the back seat of the car and driving* LESTER *crazy.*
ACE: (*Over telephone*) Hello.
GINGER: (*Sighs, into telephone*) Hi, it's me. (*Chuckling.*) Just who you wanted to talk to, right?
ACE: (*Over telephone*) Listen . . .

INT. ACE'S HOUSE, UPSTAIRS DEN – DAY

ACE *is seated at his desk.*
ACE: (*Into telephone*) . . . uh-uh-uh – I'm not gonna ask you where you are, just please, put Amy on a plane. Just put her on right away, any plane to get her here right away . . .

EXT. LOS ANGELES HIGHWAY. PHONE BOOTH – DAY

ACE: (*Over telephone*) . . . please. That's all I'm askin' you.
GINGER: (*Into telephone*) Do you . . . I mean . . . I don't think she should go by herself.

INT. ACE'S HOUSE, UPSTAIRS DEN – DAY

ACE: (*Sighs, into telephone*) What do you mean?

EXT. LOS ANGELES HIGHWAY. PHONE BOOTH – DAY

GINGER: (*Into telephone, holding back tears*) What I mean is, you think if, uh, do you think if I came back . . . do you think you could forgive me?

162

INT. ACE'S HOUSE, UPSTAIRS DEN – DAY

ACE: (*Into telephone*) Uh (*sighs*), I don't know. I gotta tell you, I
    don't know.
GINGER: (*Over telephone*) Right.


EXT. LOS ANGELES HIGHWAY. PHONE BOOTH – DAY

GINGER: (*Into telephone*) I under-understand that. I-I know I
    fucked up.


INT. ACE'S HOUSE, UPSTAIRS DEN – DAY

ACE: (*Into telephone*) What about the money? Uh, where's the
    box?
GINGER: (*Over telephone*) I gotta tell ya . . .


EXT. LOS ANGELES HIGHWAY. PHONE BOOTH – DAY

GINGER: (*Into telephone*) . . . I-I . . . made some mistakes and I
    spent some money.
ACE: (*Over telephone*) What's it . . .


INT. ACE'S HOUSE, UPSTAIRS DEN – DAY
ACE: (*Into telephone*) . . . under?
GINGER: (*Over telephone*) Pretty serious.


EXT. LOS ANGELES HIGHWAY. PHONE BOOTH – DAY

ACE: (*Over telephone*) How serious?
GINGER: It's, uh, it's under twenty-five.
ACE: (*Over telephone*) It's under . . .


INT. ACE'S HOUSE, UPSTAIRS DEN – DAY

ACE: (*Into telephone*) . . . twenty-five thousand?
GINGER: (*Over telephone*) Yeah.
ACE: (*Into telephone*) And . . .

**EXT. LOS ANGELES HIGHWAY. PHONE BOOTH – DAY**

ACE: (*Over telephone*) . . . the rest of the two million is still there?

GINGER: (*Into telephone*) Yeah, yeah, I got the rest.

**INT. ACE'S HOUSE, UPSTAIRS DEN – DAY**

ACE: (*Into telephone*) Okay, no big deal. That's okay. Yeah. He got his twenty-five. (*Sighs.*) That I'll live with. Any more I couldn't.

**EXT. LOS ANGELES HIGHWAY. PHONE BOOTH – DAY**

GINGER: (*Into telephone*) Okay?

ACE: (*Over telephone*) All right . . .

**INT. ACE'S HOUSE, UPSTAIRS DEN – DAY**

ACE: (*Into telephone*) . . . all right. Where are you? I'll send a plane for you right away.

**EXT. LAS VEGAS PRIVATE AIRPORT – NIGHT**

ACE *sees* GINGER *and* AMY *coming off the Tangiers private jet.* GINGER *wobbles a little as she comes down the ramp.*

GINGER: (*Waving brightly*) Hi, Sam.
　　(ACE *picks* AMY *up and hugs her, ignoring* GINGER. *They walk to the car and drive off.*)

**INT. ACE'S CAR – NIGHT**

AMY *looks on from the back seat.*

ACE: So, what'd ya do with it?

GINGER: With what?

ACE: With the money.

GINGER: He needed some clothes.

ACE: (*Sighs*) Twenty-five thousand for clothes.

GINGER: He wanted a watch, too.

ACE: Twenty-five thousand for clothes and a watch.
GINGER: Mm-hm.
ACE: Mm-hm.
MAÎTRE D': (*Off-screen, from following scene*) Mr R . . .

INT. VEGAS RESTAURANT – NIGHT

ACE *and* GINGER, *dressed for dinner just like any other couple, walk towards a table overlooking the colorful lights of downtown Vegas.*
MAÎTRE D': . . . good evening. Signora.
GINGER: Gino.
MAÎTRE D': This way.

ACE: (*Voice-over, as they are led to their table*) The good part was, I had Amy back. So, we went home, had the housekeeper stay over, put the kid to bed, I calmed myself down and we went to dinner. I tried to keep things nice and civil, you know. But . . . hey, twenty-five thousand for three suits? That doesn't make much sense.

ACE: (*Seated across from* GINGER *at a booth*) First of all, he's not gonna wear f– thousand-dollar suits. But let's say he did, which he won't. How you gonna get fitted for twenty-five suits in three days? I, um, I mean, how could you get fitted that fast? I can't get fitted that fast, and I pay twice as much.
GINGER: I bought him a watch too.
ACE: Yeah.
GINGER: Yeah.
ACE: But even if you bought him a watch, a really nice watch, one that he thought was nice – and he doesn't know what the fuck a good watch is – so, you go, five, ten, twelve grand?
GINGER: Yeah.
ACE: At the most, which is impossible for him.
(*She glances to the table behind them.*)
Plus, at the most, three suits, a thousand apiece. That still leaves what? Around ten thousand?
GINGER: (*Staring down at her plate, trying to restrain herself*) Would you knock it off, Sam?

ACE: I'm just tryin' to figure it out.

GINGER: There's nothin' to figure out. I'm home . . . we're
workin' it out. (*She lights a cigarette.*)

ACE: Yeah, but I've been told that before, 'We're workin' it
out.' You think that you're home . . . after what you just
put me through with Amy, is a favor to me?
(*She looks at* ACE.)
(*Pause*) So, counting the watch, let's say another four
thousand for expenses over the weekend . . . of which you
must have had a good time. I know he did. That's for sure.
I know that . . . fuckin' piece of shit had a good fuckin'
time. On my money. You might as well have fucked him,
which you probably did anyway.
(GINGER *glares at him.*)
You're lookin' at me a certain way. You – you're teary-
eyed, huh? You're upset. You're a good actress, you
know that? Good fuckin' actress. You can fuckin' get that
pity out of people. I'm not a john, you understand? You
always thought I was, but I'm not. And I'm not a sucker.
That fuckin' pimp cocksucker. He's lucky I didn't kill
him last time. Lucky he's fuckin' livin'. And if you
would've stayed with Amy . . . and you would've ran

away . . . you would've been fuckin' dead.
(GINGER *scoots out of the booth and leaves.*)
Both of you. Dead. Dead.


INT. ACE'S BEDROOM – NIGHT

*Wide overhead of* ACE *alone in bed. Off-screen, we hear* GINGER, *a little drunk, on the phone.*

GINGER: (*Off-screen, whispering into telephone*) I cannot do it anymore. I can't fuckin' live like this. It's not right.
(ACE'S *point of view as he moves towards the sound of* GINGER'S *voice. He enters frame and stops to listen.*)
(*Off-screen*) What are you? Yes, of course – He doesn't come home at night. What is the big fuckin' deal? I go – Yes, and I just – I can't fuckin' take it. Why should I fucking take it? That wasn't the deal. He acts like . . . like I'm the only one around here with a fuckin' past. He'll never let me live it down. Well . . . well, I mean, I tried. What the fuck do you think I came back here for? No, I'm not!
(ACE *slips into the foyer where he can see* GINGER'S *reflection in a glass door as she talks on the phone in the living-room.*)
(*Whispering into telephone*) I want to have him killed. Yes, I want him killed. I've fuckin' had it.


INT. ACE'S HOUSE, LIVING-ROOM – NIGHT

GINGER *is on the phone.*

GINGER: (*Into telephone*) So, are you with me on this?
(ACE *steps up behind her. She gasps, still holding the phone. Petrified.*)
ACE: You want to get rid of me? Here I am. Go ahead, get rid of me. (ACE *grabs the phone.*) Hello.
(*He hears nothing and throws the phone down near her.*
GINGER *rises and attacks* ACE.)
GINGER: (*Grunting*) Yes! I fuckin' hate you! I can't take it anymore!
(ACE *grapples with* GINGER.)
Yes, I want to kill you! I hate your fuckin' guts!

ACE: You hate my guts? I want you to come with me now.
(*He drags her by her arms across the living-room hallway, into the bedroom.*)

GINGER: Get off of me! Stop it!

ACE: Come with me now! Come with me now. Come with me now. I want you out of here.
(GINGER *screams.*)


INT. ACE'S HOUSE, BEDROOM – NIGHT

ACE: I want you out of here! I want you out of here!

GINGER: (*Starting to get up*) Let go of me! Let go of me!


INT. ACE'S HOUSE, BEDROOM CLOSET – NIGHT

*He pushes her against the closet wall, and throws an overnight bag at her.*

ACE: Take your (*kicking the bag*) fuckin' bag and get out of here!

GINGER: I'll go, but I want my money right now!
(ACE *tosses clothes at her.*)

ACE: You'll get your money! Don't worry.
(GINGER *squats down and starts to gather her stuff.*)

GINGER: The arrangement is over!

ACE: (*Tossing clothes*) No kidding. NO KIDDING!

GINGER: And I still get my money. I need some cash right now. You can't just put me in the street.

ACE: I'll get your cash. You haven't been straight with me ever since I met you! You never loved me in the first place! I need eyes in the back of my fuckin' head with you, you fuckin' bitch! (ACE *walks past her to his side of the large walk-in closet. Racks and racks of her clothes are still hanging.*)

GINGER: Love you?!
(*She tosses a pair of red shoes at him.*)
How could I love you?! How can I love you?! You treat me like I'm your fucking dog!
(ACE *leans down and opens a shoe box filled with money. He grabs as much cash as he can hold.*)

ACE: You're lower than a dog!

GINGER: Fuck you!

(*He walks up to her.*)

ACE: (*Shoving the bundles of cash in her face*) Here. Here. Is this enough money?! Huh? Will it last you two fuckin' days? Take it, greedy bitch. (*Stuffing the money in her bag.*) Take the fuckin' money you fuckin' want.

GINGER: I'm going to the bank and I'm getting my jewelry too! (*She puts on a white fur coat.*)

ACE: Yeah, no kidding. Good! It opens at 9 a.m. Be there!

GINGER: And don't you send your guys down there to stop me! I mean it.
(*She bends down to pick up her bag, but* ACE *insists on carrying it.*)

ACE: I guarantee you, I will not stop you.


INT. ACE'S HOUSE, BEDROOM/FOYER – NIGHT

GINGER *and* ACE *walk through their bedroom to the front door. He's carrying her suitcase.*

GINGER: Stop! You aren't getting rid of me with one fuckin' suitcase!

ACE: You'll come back tomorrow and get the rest. Just get out of here.

GINGER: Fine. (*Sniffs, walking back.*) I'm takin' Amy.

ACE: (*Stopping her*) You're not takin' Amy.

GINGER: I am. I'm wakin' her up right now.

ACE: You're stoned. You're a junkie. Get out of here. (*He opens the door and tosses her suitcase out.*)

GINGER: I am not! She's my daughter too! Goddamn you!

ACE: Get out of here!
(*He shoves her out the door.*)
Send my lawyers a letter. (*Slamming the door behind her.*) God-fuckin'-damn you! (*He locks the door, and peers through the peep-hole.*)

GINGER: (*Off-screen, through the doors as* ACE *walks away*) You're not getting away with this! You're not gonna fuck me out of my end!

### EXT. ACE'S HOUSE, FRONT YARD – NIGHT

GINGER *is furious. She picks up the suitcase and walks up to her sportscar.*
GINGER: Fucker! (*Sobs. She drives off.*)


### INT. ACE'S BEDROOM – NIGHT, LATER

ACE *is lying awake in bed smoking a cigarette, watching the casino's Eye in the Sky surveillance monitors. He hears a car turn into his driveway. He sees the car's headlight beams on the bedroom ceiling. The door opens.* GINGER, *wearing her long fur coat, enters and slowly walks towards the bed to lie down beside* ACE.

ACE: (*Voice-over*) The funny thing was, that after all that . . . I
    didn't want her to go. She was the mother of my kid. I
    loved her. And later . . . I realized I didn't want to give her
    the money, because if I did . . . I knew I'd never see her
    again.
    (ACE *reaches over to take* GINGER's *hand – she slowly takes
    hold of his.*)


### INT. ACE'S HOUSE, KITCHEN – DAY

GINGER *is getting* AMY *ready for school.* ACE *enters as* AMY *is on her way out. He holds her face in his hands and kisses her.*
ACE: (*Affectionately*) Oh. Have a good day at school.
AMY: Okay. (*Amy exits.*)
ACE: Okay? Okay, angel.
    (ACE *walks over to* GINGER *who turns sullenly to look at him.*)
    (*Clears throat.*) From now on, I have to know where you
    and Amy are at all times.
    (*He takes a beeper out of his coat pocket and holds it up to*
    GINGER.)
    (*Gently*) Now, here's a beeper. I want you to keep it on
    you. It's very light. So I can call you whenever I have to.
    (GINGER *reluctantly takes the beeper.*)
    (*Pause.*) Okay?
    (*She nods silently. He looks at her and turns, leaving her alone
    in the kitchen.*)

**EXT. CONSTRUCTION TRAILER – EVENING**

*A very large trailer is in the middle of an empty construction site.*
*GINGER's and NICKY's cars are parked outside.*

NICKY: (*Off-screen, from trailer*) Well, what are you supposed to
do? I mean, what do you want to do? Do you want to stay the
way you are? You want to stay like this? You can't do that.

**INT. CONSTRUCTION TRAILER – EVENING**

*GINGER and NICKY are alone in the large trailer. They are sitting*
*close together on a couch.*

NICKY: I mean, listen, two people don't get along, at some
point you gotta call it . . . I mean, it's none of my business,
but I . . . I think that's what you gotta do. You gotta take it
somewhere –

GINGER: (*Smoking a cigarette*) Oh, you're right, I know. It's . . .
well, I was just –

NICKY: What? What?

GINGER: Nothin'.

NICKY: What were you gonna say? Go ahead.

GINGER: I don't – (*Sighs.*)

NICKY: Tell me what you were gonna say. Go ahead.

GINGER: Yeah?

NICKY: Yeah.

GINGER: Well, I was thinkin', maybe . . . you know somebody
at the bank . . . could help me get my jewelry out? There's
a lot of money in there. Lot of money in there, and I'd be
willing to take care of anybody who helped me out.

NICKY: (*Pauses*) Let me think about that.

GINGER: Okay.

NICKY: See who I got in there. Gotta get somebody I can trust.

GINGER: Mm-hm.

NICKY: You know?

GINGER: Yeah. 'Cause, you know (*leaning her head back*), he's
never gonna give me my jewelry.

NICKY: Hm.

GINGER: He holds that key so tight, he's probably got it stuck
up his ass.

NICKY: (*Chuckles*) Yeah, right. That's Sammy. And he's probably got it there too. (*Takes a sip of his drink.*)

GINGER: He's so fuckin' lucky. I could have buried him. I could have gone to Europe and taken the baby. And then he'd've tracked me down and he'd've killed me.

NICKY: No, he wouldn't. I would have.

(GINGER *chuckles.*)

And he'd've been right, too. I mean, seriously.

(*She cuddles closer to him.*)

Well, there's one thing you don't do. You don't take a guy's kid and then take off.

GINGER: (*Quietly*) I didn't. (*Chuckles.*) I didn't. I mean, I did, but then I did exactly what you told me to do, and I came right back.

NICKY: You did. You're right.

GINGER: Exactly.

(NICKY *embraces her.*)

NICKY: You did. I like that. I like that. That's what I like about you. You did the right thing.

GINGER: (*Playing with his jacket*) I did what you told me to.

NICKY: Yes, you did.

GINGER: 'Cause you always tell me the right thing to do.

NICKY: Yeah. (*Pause, with his arm around her.*) Boy, he really
　　fucked himself up out here –
　　(*She caresses his face.*)
　　– didn't he?
GINGER: Sure did.
NICKY: Everything went to his head.
　　(*He sighs, rubbing her neck.*)
NICKY/GINGER: (*In unison*) Changed.
NICKY: He did. He ain't the same person, right?
GINGER: (*Whispering*) No, he's not.
NICKY: He really thinks who the fuck he is, I'll tell you that.
GINGER: (*Holding back tears*) Exactly. (*Sighs.*) He hates me.
　　(*She rests her head on* NICKY's *shoulder, starting to weep.*)
　　He hates my fuckin' guts.
NICKY: Come on, come on, you're a toughie. You can take this.
　　(*Runs his hand down her cheek.*)
　　Don't cry.
GINGER: (*Crying*) I'm not as tough as you think I am.
NICKY: Yes, you are.
GINGER: (*Sobbing*) I'm not and he scares the shit out of me. I
　　never know what he's gonna do.
NICKY: (*Whispering*) Come on. Don't be scared.
GINGER: (*Softly, through tears*) I need some help. I do. I need
　　some help.
　　(*Strokes his chest.*)
　　You gotta help me. I need a new sponsor, Nicky.
　　(GINGER's *sobs subside a little and her hand starts to stroke*
　　NICKY's *neck.*)
　　(*Whispering*) I do. I need a new sponsor.
NICKY: (*Quietly, cheek to cheek*) Is that what you want?
GINGER: Yeah.
NICKY: A sponsor.
GINGER: Yeah.
NICKY: Mm . . . okay. Don't worry about it. Nobody'll fuck
　　with ya anymore. I'll take care of ya.
GINGER: (*Whispering*) Nicky, please . . .
NICKY: Yes, I will. It's what you want, isn't it? Huh?
GINGER: (*Sobbing*) Thank you. Yeah, yeah, yeah.
NICKY: It's what you want?

GINGER: Yeah. Uh-huh –
>   (NICKY *interrupts and kisses her. She kisses him back. He pushes her head down to his lap.*)

EXT. CONSTRUCTION TRAILER – NIGHT

NICKY *opens the door to the trailer and peers out to make sure no one is watching.*

EXT. FBI SURVEILLANCE CAMPER – NIGHT

*We see past a chain-link fence to a camper. We hear the sound of photos being taken by a high-speed camera.*

EXT. CONSTRUCTION TRAILER – NIGHT

*We see* GINGER *and* NICKY *slip out of the trailer in the deserted work site.*
FBI AGENT #1: (*Off-screen*) You see that?

EXT. FBI SURVEILLANCE CAMPER – NIGHT

FBI MEN *with long-lens cameras are recording the event on film.*
FBI AGENT #1: That's Ace's wife.
>   (*Still photos:* NICKY *and* GINGER *steal a kiss.*)
>   Fantastic!
>   (*Still photos: Click. Click.* GINGER *and* NICKY *embrace.*)

EXT. CONSTRUCTION TRAILER – NIGHT

*The* AGENTS *watch as* GINGER *and* NICKY *move towards their separate cars.*

EXT. FBI SURVEILLANCE CAMPER – NIGHT

FBI AGENT #1: This is great for the boss.

EXT. CONSTRUCTION TRAILER – NIGHT

GINGER *gets into her car.*
*(Still photos: Click:* GINGER *getting into her car. Click:* NICKY *getting into his car.)*


EXT. CONSTRUCTION TRAILER – NIGHT

NICKY *and* GINGER *drive off.*


INT. ACE'S KITCHEN – NIGHT

ACE *is waiting for* GINGER. *He hears a car pull into the drive-way, he gets up and looks out the sliding glass door. It's* GINGER. *He sits back down, motionless with a glass of milk. She walks in with a sack of groceries and some dry cleaning.*
GINGER: Hi. *(She puts her purse and the groceries down on the kitchen counter, and hangs up the dry cleaning.)*
ACE: Hi. You didn't answer your beeper.
GINGER: I threw it away.
ACE: You threw it away?
GINGER: *(As she puts some items away)* Look, I tried to do this thing. I know that you want me to, but it's just – You know, I'm driving down the freeway and the fuckin' thing's 'beep-beep-beep-beep'. You know, I'm in a restaurant and it's – it's embarrassing. I don't want to do it anymore. *(Stopping suddenly.)* Where's Amy?
ACE: I put her to bed.
GINGER: Oh. *(Walking away towards their bedroom.)* I got your cigarettes.


INT. ACE'S HOUSE, BATHROOM – NIGHT

GINGER *sets some items down on her dressing-table, in front of a mirror.*
GINGER: Oscar wants you to call him.
ACE: So, who'd you go to lunch with?
GINGER: With Jennifer.
ACE: And where'd you go?

GINGER: To the Riviera.

ACE: (*Pause*) What'd you have?

GINGER: I had a . . . salad.

ACE: What did Jennifer have?

GINGER: (*Turning to* ACE) She had the same.

ACE: (*Pause*) Okay. I want you to call Jennifer and I want you to tell her to tell you what she had for lunch, and I'm gonna listen in on the other line.

GINGER: Why do you want to do that?

ACE: You know why I want to do it. Just do it.

GINGER: Fine. (*Walking out and down the hall.*) Just gonna get the bowl for my thing.

ACE: Mm.


INT. ACE'S HOUSE, LIVING-ROOM – NIGHT

GINGER *is on the hall phone, dialing. We hear a phone ring through the earpiece. She waits a few seconds and hangs up.*

GINGER: The line's busy. There's nobody there.

    (*She starts to walk away.* ACE *stops her, picks up the phone and dials. We hear* JENNIFER *answer.*)

JENNIFER: (*Over telephone*) Hello.

ACE: (*Into telephone*) Hello, Jennifer, it's Sam –

    (*Tight on* GINGER'S *fingers cutting off the call.*)

GINGER: All right . . . I didn't have lunch with Jennifer.

ACE: (*Hanging up*) Who were you with?

GINGER: (*Quietly*) I was with somebody.

ACE: I know you were with somebody. Who was it? (*Pause.*) I just hope it's not someone who I think it might be. (*Sighs, then whispers:*) I just hope it's not them.

ACE: (*Voice-over, quietly*) I knew she fucked around. (*Sighing.*) You know . . .


INT. ACE'S BEDROOM – NIGHT

*The two of them are seated separately.* GINGER *is on the floor leaning against a chair, crying softly.*

ACE: (*Voice-over*) . . . she did what she did and I did what I had to do. But, Jesus, Nicky was the worst thing she could've done.

ACE: What if he won't stop?

ACE: (*Voice-over*) I mean, it could get us both killed.

GINGER: I can back him off.
(ACE *sighs.*)

ACE: (*Voice-over*) She was very convincing . . .

EXT. LA CONCHA MOTEL – DAY

*A neon signs reads: LA CONCHA MOTEL.*

ACE: (*Voice-over*) . . . when she wanted to be.
(*We see a canted angle of a room and balcony with drawn curtains.*)
And . . . this . . . this is how she backed him off.

INT. LA CONCHA MOTEL – DAY

GINGER *and* NICKY *are making love on the bed, panting, grunting and gasping.*

INT. LA CONCHA MOTEL – DAY, LATER

*They have finished making love.* NICKY *is zipping up his pants.*
GINGER *still sits on the bed smoking a cigarette.*
NICKY: Hey, Ginger . . . don't forget, if you're challenged, you know, if he asks anything, deny everything.
(*He walks up to her.*)
Do you understand? I don't want him bringin' beefs back home . . . 'cause that could be a problem. You gotta be careful. He's not dumb, you know? You hear what I'm sayin', right?
(*Her arm and thigh are bruised.*)
GINGER: I know. You don't have to tell me that. What do you think (*chuckling*), I'm stupid? (*She takes a drag off her cigarette.*)

177

NICKY: Do I think you're stupid? No, I think you're beautiful.
(*He bends down and kisses her.*)
But I gotta go. (*He exits.*)

ACE: (*Voice-over*) By this . . .

EXT. ALL–AMERICAN GAS STATION, BACK HOME – DAY

*A car moves into the station and stops at a gas pump.*

ACE: (*Voice-over*) . . . time, Nicky had things so fucked up on the
streets, that every time Marino went back home, the . . .

INT. ALL-AMERICAN GAS STATION, OFFICE AND GARAGE – DAY

*Slow-motion of MARINO walking through the front office past a few
men. He tosses his cigarette butt and puts it out with his shoe. He
looks nervous.*

ACE: (*Voice-over*) . . . packages got smaller and smaller. It
got . . .

INT. ALL-AMERICAN GAS STATION, GAGGI'S BACK OFFICE –
DAY

MARINO *takes a small stack of cash out of his coat. A seated* GAGGI
*nods for one of his men to take the money.*

ACE: (*Voice-over*) . . . to the point when he walked into the place
. . . he didn't know whether he was gonna be kissed or
killed.

(GAGGI's *man takes the money.*)
GAGGI: (*Off-screen*) Frankie, I want to ask you something.
GAGGI: It's private . . . but I want you to tell me the truth.
MARINO: Of course, Remo.
GAGGI: I want you to tell me the truth, mind you.
MARINO: I always tell you the truth, Remo.
GAGGI: Frankie . . . the little guy, he wouldn't be fuckin' the
Jew's wife, would he? Because if he is . . . it's a problem.
(*Freeze frame of* MARINO.)

178

MARINO: (*Voice-over*) What could I say? I knew if I gave the
wrong answer, I mean, Nicky, Ginger, Ace, all of 'em
could've wound up gettin' killed.
(*Freeze frame of* GAGGI.)
Because there's one thing about these old timers: They
don't like any fuckin' around with the other guy's wives.
It's bad for business.
(*On* MARINO's *freeze frame.*)

MARINO: So, I lied . . . even though I knew that by lyin' to
Gaggi, I could wind up gettin' killed too.
(*Unfreeze – live action continues.*)
(*To* GAGGI) No. I ain't see anything like that.

GAGGI: Are you sure?

MARINO: I'm positive. Remo . . . things are very fucked up
down there, you know?

GAGGI: Yeah, I know. That's why I'm asking. You see, my main
concern is Nicky.

MARINO: Hm.

GAGGI: I want to know . . . if he's doin' all right. If he's okay.

MARINO: He's good. He's fine.

GAGGI: I'm askin' you, Frankie, to keep an eye on Nicky. Do it
for me.

MARINO: No problem.

GAGGI: You see . . . I wouldn't want to be jeopardizing
anything for people who are our friends. You
understand?

MARINO: I understand.

GAGGI: Okay. (*Pause.*) Frankie, you're a good boy. (*Pats*
MARINO's *hand.*)

MARINO: Thanks, Remo.
(GAGGI *drinks from his espresso cup. So does* MARINO, *looking
over cautiously at the old man.*)

ACE: (*Voice-over*) By now, Nicky and his crew had already hit
rock bottom. I mean, Vegas really got to him.


EXT. BAR PARKING LOT, LAS VEGAS – NIGHT

NICKY *is punching a man who is leaning against a car. They are surrounded by* MARINO, FUSCO, BLUE *and* HARDY. *The man remains erect.*

ACE: (*Voice-over*) The booze, the coke, the broads . . . I mean, he got sloppy. He just wasn't the same Nicky anymore.
(DOMINICK *takes over. Exhausted,* NICKY *walks to his car and leans on the open car door.*)

MARINO: (*To* NICKY) You must have drank too much.
NICKY: Go fuck yourself.

ACE: (*Voice-over*) I heard one night he had to belt a guy three times before he finally went down.
(DOMINICK *finally knocks the man down.*)
In the old days, Nicky would've decked him with one shot.


INT. ROOM – NIGHT

*Extreme close-up of a camera following a line of cocaine as it is sucked up into a straw.*

ACE: (*Voice-over*) You add this into the mix . . .
(*Extreme close-up looking through the straw as the coke is sniffed.*)
Maybe Vegas just got . . .


EXT. BAR PARKING LOT – NIGHT

NICKY *and his crew get into their cars.*

ACE: (*Voice-over*) . . . to all of us. And his crew followed him right over the edge.
(*The man is left alone on the ground of the dingy parking lot.*)
They were all tuned up half the time on coke. I mean, they started doin' . . .


EXT. BERNIE BLUE'S HOUSE, RESIDENTIAL STREET – NIGHT

BLUE *gets out of his car with an aluminium foil package to confront the police.*

ACE: (*Voice-over*) . . . stupid things.

COP #1: Watch it, partner, watch it!

ACE: (*Voice-over*) The worst was Blue.

BLUE: (*Belligerent*) Hey, what do you guys want out of my life, huh?

COP #1: Police! Stay in the fuckin' car!

ACE: (*Voice-over*) He never knew when to keep his fuckin' mouth shut.

COP #2: He has a gun!

COP #1: Drop your gun or I'll –!

BLUE: Hey, fuck you!

COP #1: Drop the gun!
> (BLUE *is shot several times by both* COPS. *He falls on the ground, dead.*)

ACE: (*Voice-over*) The cops shot him. They shot Blue . . .


FLASHBACK – A LITTLE EARLIER

BLUE *is yelling back at the* COPS, *holding the foil package.*

ACE: (*Voice-over*) . . . because they thought his hero sandwich was a gun!
> (*Freeze frame as the camera moves in on the wrapped sandwich in his hand.*)
> You know, they could have . . .
> (*The* COPS *walk up to* BLUE, *who is on the ground amid shattered glass.*)
> . . . been right, but who knows?

COP #1: Jesus Christ! What gun? He's got a fuckin' hero sandwich here.

COP #2: What do you want? It – It's pitch-black out here. It's tin foil.

COP #1: Pitch-black?! It –

COP #2: It looked like a fuckin' gun!

COP #1: You – You fuckin' moron, I'll be filling out paper work for the next two months because of you and this piece of shit, you . . .

COP #2: Oh my God, what are we gonna do? I'm sorry.

COP #1: . . . fuckin' jerk-off.

ACE: (*Voice-over*) And to make matters worse, to get even, Nicky's crew got stoned one night and they started shootin' up the cops' houses.
(COP #1 *plants a gun on the ground next to* BLUE's *legs using a handkerchief to avoid leaving fingerprints.*)


EXT. DETECTIVE'S HOUSE – NIGHT

*The house explodes as gunfire riddles the front of a detective's home.* MARINO, DOMINICK, FUSCO, HARDY *and three* HOODS *in another car are spraying the home with machine-guns and shotguns.*


EXT. GOLD RUSH – DAY

NICKY *and* MARINO *emerge from the shop.*

ACE: (*Voice-over*) I mean, it got to the point where they couldn't even talk in the Gold Rush anymore because the Feds put a wire in the wall.


EXT. FBI STAKEOUT POST: MOTEL ACROSS FROM THE GOLD RUSH – DAY

*Two* FBI AGENTS *with binoculars are watching* NICKY *and* MARINO, *trying to read their lips.*

ACE: (*Voice-over*) And even when they talked outside, they had to cover their mouths because . . .

LIP-READER: (*Lowering his binoculars*) Jeez, he's coverin' up again. (*He raises the binoculars and looks through again.*)

ACE: (*Voice-over*) . . . the Feds brought in lip-readers.


EXT. GOLD RUSH – DAY

NICKY *and* MARINO *are outside talking. They are covering their mouths with their hands and constantly looking around.*

ACE: (*Voice-over*) Nicky found out about it from a teller who
  owed him money. This guy worked . . .
  (*Voice-over trails off.*)

MARINO: He asked me again about you and the Jew's wife.
NICKY: Walk, walk, walk. What'd you say?
MARINO: He asked me again about you and the Jew's wife.
NICKY: Yeah, what'd you tell him?
MARINO: I told him I didn't know nothin'. But Jiggs and, uh,
  Tony Gorilla said if you did anything, you're fucked up.
NICKY: You think he's goin' home, makin' a beef behind my
  back?
MARINO: Nah. You would've heard somethin'.
NICKY: Yeah, what's to stop him?
MARINO: I know. I know.
NICKY: I don't trust him anymore. But they'd never okay
  anything, you know?
MARINO: Yeah, but they keep askin' about it.
NICKY: Well, now, sure they're askin'. They earn with the
  prick. I got a funny feelin' he's gonna start a fuckin' war or
  somethin'. (*Pause.*) I'm not sure yet, you know. But I w–
  You know, but you know what I want you to do?
MARINO: What?

(NICKY *looks suspiciously at a man walking by them.*)

NICKY: Who's this guy? Who's this guy?

MARINO: Oh, he ain't nobody.

NICKY: You know what I want you to do? Get a couple of guys to dig a hole in the desert, then let 'em show you where it's at.

MARINO: Angelo and Buster.

NICKY: Yeah, but I'm not sure yet.

MARINO: They'll do it.

NICKY: And when I'm ready, I'll say the words, 'Go see the Jew.'

MARINO: Yeah.

NICKY: And you make it disappear, you know what I mean?

MARINO: Yeah, just let me know. But you gotta be ready. You know what I'm talkin' about?

NICKY: Did I say to do anything yet? I said I'm not sure . . . I'll let you know. I want to think about it. Where're these pricks at? (*Looks for the* FBI AGENTS.)

MARINO: Don't know.

NICKY: Dominick said they're in the motel?

MARINO: Yeah, either that or in the fuckin' bank. I don't know. They're all over the joint.


INT. JUBILATION NIGHTCLUB – NIGHT

ACE *is seated at a table with* SHERBERT, TRUDY, OSCAR *and two showgirls.* ACE *is on the phone. It rings and rings, but there's no answer.*


INT. ACE'S HOUSE – DAY

*The camera pans from the bedroom hallway to the living-room as the phone rings.*


INT. JUBILATION NIGHTCLUB – NIGHT

ACE *hangs up.*

ACE: (*Getting up from the table*) Be right back. I'll be right back. (*He walks over to* RUDY, *the maître d'.*)

Rudy, any calls for me, just give 'em to Mr Sherbert. I'll be right back.

RUDY: Sure, Mr Rothstein. You'll be back . . . ?

ACE: I'm going home for a few seconds. I'll be right back.

(ACE *hurries out.* RUDY *picks up the phone and dials a number.*)

RUDY: (*Into telephone*) He's on his way home.


INT. LEANING TOWER – NIGHT

NICKY *is on the phone. The place is jumping in the background.*

RUDY: (*Over telephone*) Yeah, he just left.

NICKY: Yeah? All right.

(*He hangs up the phone and looks across the room at* GINGER, *who is seated in a booth smiling at him and picking the olive out of a Martini.*)


INT. ACE'S HOUSE – NIGHT

ACE *gets home and can't find* GINGER.

ACE: (*Looking around the house*) Hello? Hello! Ginger.

AMY: (*Faintly, from her bedroom*) Help, Daddy!

(*Fear strikes him and he runs to his daughter's room.*)

(*Knocking, turning the doorknob*) Amy! Amy, open the door!

AMY: (*Off-camera, from her room*) I can't! I'm tied!

ACE: Wh-wh –

(ACE *slams his shoulder against the door, trying to knock it down.*)


INT. ACE'S HOUSE, AMY'S BEDROOM – NIGHT

ACE *forces it open and sees that* AMY'*s arms have been tied to her bed with stockings.* AMY *screams.*

AMY: Dad!

ACE: What happened? What happened? Who did this to you?

AMY: Mommy.

ACE: I'm gonna get a knife and cut you loose, honey, I'll –

AMY: (*Panting*) Oh, no, please, please. (*She tries to keep him from leaving her.*)

185

ACE: (*Bending down, kisses her*) Okay, I'll be right back.

    (ACE *cuts* AMY *loose with a knife.*)

    When did this happen, honey?

AMY: I don't know.

    (*She gets up and hugs her father.*)

ACE: You don't know? What time did your mother do this?

    When did she leave?

AMY: I don't know.

ACE: (*Comforting* AMY *as she moans*) Ohhh . . .

    (*He kisses her. They get up from the bed when the phone rings.*)


INT. ACE'S HOUSE, LIVING-ROOM – NIGHT

ACE *walks to the phone.*

ACE: (*Into telephone*) Hello.

NICKY: (*Over telephone*) Sammy.

ACE: (*Into telephone*) Yeah, uh, who's this?

NICKY: It's me.

ACE: (*Into telephone*) Nick?


INT. LEANING TOWER – NIGHT

DOMINICK *looks on as* NICKY *talks on the phone.*

NICKY: (*Into telephone*) Yeah, what are you doin'? You okay?

ACE: (*Over telephone*) No, I'm not okay.


INT. ACE'S HOUSE, LIVING-ROOM – NIGHT

ACE: (*Into telephone*) How'd you know I was here?

NICKY: (*Over telephone*) Well . . .


INT. LEANING TOWER – NIGHT

DOMINICK *and* MARINO *look on.*

NICKY: (*Into telephone*) . . . uh, you know, I just wanted to talk
    to you a minute.

ACE: (*Over telephone*) Well . . .

INT. ACE'S HOUSE, LIVING-ROOM – NIGHT

ACE: (*Into telephone*) . . . Ginger's missing and she tied Amy up and she locked her in her room. I gotta find her. I don't know where the hell she is.

INT. LEANING TOWER – NIGHT

NICKY: (*Into telephone*) Yeah? Well, listen, Ginger's over here at the Leaning Tower with me.

INT. ACE'S HOUSE, LIVING-ROOM – NIGHT

ACE: (*Into telephone*) She's there with you? (*Getting angry.*) She's there with you?
NICKY: (*Over telephone*) Yeah, she's here.
ACE: (*Into telephone*) I'll be right there. (*He hangs up and starts to leave.*)

INT. LEANING TOWER – NIGHT

NICKY: (*Into telephone*) Uh, all right.
(*He hangs up and steps over to* DOMINICK *and* MARINO.)
He's comin' over.
DOMINICK: Great!

EXT. LEANING TOWER – NIGHT

*High angle past the restaurant's neon sign to* ACE's *car screeching to a halt by the main entrance. He storms in.*

INT. LEANING TOWER – NIGHT

ACE *is stopped by* NICKY *in the foyer.*
NICKY: (*Trying to calm him*) Ace don't . . . listen, don't . . . don't make a scene, all right?
ACE: I want to just talk. I want to talk to that Irish bitch.
NICKY: She didn't know who to turn to. (*Raising his hand almost in a plea.*) She . . . she didn't know where to turn.

She was tryin' to save your marriage.

ACE: Yeah? Nicky, I want to talk to that fuckin' bitch.

NICKY: (*Menacing*) Hey, be fuckin' nice. Calm. Be nice. Don't fuck up in here.

(ACE *pauses for a beat, realizing that* NICKY *is standing in his way and could be dangerous.* ACE *gives him a wide berth.*

*We follow* ACE *through the crowd to* GINGER, *seated in a booth. He sits down angrily across from her.*)

GINGER: (*Stoned, smoking a cigarette*) Hi, Sam.

ACE: (*Quietly*) I mean, you tie up our kid and you lock the fuckin' door? Are . . .

GINGER: Oh . . .

ACE: . . . you out of your mind? That's our child. Are you out of your fuckin' mind?

GINGER: It's just for a little while, Sam. The baby-sitter wasn't there.

ACE: I ought to fuckin' have you committed. You fuckin' do that again (*pointing his finger at her*), I'll f–, I'll f–

GINGER: She wasn't gonna get up. I was just gonna be out for a little while.

ACE: I should have –

GINGER: I mean, she was asleep. I was going to be right back before she even woke up.

ACE: Listen to me, listen to me, listen to me. (*Pounding his fist on the table.*) Listen, you fuckin' cunt.

GINGER: Oh, sh–

ACE: Listen to me.

GINGER: Fuck you.

ACE: (*Knocking her drink over*) Let me tell you something. (*Pointing.*) Listen to me.

GINGER: I w– I was gonna be back before she woke up.

ACE: You listen carefully! You ever fuckin' touch her again, you ever do anything like that again, I'll fuckin' kill you. Pure and simple. Do you hear me? Pure and fuckin' simple, I'll fuckin' kill you, you bitch.

GINGER: (*Leaning in to him*) Why don't you just let me go, Sam?

ACE: You fuckin' whore!

GINGER: I'll sign anything you want me to sign, okay?

188

ACE: You understand? What? Let you go?

GINGER: I just want the key to my jewelry, and I want you to let me go.

ACE: You want your jewelry?

GINGER: I want you to let me go.

ACE: And what? And let you disgrace me, you fuckin' pig? And let you disgrace me? Get up. Get up and be a mother. Get in the car and go to the house . . .

(GINGER *darts a look to* NICKY *who is at the bar, watching anxiously. He gestures with his head for her to leave.*)

. . . right now. Get up and –

(ACE *notices her look at* NICKY *but when he turns to see what she's looking at, he just misses* NICKY's *gesture.* ACE *grabs* GINGER *by her collar.*)

Get – Get up! Get up!

GINGER: I wou– I wouldn't do that if I were you.

ACE: Get – get up!

GINGER: I wouldn't do that . . .

ACE: Get up! Get going! (*Pushing the table.*) Get up!

(NICKY *gestures to her again.*)

GINGER: I wouldn't –

ACE: Get the fu– (*Shaking the table.*) You threatening me? (*Making a fist.*) I'll fuckin' kill you in this place! (*Pointing to her.*) Get up and go home right now.

(GINGER *gets up and leans in to shout at* ACE.)

GINGER: (*Barking*) I'm going. I'm going, you –!

(*She grabs her purse and leaves. Patrons stare as* ACE *follows her out.*)

INT. ACE'S HOUSE, FOYER – NIGHT

GINGER *follows* ACE *through the door. As soon as she closes the door behind her,* ACE *turns to face her.*

ACE: Now you need approval from him to go home?

GINGER: So what? So who fuckin' blew you in the parking lot before you came in . . . huh?

ACE: (*Disgusted*) You make me sick, you fuck. Once a fuckin' hooker, always a hooker.

GINGER: Oh, fuck you! Fuck you, Sam Rothstein! (*Opening the*

189

*door.*) Fuck you! (*A furious* GINGER *turns around and storms out, slamming the door.*)

INT. ACE'S HOUSE KITCHEN – NIGHT

*Through the kitchen sliding glass door:* GINGER's *engine roars and tires screech as she tears away in her sportscar.* ACE *dials the phone.*
ACE: (*Into telephone*) Yeah, Billy Sherbert, please. Put him on.
SHERBERT: (*Over telephone*) Who's this?
ACE: (*Into telephone*) Yeah, Billy, listen, I'll explain to you later. Just – You – You got a gun at home? Yeah. Bring it over here right away.

INT. JUBILATION NIGHTCLUB – NIGHT

SHERBERT *is still at the discothèque.*
SHERBERT: (*Into telephone*) Okay. Just take it easy.
ACE: (*Over telephone*) Right away. Okay?
SHERBERT: (*Into telephone*) I-I'll do it.

INT. ACE'S KITCHEN – NIGHT
ACE: (*Into telephone*) Okay. (*He hangs up.*)

EXT. LEANING TOWER – NIGHT

GINGER's *car screeches into the parking lot and she jumps out, leaving her car door open and engine running. A valet parker approaches.*
GINGER: (*To* VALET PARKER) Leave it where it is.

INT. LEANING TOWER, FOYER – NIGHT

GINGER *bursts in.* MARINO *tries to calm her down.*
GINGER: Where is he? Goddamn it! I want that Jew bastard killed! I have fuckin' had it!
    (NICKY *walks in from the restaurant.*)
MARINO: Calm down, calm down. Shh!

NICKY: Shh. (*To* MARINO.) Hide her car in the back!
    (*He pulls her by her arm to a storage room upstairs.*)
GINGER: There's no reason to hide my car. He already knows!
    (*Walking up the stairs.*) He threw it in my face! The second
    I get out of here, I –


INT. LEANING TOWER, UPSTAIRS STORAGE ROOM – NIGHT

GINGER *is enraged and panting.*
NICKY: What did I tell you? Supposing he goes back home and
    makes a fuckin' beef? I gotta know exactly what you said.
    Tell me what you said to him.
GINGER: Me? I said . . . nothin'. I said, I said, 'No, no, no.'
    Everything he said, I just kept sayin' no.
NICKY: I told you this was fuckin' dangerous. Remember I said,
    'Ginger, this is a dangerous situation. Be very careful.' You
    fuckin' yessed me to death.
GINGER: If it's so fuckin' dangerous, then why don't you kill him?
NICKY: I'm not gonna kill him. Shut the fuck up. What, do you
    know what you're talkin' about? I'm not killing anyb–
GINGER: (*Interrupting*) Oh, well, then, have him killed and get it
    over with.

NICKY: (*Loud and angry*) Hey, don't be such a fuckin' smart-ass, will you? I mean, I know the fuckin' guy thirty-five years, I'm gonna fuckin' whack him for you? Fuck . . . motherfucker! I knew this, I knew it.

GINGER: What about my money?

NICKY: (*Raising his voice even more*) How the fuck am I gonna get your fuckin' money now? You think he's gonna give you fuckin' money? Are you out of your mind?! Look what you did to this fuckin' guy! If you would have just kept your fuckin' mouth shut! (*Walking away.*) Ah, what the fuck is the use? I should've never got invol–
(GINGER *screams and attacks* NICKY.)
(*Grappling with her*) What? Hey! Hey! What the fuck are you . . . ?
(NICKY *slaps her roughly across the face, grabs the back of her jacket and forcefully leads her to a stairway.*)

GINGER: Ah, you fuck! You're such a fuckin' asshole!

NICKY: Get the fuck out of here. Get out! Get the fuck out!
(*Shoves her down the stairs.* GINGER *yells and gasps on her way down.*)

MARINO: (*Off-camera, from bottom of stairway*) Whoa. Calm down.

NICKY: (*Behind* GINGER) Get out. Get out! Get out!

MARINO: (*Off-camera*) Take it easy!

NICKY: Why'd I get involved with this fuckin' nut in the first place? Get out!

MARINO: You're gonna fuckin' kill her. Take it easy.

NICKY: (*Pushing a sobbing* GINGER *out the back door*) Get her the fuck out of here. Get her out of here.


EXT. LEANING TOWER, BACK DOOR/REAR PARKING LOT –
NIGHT

MARINO *throws* GINGER *out the back door. She falls on her side, crying.*

NICKY: Get the fuck out of here.

GINGER: (*Sobbing, getting up*) I don't need you! I have my own fuckin' money!

NICKY: All right, all right.

(*She stumbles to her car.*)

GINGER: I'm goin' to the FBI! I'm not scared anymore!

NICKY: All right. Be careful.

GINGER: You fucked with me for the last time!

NICKY: Okay, yeah.


INT. LEANING TOWER, BACK DOOR – NIGHT

*NICKY and MARINO are at the back door watching GINGER screech out of the parking lot.*

NICKY: Be careful. (*To MARINO.*) Hey, come on. Get inside.

(*They turn and walk back inside. MARINO leans on a wall next to the kitchen. NICKY has scratches on his hand and face.*)
Can you fuckin' believe that? (*Showing MARINO his scratches.*) Look at this motherfucker.
(NICKY *sits on the bottom step across from* MARINO, *who sighs. Cooks mill around in the background.*)
I fucked up, Frankie. I fucked up good this time. Should have never started with this fuckin' broad.

MARINO: Take it easy. What could you do? I mean, she threw herself at you, right?

NICKY: I'm in a bad fuckin' spot here. You know that? Bad fuckin' spot. (*He puts his head in his hands.*)


INT. ACE'S HOUSE, KITCHEN – NIGHT

*We see SHERBERT approach the sliding glass door holding a shotgun. ACE lets him in, locks the door and grabs the gun from him.*


EXT. ACE'S HOUSE, LIVING-ROOM – NIGHT

*Through the sliding patio doors, we see ACE and SHERBERT making sure all the doors are locked and the lights are turned off.*

ACE: (*Voice-over*) I already left the kid with neighbours and I had about a million in cash and jewels that I gave to Sherbert to lock up in the hotel.

ACE: (*Off-screen, from following scene*) Put this in the . . .

INT. ACE'S HOUSE – NIGHT

ACE *leads* SHERBERT *to the front door as he stuffs a shoebox filled with cash and jewels in a bag and hands it over to him.*
ACE: . . . hotel safe, then I want you to come right back. (ACE *shuts the door behind him and switches off a light. The room goes black.*)


EXT. ACE'S HOUSE – MORNING

*A crisp, sunny morning.* SHERBERT'S *car is parked on the street in front of the house.*


INT. ACE'S HOUSE, UPSTAIRS DEN – MORNING

*An exhausted* ACE, *in his robe, and* SHERBERT *are seated across from each other at the bar with the shotgun displayed prominently on the counter between them.*


EXT. NEIGHBORHOOD STREET, ACE'S HOUSE – MORNING

*Camera pans with* GINGER'S *car as it approaches the driveway and crashes into the back of* ACE'S *parked car.*


INT. ACE'S HOUSE, UPSTAIRS DEN – MORNING

ACE *and* SHERBERT *react to the noise.* SHERBERT *grabs the shotgun.* ACE *looks out the window at* GINGER *ramming her car into his.*
ACE: She, she's alone. Just go. Take the gun and go into Amy's.
GINGER: (*Screaming; off-screen*) You get down here!
ACE: (*To* SHERBERT *as he walks around the bar with the gun*) Just wait there for me!
GINGER: (*From driveway*) Get down here and talk to me, goddamn it! Don't fuckin' ignore me! You motherfucker! (SHERBERT *exits.* ACE *runs over to the stairs and starts down them.*)

EXT. ACE'S HOUSE – MORNING

GINGER *repeatedly smashes into* ACE's *car.*

GINGER: (*From her car*) I mean it!

> (ACE *emerges from the front door, taking cover behind a brick column.*)

> You come down here right now! Come down here and talk to me, goddamn it! Fuck you! Goddamn you, come out here! I'm gonna drive this fucking car through the living-room!

> (*She starts to drive it across the lawn.* ACE *darts back towards the front door.* GINGER's *car stops in front of the porch.*)

> (*Getting out of the car to confront* ACE) You fucking coward! You motherfucker! (*She slips and falls on the lawn.*) You come out here and talk to me, you fucker!

ACE: (*From the porch*) Will you stop it? You're drunk, you're on drugs. You're gonna –

GINGER: I am not!

ACE: (*Pointing to her*) You're gonna be sorry if you don't stop that.

GINGER: Don't you threaten me!

ACE: You'll wake the whole neighborhood!

GINGER: (*Kicking the hedges*) Don't you threaten me!


EXT. NEIGHBOR'S HOUSE ACROSS THE STREET – MORNING

*A female neighbor walks out of her house. A man from the house next door does the same. We see* AMY *watching from the neighbor's window.*

GINGER: (*Off-camera*) You are not threatening me anymore!

ACE: (*Off-camera*) I'm not –


EXT. ACE'S HOUSE – MORNING

GINGER *is bending down, breaking off branches from some plants and throwing them at* ACE.

GINGER: You fuck! You fuck! I'm sick of you!

> (ACE *flinches as a handful of leaves hit his face.*)

> I am fuckin' Nicky Santoro! I am! He's my new sponsor!

(ACE *gestures towards the neighbors who are watching. A squad car pulls into the driveway.*)
(*Off-camera: to* ACE) What about that, you fuckhead?!
(*To neighbors.*) What are you looking at? Fuck off!
(*Two* COPS *walk up the driveway towards* GINGER.)
COP #1: Hey!
COP #2: Hey!
GINGER: (*To neighbors*) Go back inside! This is none of your
  business! (*To* ACE.) I don't have to take your shit all the
  time anymore.
COP #1: Hey.
GINGER: I'll go to the FBI!
COP #2: Mrs Rothstein, hey.
GINGER: I will go to the police! I am not (*kicking hedge*)
  protecting you anymore, you fuck!
COP #1: Mrs Ro– Mrs Rothstein! Okay, shh!
GINGER: He won't . . .


EXT. FBI SURVEILLANCE CAMPER – MORNING

*An* FBI AGENT *is parked down the block, photographing the scene
through a long-lens camera.*

GINGER: (*Off-camera*) . . . let me inside!

INT. FBI SURVEILLANCE CAMPER – MORNING

*On the* FBI AGENT *and his camera as he photographs the scene.*
GINGER: (*Off-camera*) He won't let me in my own house!

EXT. ACE'S HOUSE – MORNING

*Freeze frame:* COP #1 *tugging at* GINGER's *jacket.*

*Unfreeze: live action continues as she pulls away from him.*
COP #1: Mr Rothstein. Mr Rothstein, I'm sorry. We've got
    some complaints about – about the noise.
GINGER: I'm just trying to get in my house!
COP #1: I understand.
GINGER: He won't let me go in my house!
ACE: I won't let her in. I'm sorry, Randy, I'm not gonna let her
    in. She – Well, I'm not gonna let her in, the way she's
    behaving. I'm – I'm –
GINGER: Not gonna let me in?
ACE: Who knows what you're gonna do in there? I don't want
    you –
GINGER: What do you mean, what am I gonna do? I'm in the
    same clothes for two days! I want to get a few of my things!
    Big deal!
COP #1: All right. Okay, okay.
COP #2: Mr Rothstein, why don't we just let her in the house
    and get a few of her things? That way she'll get out of here.
    This is half her house anyway.
ACE: I'm afraid to let her in the house.
GINGER: Oh, you are . . .
ACE: I'm afraid she's gonna destroy stuff.
GINGER: (*Kicking, pulling up plants and throwing them at* ACE)
    Let me in the house! Fucker!
    (COP #1 *holds her back.*)
    Fucker!
COP #1: Please.
ACE: Should I let her in like – ?

GINGER: You ought to be afraid, the way you fuckin' treat me!

COP #1: Hey, Mr Rothstein, it'll make it a lot easier on everybody here if we just let her in the house.

COP #2: If we let her get a few of her things we'll be out of your hair.

ACE: If she calms down, I will let her in the house.

GINGER: (*Pants, yelling*) I am calm!

ACE: If she calms down . . .

COP #1: (*To* GINGER) No, you're not calm.

ACE: . . . I will let her in the house for five minutes if you gentlemen will escort her out if she happens not to want to leave. Because I don't – I –

GINGER: (*To* COP #1) Can I go in?

COP #1: That's not a problem, that's not a p–

GINGER: Can I go in?

COP #1: Jeff, would you go in with her?

(GINGER *walks toward the front door.*)

COP #2: We can do that. Absolutely. Yes. Absolutely.

GINGER: Yes, fine! Fine! (*In* ACE's *face as she brushes past him.*) Fuck you!


EXT. FBI SURVEILLANCE CAMPER – MORNING

*The* FBI AGENT *taking photographs.*

*We see a series of surveillance photos of* GINGER, ACE *and the* COPS *on the front lawn.*


EXT. NEIGHBOR'S WINDOW – MORNING

AMY *is watching her parents and the* COPS *across the street, until the housekeeper pulls her away into the house.*

GINGER: (*Off-camera, from following scene*) You wouldn't believe how mean he's been to me. He's locked up . . .


INT. ACE'S HOUSE, UPSTAIRS DEN – MORNING

GINGER *races up the stairs, trailed by* COP #2.

GINGER: . . . most of my important stuff, all my papers and

things. And I have to get 'em. (*She walks across the room to* ACE*'s desk.*) So don't let him come in here 'cause I know they're in here in the desk and he's – (*She tries to open the middle drawer but it's locked.*) Fuck! (*Going through a couple of drawers.*) Just pay attention. He could come up here at any time. (*Pants. She spots a pair of scissors on the desk. She tries to open the drawer with them. Then, to* COP #2:) Are you watching for him? (*She finally pries the drawer open, breaking the tip of the scissors.* GINGER*'s hands open the drawer and she picks up the safe deposit keys.*) Got 'em.
(*Freeze frame on the glimmering keys.*)

EXT. ACE'S HOUSE – MORNING

ACE *and* COP #1 *are on the front porch talking.*

ACE: (*Smoking, checking his watch*) Yeah, I don't want her in there more than a few more minutes.

COP #1: No, it's – it'll just be a couple of minutes. We got other things to do too, you know. He'll hurry her up. How's everything else besides this?

ACE: Fine, fine. How's your family?

COP #1: Not bad, not bad. In fact, uh, my wife's pregnant again.

ACE: Oh, good.

COP #1: Yeah.

ACE: Congratulations.
(ACE *shakes his hand.*)

COP #1: Thanks, yeah . . . I'm kind of happy about this, you know.

INT. ACE'S HOUSE, BEDROOM CLOSET – MORNING

GINGER *runs into the closet, bending down to search through the shoe boxes that usually contain money but are now empty.*

GINGER: (*Kneeling, to* COP #2) I just have to get this one more thing and then we'll be – We can go. (*She picks up an empty shoe box.*) Shit! (*Gets up, picking up a pair of* ACE*'s shoes and tossing them on the floor.*) God, fuck! Shit! God! (*She runs out, taking a fur coat off a hanger. Then, grunting:* Really

pisses me off . . . (*To* COP #2.) Don't worry about it.
(COP #2 *follows her out of the closet.*)


EXT. ACE'S HOUSE – MORNING

ACE, COP #1 *and several neighbors wait as* GINGER *storms out with* COP #2 *carrying a small overnight bag.*

GINGER: (*To the* COPS *but looking at* ACE) And it would be great if you guys could follow me out of here, because *he's* been threatening me. (GINGER *walks to her car.*)

COP #2: (*To* COP #1) Come on. I'm sorry.

COP #1: Okay.

ACE: (*To* COP #1, *shaking hands*) Okay, Randy. Thank you.

COP #1: All right, take care.

(GINGER *backs her car out, smashing into* ACE's *car once again.*)


EXT. ACE'S HOUSE, KITCHEN WINDOW – MORNING

SHERBERT *watches from a small, curtained window.*


EXT. NEIGHBORHOOD STREET – MORNING

GINGER *drives down the street followed by the police car. The FBI camper pulls out and follows the squad car following* GINGER.


EXT. GINGER'S CAR – MORNING

GINGER *is driving and crying.*

GINGER: (*To herself, panting*) I can't believe this. (*Sighs.*)


EXT. VEGAS BANK – MORNING

GINGER *swerves into the bank, parks in front of the main entrance and gets out of her car. The* COPS *park behind her.*

GINGER: (*To* COPS, *rushing inside*) I just need to pick up a little cash inside. Could you come with me?

EXT. FBI SURVEILLANCE CAR, ACROSS THE STREET – MORNING

*Two more* FBI AGENTS, *with binoculars and a camera, photograph* GINGER *as she walks into the bank.*


INT. VEGAS BANK VAULT – MORNING

*A bank employee is helping* GINGER *unlock a safe deposit box. She pulls it out hurriedly.*


INT. ACE'S HOUSE, UPSTAIRS DEN – MORNING

ACE *is on the phone talking to* CHARLIE CLARK. *He's looking at the jimmied drawer, broken scissors and the missing keys.*
ACE: (*Into telephone, throwing the scissors into the open drawer*)
     Charlie, you've gotta – you've gotta stop her!
CHARLIE CLARK: (*Over telephone*) I-I'm sorry, Sam.
ACE: (*Into telephone*) You've got to stop her.
CHARLIE CLARK: (*Over telephone*) What can I do?
ACE: (*Into telephone*) She's a fuckin' junkie. She's out of her
     fucking mind. Do you unders–
     (SHERBERT *is behind* ACE, *listening.*)
CHARLIE CLARK: (*Over telephone*) She has . . .


INT. VEGAS BANK – MORNING

CHARLIE CLARK *is on the phone.* GINGER, *in the background, comes out of the vault and carries one of her boxes to a cubicle.*
CHARLIE CLARK: (*Into telephone*) . . . the keys, and it's still in
     both your names.
GINGER: (*Carrying the box, slipping but catching herself*) Whoa.
CHARLIE CLARK: (*Into telephone*) I'm sorry, there's nothing I
     can do. I'd like to help . . .


INT. ACE'S HOUSE, UPSTAIRS DEN – MORNING

CHARLIE CLARK: (*Over telephone*) . . . but I can't.
ACE: (*Into telephone*) Legally, she can't take that stuff. Legally,
     she can't take the stuff.

CHARLIE CLARK: (*Over telephone*) No, Ace.

ACE: (*Into telephone*) Half of everything is mine.

CHARLIE CLARK: (*Over telephone*) Ace, listen to me.

ACE: (*Into telephone*) Half – I'm comin' down. (*He hangs up.*)


EXT. ACE'S HOUSE, DRIVEWAY – MORNING

ACE *and* SHERBERT *get into* ACE'*s damaged car. A metal strip dangling from* SHERBERT'*s door scrapes the pavement as they pull out.*


INT. VEGAS BANK – DAY

GINGER *opens the safe deposit box, which is filled with bound stacks of cash. She grabs handfuls in a frenzy, some fall off the counter to the floor.*

GINGER: Shit! Oh, goddamn it! (GINGER *gets down on the floor to pick them up. Then, to* COPS *who are watching:*) Um, I'm gonna need a bag. If you could just ask the guy for a big bag, okay?

COP #1: (*To* COP #2) Go get a bag, man.

GINGER: (*Looking up, offering* COP #1 *some cash*) And here. Here.

COP #1: Lady, I can't. I can't. I ca–
(COP #2 *exits.*)

GINGER: No, you can, you can. (*Sobbing.*) You've been so nice to me.

COP #1: (*Taking the money*) I can't.


INT. VEGAS BANK – MORNING, A LITTLE LATER

COP #2 *holds open a large canvas bag for* GINGER.

COP #2: (*To* GINGER) Like this?

GINGER: (*Struggling with two handfuls of cash*) Yeah, just hold the top open, all right, and I can – (*She starts to stuff the money in the bag.*)

**EXT. FBI SURVEILLANCE CAR, ACROSS THE STREET – MORNING**

*The* FBI AGENTS *photograph* GINGER *leaving the bank.*


**EXT. VEGAS BANK – DAY**

GINGER *throws the canvas bag into the trunk of her car when,*
*suddenly, she sees* ACE'*s beat-up Cadillac approaching. She gasps.*
GINGER: Oh, God. It's him. (*To* COPS.) You have to stop him.
　　　You have to – 'Cause he said he was going to kill me.
　　　(ACE *jumps out of his car and runs toward* GINGER,
　　　SHERBERT *follows him out.* ACE *is intercepted by the* COPS *who*
　　　*hold him back.*)
　　　You just – Just stop him.
COP #1: Mr Ro– Mr Roth– Mr Rothstein, where you goin' –
ACE: Stop –
COP #1: Wait, hold on a second.
ACE: Hey!
COP #1: Hold on a second.
　　　(*The* COPS *huddle around* ACE *and* SHERBERT *until* GINGER'*s*
　　　*car pulls out of the bank.*)
　　　Nothin' we can do about it. Nothin' we can do. There's
　　　nothin' we can do.
　　　(ACE, *unable to pursue, watches* GINGER *speed away.*)
ACE: Look, look. You can't stop her for speeding? I mean, look
　　　what the hell she's doing.
COP #1: Speeding?
COP #2: We're talkin' to you right now.
　　　(GINGER'*s car disappears into traffic. The FBI car across the*
　　　*street follows right behind her.*)
　　　There's nothing we can do. She had the key.
COP #1: She's on the account. There's nothing we can do.


**EXT. FBI SURVEILLANCE CAR – MORNING**

*The* AGENTS *are following* GINGER.
FBI AGENT #1: Let's pull her over at that Citgo Station.
FBI AGENT #2: (*Driving*) Okay, let's do it.
　　　(FBI AGENT #1 *puts a siren on top of the car's roof.*)

**EXT. VEGAS STREET, CITGO STATION – MORNING**

GINGER *pulls over at a gas station, the FBI car with siren blaring right behind her.*

**EXT. VEGAS BANK – MORNING**

*A powerless* ACE *and* SHERBERT *are still standing in front of the bank with the* COPS. COP #2 *gives* ACE *a 'sorry' gesture.*

**EXT. CITGO STATION – MORNING**

GINGER *and the* FBI AGENTS *are standing by her car. She is distraught.*

FBI AGENT #2: We're – we're placing you under arrest for –

GINGER: (*Sobbing*) For what?

FBI AGENT #2: We're placing you under arrest for aiding and abetting –

GINGER: (*Through tears*) What?

FBI AGENT #2: We're placing you under arrest for aiding and abetting a –

GINGER: (*Crying*) But I'm just trying to leave.

ACE: (*Voice-over*) After all the threats and all the bullshit, it turned out Ginger didn't tell 'em anything. But by then, the Feds didn't need her, anyway.

GINGER: (*Sobbing*) But it was just mine.

ACE: (*Voice-over*) They had all the pieces they needed.

FBI AGENT #1: Come on.

GINGER: But I didn't do anything.

(*The* AGENTS *escort* GINGER *to their car.*)

ACE: (*Voice-over*) And everybody . . .

**EXT. GOLD RUSH – NIGHT**

*Twelve* FBI AGENTS *with rifles, wearing 'FBI' armbands, charge into the parking lot and rush through the front door.*

ACE: (*Voice-over*) . . . began to tumble.

FBI AGENT #3: FBI! We have a warrant!

ACE: (*Voice-over*) . . . one after the other . . . just like dominoes. Between Piscano complaining on a wire.


EXT. GOLD RUSH – NIGHT, A LITTLE LATER

*The* FBI AGENTS *escort* DOMINICK, HARDY, FUSCO *and* MARINO *out of the front of the shop.*

ACE: (*Voice-over*) Between Nicky, Ginger, me and my license . . . paradise . . . we managed to really fuck it all up.


INT. NICKY'S HOUSE – NIGHT

*We hear a doorbell ring.* LITTLE NICKY, *now ten years old, sees* FBI AGENTS *approaching the house.*

LITTLE NICKY: (*Getting up from the couch*) Mom!

JENNIFER: (*Off-camera, into telephone*) Yeah, well, someone's at the fuckin' door now.
(*Jennifer's cousin opens the door; seven* AGENTS *storm in.*)

FBI AGENT #4: FBI. We have a federal search warrant.

NICKY: (*Voice-over*) Right away, I got wind of the pinches comin' down, so I took off. Who needs to hang around for that bullshit?

FBI AGENT #4: (*To* JENNIFER, *showing his badge*) My name is Marc Casper, Special Agent, FBI.

JENNIFER: (*Defensive*) Yeah, well (*grabbing the phone and walking away*), can I make a fuckin' phone call?

FBI AGENT #4: (*Blocking her way as she tries to get by him*) Hey, ho-hold it for a minute. You can make a phone call, but you don't have to talk to us like that.

JENNIFER: (*Slamming the phone down on a table*) Hey –


INT. TANGIERS CASHIER'S CAGE – DAY

NANCE *is talking to a cashier behind the cage when* FBI AGENTS *with Gaming Board investigators* DUPREY *and* AUSTIN *enter the casino.*

FBI AGENT #5: FBI! Don't be alarmed.
    (NANCE *rushes out a back door.*)

NICKY: (*Voice-over*) But they got almost everybody else.

FBI AGENT #5: This area is seized.
DUPREY: Grab everything in sight.
FBI AGENT #6: Right.
DUPREY: (*Walking through a door into the cage*) Get the master account list!
AUSTIN: I want all those papers seized, regardless of what they are.
    (*As* AUSTIN *and the others make their way into the soft count room, an* AGENT *puts up a yellow crime banner across the front of the cashier's window.*)
    I want this area off-limits to everybody.

INT. TANGIERS SOFT COUNT ROOM – DAY

*The counters look on as several* AGENTS *seize the money boxes and stacks of cash from the glass table.* DUPREY *sifts through the Count Room Executive's notebook.* AUSTIN *is at a cabinet looking through a ledger.*

AUSTIN: (*Holding the book*) Ah, yes, here we are. A little craps figures.[1] Hey – Hey.

ACE: (*Voice-over*) Green?

INT. GREEN'S MALIBU HOUSE – NIGHT

GREEN, *wearing a tennis outfit and holding a racquet, is being questioned by* FBI AGENT #8 *who's showing him confiscated papers. Several* AGENTS *are searching the house.*

ACE: (*Voice-over*) Don't even ask.

FBI AGENT #8: Thirty thousand dollars . . .
GREEN: No, he didn't. And that's why it wasn't valid. I was

1 Actual amount taken from craps tables before the skim.

being extorted, all right? I'm willing to tell you whatever
you want to know. I've got nothin' to hide here.

NICKY: (*Voice-over*) Now, for the best . . .


INT. PISCANO'S HOUSE, LIVING-ROOM, KANSAS CITY – DAY

FBI AGENT #9 *removes some ledgers from a filing cabinet.*

NICKY: (*Voice-over*) . . . and I couldn't believe this shit.
Piscano's expense reports took the cake.

(AGENTS *are wandering around the house, looking for
evidence.*)
FBI AGENT #9: Oh, this is good. Bingo!

NICKY: (*Voice-over*) He might as well have given them a fuckin'
blueprint. Everybody's names, addresses, dates,
everything.

FBI AGENT #9: (*Crossing the room to* PISCANO) Look at this!
Thank you so much, Mr Piscano. How considerate of you.
Appreciate it.
PISCANO: Those are my m– those are my mother's books.
FBI AGENT #10: You're under arrest.

NICKY: (*Voice-over*) What a fuckin' balloon head.

(PISCANO *gets more and more agitated as* FBI AGENT #10 *gets
one cuff on him.*)
PISCANO: What are you guys doin'?!
(PISCANO *gasps and clutches his chest, having a heart attack.
The* AGENT *drops the cuffs and tries to help* PISCANO *as he
collapses onto the floor.*)
FBI AGENT #10: Take it easy, Artie. We just want to talk to you.
(PISCANO'S WIFE *and the* FBI AGENTS *kneel down beside
him.*)
PISCANO'S WIFE: (*Screaming*) Artie, are you okay? Sweetheart?
Honey? Wait a minute! He's sick! Artie! Oh, God!
(*She continues to scream as the* AGENTS *try to revive him.*)
FBI AGENT #10: (*To* PISCANO'S *wife*) Move back! Come on!
FBI AGENT #9: Dave!

PISCANO'S WIFE: He's sick! It's his heart!

FBI AGENT #9: CPR! Now!

PISCANO'S WIFE: Oh, God, is he breathing? He's not breathing!
(*An* FBI AGENT *gives him mouth-to-mouth.*)

ACE: (*Voice-over*) Poor Artie. He got so upset he had a heart attack and dropped dead right there in front of his wife.

(FBI AGENTS #9 *and* #10 *restrain* PISCANO's *hysterical* WIFE.)

PISCANO'S WIFE: Artie!

FBI AGENT #10: Calm down! Calm down!

PISCANO'S WIFE: No, I won't calm down! He's my husband!

FBI AGENT #10: Stay out of the way!

PISCANO'S WIFE: Artie! Artie!

FBI AGENT #10: We can't help him if –


EXT. ACE'S HOUSE – DAY

ACE *opens his front door and is confronted by two* FBI AGENTS. *He is shown pictures of* NICKY *and* GINGER *at the construction site.*

ACE: (*Voice-over, quietly*) And at the end of the day, they finally came to see me with the pictures.

FBI AGENT #1: (*Pointing to the pictures*) Why protect a friend who betrayed you like that?

ACE: (*Voice-over*) But I didn't want to look at 'em. I didn't want to look at the guys who brought 'em, either.

(ACE *refuses to look at the photos and quietly closes the door on the* AGENTS.)


INT. FEDERAL COURT-HOUSE – DAY

GAGGI, FORLANO, BORELLI *and* CAPELLI *are all in court.* FORLANO *and* CAPELLI *are breathing through masks and oxygen tanks with nearby doctors and nurses.* GAGGI *has a cane in front of him. Several court spectators look on. We hear the bosses' lawyer speak.*

LAWYER: Your Honor, as you can see, my clients are elderly

and infirm. Any incarceration could pose a serious health risk. They are no danger to the community and they pose no flight risk.

NICKY: (*Voice-over*) When the bosses were arrested, some of 'em were so old they needed doctors at their arraignment.

LAWYER: And Pre-trial Services recommends that bail remain as presently set.

JUDGE: (*Calling a recess*) We're going to take a ten-minute recess.
(*The* JUDGE *pounds his gavel.*)

NICKY: (*Voice-over*) And when it looked like they could get twenty-five years . . .

(*The* BOSSES, *their nurses and lawyer file through a side court door.*)
. . . to life in prison, just for skimmin' a casino . . . sick or no fuckin' sick, you knew people were gonna get clipped. So, the day of the arraignment, they had this meeting right in the back of the court-house.


INT. COURT-HOUSE CONFERENCE ROOM – DAY

*The* BOSSES *are gathered around a conference table as the lawyers and nurses silently walk out the door as if on cue.*

NICKY: (*Voice-over*) See, when something like this happens, you know how things are gonna work out. It's always better with no witnesses. So, what about Andy?

(*The camera pans from one* BOSS *to the other.*)

FORLANO: (*Putting down his oxygen mask once the door behind him is shut*) He won't talk. Stone is a good kid. Stand-up guy, just like his old man. That's the way I see it.

BORELLI: I agree. He's solid. A fuckin' Marine.

CAPELLI: (*Holding his oxygen mask*) He's okay. He always was. Remo, what do you think?

GAGGI: (*Pause*) Look . . . why take a chance? At least, that's the way I feel about it.

EXT. BACK HOME RESTAURANT, STRIP MALL PARKING LOT –
DAY

ANDY STONE *and his* LAWYER *are walking toward their car.*
STONE: You call Artie . . . and you tell him I don't care what,
he's gotta be in my office Thursday morning before eleven
o'clock.
LAWYER: It's done.
(*His* LAWYER *veers to the left, walking away from* STONE *who
keeps talking.*)
(*Off-camera*) It's done.
STONE: (*To himself*) It's terribly important. I gotta have a
conversation with this guy. That's all.
(GAGGI'*s men,* CURLY *and* BEEPER, *appear from behind*
STONE *and shoot him dead. They empty their silent half-load
rounds into* STONE *even after he's down on the snowy ground.
They walk away discreetly, leaving him partially hidden
between cars.*)

NICKY: (*Voice-over*) As much as they liked him, I mean, he
wasn't one of us. He wasn't Italian. As far as they knew,
he could have talked. Otherwise, Stony might still be
alive.

MONTAGE OF MURDERS:


EXT. NANCE'S COSTA RICAN HOUSE – DAY

TITLE IN: COSTA RICA

*The camera moves down a waterfall to reveal* NANCE'*s Spanish-style
house.*

NICKY: (*Voice-over*) The first one to skip was John Nance. He
found a nice, warm secluded place in Costa Rica. He
thought nobody would find him there.
(*Several gunshots are heard.* NANCE *emerges from the house
through a door and runs along a verandah to another door. He
breaks a pane of glass, unlocks another door and runs in.*
BEEPER *emerges from the first door and follows him back into
the house. Several more shots are heard.* NANCE *emerges from*

210

*yet another door, only this time he's been shot in the stomach.*
*He painfully staggers away from the hitmen.*)
But, then, his kid got nabbed by the Feds for drugs, and so
naturally the bosses were afraid he'd come out of hidin'
just to save his kid and give 'em all up. So . . .

(CURLY *and* BEEPER *come out of the house and approach*
NANCE *from behind.*)
CURLY: Hey, where you goin', jag-off?
(NANCE *kneels down.* CURLY *points his gun expertly at the*
*top of* NANCE'*s head and fires. Blood splatters from*
NANCE'*s mouth and he falls to the ground. The gunmen*
*walk away.*)

NICKY: (*Voice-over*) But anyway, they, you know, they all had to
follow.


EXT. HOLE IN THE DESERT – DUSK

*A bound* COUNT ROOM EXEC *and a* CLERK *are kneeling next to a*
*large pit in the desert ground in front of* BEEPER *and* CURLY.

NICKY: (*Voice-over*) Everybody went down.

(*The* CLERK *groans as he's shot in the head by* BEEPER. *Blood*
*splatters and he falls right into the pre-dug hole.*)
COUNT ROOM EXEC: Go ahead, fuck –
CURLY: Fuck you.
(CURLY *shoots the* EXEC *in the head, he too falls backward into*
*the pit. The gunmen fire more rounds into the bodies, then toss*
*their guns into the hole.*)

NICKY: (*Voice-over*) Before you knew it . . .


EXT. PARKING LOT – NIGHT

RICHIE, *a sharply dressed Tangiers* EXEC, *is getting into his new*
*Lincoln.*

NICKY: (*Voice-over*) . . . anybody who knew anything wound up
gettin' whacked.

(CURLY *sneaks up from behind and hits the* EXEC *with a lead pipe. He puts a plastic bag over his head and begins to choke him to death. The* EXEC *struggles a bit but the bag soon fills with blood.* CURLY *strikes him with the pipe one last time.*)

INT. BEVERLY SUNSET MOTEL – NIGHT

*The camera pans away from an empty registration desk to a motel corridor.*
GINGER: (*Off-camera, gasping*) Oh! Oh, no! No . . .
   (*The camera moves past several rooms along a cinder block wall.*)

ACE: (*Voice-over*) After Ginger took off, she wasn't much help to anybody. She found some pimps, low-lifes, druggies and bikers in LA. And in a few months, they went through all the money and all the jewels.

(*Suddenly, a door opens and* GINGER *overdosing, staggers into the hall looking for help. She gasps, goes halfway down the seedy corridor towards the desk, but collapses and dies.*
   *Freeze frame on* GINGER *sprawled out on the motel carpet.*)

After they found her body . . . I had a private doctor do

another autopsy. He said they gave her . . . a hot dose. In the end . . . all she had left was thirty-six hundred in mint-condition coins.

END OF MONTAGE

EXT. TONY ROMA'S RESTAURANT PARKING LOT – DAY

ACE *emerges from the restaurant, smoking a cigarette as in the first scene in the film. He gets into his car to start the ignition.*

ACE: (*Voice-over*) No matter what the Feds or the papers might have said about my car bombing . . .

(*Flames surge from the windshield, concealing* ACE *behind the wheel.*)

FLASHBACK: EXT. TONY ROMA'S RESTAURANT PARKING LOT – DAY

*The sign above him reads: 'Tony Roma's a Place For Ribs'.* ACE *is leaving the restaurant and walking to his car.*

ACE: (*Voice-over*) . . . it was amateur night, and you could tell. Whoever it was, they put the dynamite under the passenger side. But what they didn't know, what nobody outside the factory knew, was that that model car was made with a metal plate under the driver's seat. It's the only thing that saved my life.

(ACE *opens his car door and gets in.*)

INT. ACE'S CAR, TONY ROMA'S RESTAURANT PARKING LOT – DAY

ACE *turns on the ignition and we see two- and three-inch flames come out of the defroster vents. Everything goes silent as he is suddenly engulfed in flames.*

*The car explodes in flames two storeys high. The screen fills with the rising explosion of smoke and fire.*

ACE: (*Voice-over*) The bombing was never authorized, but I suspect I know who lit the fuse.


EXT. MIDWEST CORNFIELD – DAY

NICKY, DOMINICK *and* MARINO *get out of a car on a farm road for a meeting.* FAT SALLY, *a heavy-set wiseguy, is already there.*

FAT SALLY: (*Off-camera*) Hey, Nicky.

ACE: (*Voice-over*) And so did the powers that be.

NICKY: Hey, Mikey, how's your hernia?
    (*They shake hands.*)

FAT SALLY: How you doin'?
    (MARINO *approaches* NICKY *from behind.*)

NICKY: (*Voice-over*) It took months for . . .


FLASHBACK: EXT. MIDWEST CORNFIELD – DAY

NICKY's *car drives up the farm road to meet his crew.*

NICKY: (*Voice-over*) . . . everything to calm down, but finally my guys got out on bail and the bosses wanted me to send my brother Dominick out to Vegas. Always the dollars, always the fuckin' . . .
    (NICKY, DOMINICK *and* MARINO *get out of the car to greet* FAT SALLY. HARDY, FUSCO *and* BEEPER *are also waiting there, smiling.*)
. . . dollars. I mean, it was still way too hot for me to even go near Vegas, so I set up a meeting with the guys way out in the sticks. I didn't want my brother to get fucked around.
    (NICKY *shakes hands with* SALLY. FUSCO *walks up to say hello.*)
I mean, what's right is right. They don't give a fuck about – urgghh!

(MARINO *hits* NICKY *in the back with a bat.* FAT SALLY *grabs him by the throat.*
    HARDY *and* BEEPER *hold* DOMINICK *by the arms.*

214

MARINO *hits* NICKY's *legs with the bat.*)
FAT SALLY: Huh? Come on, you fuckin' rat.
DOMINICK: Fuck! You . . .
> (FUSCO *and* FAT SALLY *pin* NICKY *down and hold his face
> straight ahead, forcing him to watch his brother being beaten.*)
> (*To* MARINO) . . . rat motherfucker! You rat mother–
> (MARINO *hits* DOMINICK *in the shoulder with the bat.*)
MARINO: Tough guy! You and your f– (*he strikes* DOMINICK's
*chest*) fuckin' brother!
DOMINICK: Oh, you – !
> (NICKY *tries to look away.*)
MARINO: No more!
FAT SALLY: Get him, Marino!
MARINO: (*Hitting* DOMINICK *across the neck*) You fuckin'
scumbag!
> (*The wiseguys hold* NICKY's *face so he has to see his brother.*)
> (*Lunging the bat into* DOMINICK's *stomach*) No more.
> (*He swings the bat across his head, knocking* DOMINICK *on the
> ground.*)
NICKY: (*Still pinned, screaming*) Frankie!
MARINO: (*Looking at* NICKY *as he strikes* DOMINICK) No more!
You see? Watch!
> (HARDY *and* BEEPER *join* MARINO. *All three are beating*
> DOMINICK *with baseball bats.*)
NICKY: (*Held down by his neck*) Frankie! Frankie, you piece of
shit!
MARINO: Fuck you, you motherfuck!
> (*The camera tilts down to* DOMINICK's *bloody face as the three
> continue to beat him to death.*)
NICKY: Fuckin' punk, motherfucker! Piece of shit!
> (NICKY *tries to stand up but* FAT SALLY *and* FUSCO *keep him
> down.*)
MARINO: No more fuckin' dirty work!
NICKY: (*Rolling over on his back in pain*) No, no, no, no!
MARINO: (*To* HARDY *and* BEEPER) Take him out! Take this
motherfucker out!
> (*They drag* DOMINICK *by his feet.* MARINO *swings at him with
> two bats as he's taken away into the cornfield.*)

### EXT. MIDWEST CORNFIELD, GRAVE SITE – DAY, A LITTLE LATER

DOMINICK *is battered and bloody.* MARINO, HARDY *and* BEEPER *stand over him, still swinging their bats.*

NICKY *is on his side, still held down by* SALLY *and* FUSCO. *His face is a little bloody.*

NICKY: (*Whimpering, as they beat* DOMINICK) Dominick! Oh, Dominick. Oh, Dom. Frankie. (*Pleading for his brother's life.*)

Frankie, leave the kid alone. He's still breathin'. He's still breathin'. Leave him alone. Frankie.

(MARINO *swings two final blows to* DOMINICK's *head.* NICKY *looks away, sobbing.*)

MARINO: All right. Strip him.

(MARINO *and his hoods remove* DOMINICK's *pants and shirt.*)

NICKY: (*Sobbing as they undress his brother*) No balls, you got no fuckin' balls. Oh, Dominick. Oh, Dom.

(NICKY *sobs. They drag* DOMINICK *toward a freshly dug grave and toss his limp, barely conscious body into it.*)

(*Crying quietly*) Dominick. Dominick. (*Sobs.*) Dominick.

(NICKY *looks up to* MARINO. *They share a look before*

MARINO *swings his bat, striking* NICKY's *head.*
*Freeze frame on* MARINO.
*Unfreeze – live action continues.*
MARINO *and his men start beating* NICKY, *who groans and spits blood as he is struck.*)


EXT. MIDWEST CORNFIELD, GRAVE SITE – DAY, A LITTLE
LATER

NICKY *is stripped down to his underwear.* HARDY *and* FUSCO *drag him to the grave and dump him over* DOMINICK.
MARINO: Come on, come on. Bury 'em.
    (MARINO *and* BEEPER *look on as the other hoods begin the tedious work of tossing dirt on to the bodies, shovel by shovel, until they are covered up to their necks.*
    *We see* NICKY's *face, bloodied and battered. He's still breathing and groaning.*)
ACE: (*Voice-over*) How much were they gonna take? So, they made an example of him and his brother. They buried them while they were still breathing.

    (*A full shovel of dirt lands upon* NICKY's *face and chest with a thud.*)


INT. ACE'S CAR, TONY ROMA'S RESTAURANT PARKING LOT –
DUSK

ACE *is engulfed in flames. His jacket sleeve catches fire. He opens the door and rolls out onto the pavement, barely escaping a smaller explosion. He lies on the floor as a ball of fire rises behind him. Two men pull him away from the car.*
MAN #1: Mister, you all right?
MAN #2: Watch out, the –!
    (ACE *watches as his car explodes in flames. Ashes and debris fall on* ACE *and the two men.*)
    Mister, you all right?
ACE: (*Dazed*) Yeah.

ACE: (*Voice-over*) They had other ideas for me.

### EXT. TONY ROMA'S RESTAURANT PARKING LOT – NIGHT

ACE *is being wheeled to an ambulance on a stretcher. There are firemen and policemen in the background.*

AMBULANCE DRIVER: (*As* ACE *is wheeled into the rear of the ambulance*) You sure are lucky, mister.
(ACE'*s face disappears into the ambulance.*)

### FLASHBACK: EXT. TONY ROMA'S RESTAURANT PARKING LOT – DAY

ACE'*s car explodes.*

*Music in: J. S. Bach – 'St Matthew Passion'.*

### EXT. THE DUNES HOTEL AND CASINO – NIGHT

*The casino is being leveled – actuality footage.*

### EXT. THE MGM GRAND HOTEL AND CASINO – NIGHT

*The brand-new 5,000-room hotel with its entrance shaped like the MGM lion's head.*

ACE: (*Voice-over*) The town will never be the same. After the . . .

EXT. THE DUNES HOTEL AND CASINO – NIGHT

*The hotel and casino implodes, filling the screen with fire and smoke.*

ACE: (*Voice-over*) . . . Tangiers, the big corporations took it all over. Today it looks like . . .

INT. CASINO – DAY

*Slow motion of tourists walking into a casino looking like the living dead.*
ACE: . . . Disneyland.

INT. TREASURE ISLAND HOTEL AND CASINO – NIGHT

*A crowd gathers to watch a mock pirate ship sink in a tank.*

ACE: (*Voice-over*) And while the kids play cardboard pirates, Mommy and Daddy drop the house payments and Junior's college money . . .

EXT. THE DUNES HOTEL AND CASINO – NIGHT

*The casino is destroyed floor by floor by explosions.*

ACE: (*Voice-over*) . . . on the poker slots.

EXT. THE EXCALIBUR HOTEL AND CASINO – NIGHT

*Another 5,000 room hotel built like an Arthurian castle.*

ACE: (*Voice-over*) In the old days, dealers knew your name, what you drank, what you played. Today, it's like checkin' into an airport. And if you order room service, you're lucky if you get it by Thursday.

**EXT. THE DUNES HOTEL AND CASINO – NIGHT**

*The casino marquee topples to the ground in flames.*

ACE: (*Voice-over*) Today, it's all gone. You get a whale show up
    with four million in a . . .

**INT. CASINO – DAY**

*The living dead walk down a few steps, marveling at the huge
casino.*

ACE: (*Voice-over*) . . . suitcase, and some twenty-five-year-old
    hotel school kid is gonna want his Social Security Number.

**EXT. THE DUNES HOTEL AND CASINO – NIGHT**

*The casino collapses into smoke and dust.*

ACE: (*Voice-over*) After the Teamsters got . . .

**EXT. THE MIRAGE HOTEL AND CASINO – NIGHT**

*A 4,000 room hotel with a 60-foot volcano out front. Tourists watch it
belch smoke and flames.*

ACE: (*Voice-over*) . . . knocked out of the box, the corporations
    tore down practically every one of the old casinos. And
    where did the money come from . . .

**EXT. THE LUXOR HOTEL AND CASINO – NIGHT**

*A giant glass pyramid 30 storeys high with a huge sphinx outside.*

ACE: (*Voice-over*) . . . to rebuild the pyramids? . . . Junk
    bonds.

**EXT. ACE'S SAN DIEGO LUXURY HOME – DAY**

**TITLE IN: SAN DIEGO**

*A house very much like* ACE's *house in Vegas, including the fact that it backs up on a golf course. We see* ACE *inside talking on the phone with a bookie.*

ACE: (*Into telephone*) Still not sure?


INT. ACE'S SAN DIEGO LUXURY HOME – DAY

*An older, grayer* ACE *is alone in his living-room with TV sets, fax machines and multiple phone lines. He is surrounded by newspapers and files. He is very much the way we saw him during his earlier handicapping days.*

RACE ANNOUNCER: (*From a television set*) They're off and
 running . . .

ACE: (*Into telephone*) Probable, but may be questionable. All
 right. Well, let me know as soon as you can find out. (ACE
 *sets his cordless phone down and jots down a few notes on a
 racing form. A television set shows a football game in the
 background.*)

ACE: (*Voice-over*) But in the end, I wound up right back where I
 started. I could still pick winners, and I could still make
 money for all kinds of people back home. And why mess
 up a good thing? And that's that.

(*He takes off his glasses, and gazes ahead.*)

(*Fade to black.*)

# Music Featured in *Casino*

Final Chorus from 'St Matthew Passion'
Composed by J. S. Bach
Performed by the Chicago Symphony Orchestra,
Sir Georg Solti
Courtesy of the Decca Record Company Limited, London
by Arrangement with the PolyGram Film & TV Licensing

'Zooma Zooma'
Written by Paolo Citarella and Louis Prima
Performed by Louis Prima
Courtesy of Capitol Records
under License from CEMA Special Markets
Published by Shapiro, Bernstein & Co., Inc.

'Moonglow'/Love Theme from *Picnic*
Written by Eddie DeLange, Will Hudson, Irving Mills/
Morris Stoloff
Courtesy of MCA Records
Published by EMI Mills Music, Inc./Scarsdale Music Corp. –
Shapiro, Bernstein & Co., Inc. – Film Division

'You're Nobody 'Til Somebody Loves You'
Written by Russ Morgan and Larry Stock
Performed by Dean Martin
Courtesy of Capitol Records
under License from CEMA Special Markets
Published by Shapiro, Bernstein & Co., Inc./Southern Music
Publishing Co., Inc.

'Sing, Sing, Sing (with a Swing)'
Written and Performed by Louis Prima
Courtesy of Capitol Records
under License from CEMA Special Markets
Published by EMI Robbins Catalog Inc.

'Love Me the Way I Love You'
Written by Charles Tobias
Performed by Jerry Vale
Courtesy of The Robert Vale Record Co.
Published by Ched Music Corp. and Ritvale Music Corp.

'Let's Start All Over Again'
Written by Arthur Behim and Joseph Howard
Performed by The Paragons
Courtesy of Collectible Records
Published by Shawnee Press, Inc. and EMI Miller Catalog Inc.

'Sweet Virginia'
Written by Mick Jagger and Keith Richards
Performed by The Rolling Stones
Courtesy of Promotone B.V.
Published by ABKCO Music, Inc.

'Basin Street Blues/When It's Sleepy Time Down South'
Written by Spencer Williams/Clarence Muse, Leon Rene,
Otis Rene
Performed by Louis Prima
Courtesy of Capitol Records
under License from CEMA Special Markets
Published by Edwin H. Morris & Company, a division of
MPL Communications, Inc./EMI Mills Music Inc. and
Screen Gems-EMI Music Inc.

'Stella By Starlight'
Written by Ned Washington and Victor Young
Performed by Ray Charles
Courtesy of Ray Charles Enterprises, Inc.
Published by Famous Music Corportion

'Boogaloo Down Broadway'
Written by Jesse James
Performed by The Fantastic Johnny C.
Courtesy of Phil-L.A. of Soul Records
Published by Dandelion Music

228

'Nights in White Satin'
Written by Justin Hayward
Performed by The Moody Blues
Courtesy of Threshold/Polydor/Atlas Records
by Arrangement with PolyGram Film & TV Licensing
Published by TRO-Essex Music, Inc.

'Walk on the Wild Side'
Written by Elmer Bernstein and Mack David
From the Columbia Film *Walk on the Wild Side*
Performed by Jimmy Smith
Courtesy of Verve Records
by Arrangement with PolyGram Film & TV Licensing
Published by Shapiro, Bernstein & Co., Inc. – Film Division

'Gimme Shelter' (Live Version)
Written by Mick Jagger and Keith Richards
Performed by The Rolling Stones
Courtesy of Promotone B.V.
Published by ABKCO Music, Inc.

'Gimme Shelter'
Written by Mick Jagger and Keith Richards
Performed by The Rolling Stones
Published by ABKCO Music, Inc.
by Arrangement with ABKCO Records

'EEE-O Eleven'
Written by Sammy Cahn and Jimmy Van Heusen
Performed by Sammy Davis, Jr.
Published by Maraville Music Corp.

'I'll Walk Alone'
Written by Julie Styne and Sammy Cahn
Performed by Don Cornell
Courtesy of MCA Records
Published by WB Music Corp. o/b/o Cahn Music Co.

'Sunrise' (Prelude from *2001: A Space Odyssey*)
Composed by Richard Strauss
Performed by the Chicago Symphony Orchestra
Courtesy of RCA Victor Red Seal, a Division of BMG Classics

'That's the Way I Like It'
Written by Harry Wayne Casey
Published by Windswept Pacific Entertainment Co. dba
Longitude Music Co.

'Venus'
Written by Edward H. Marshall
Published by ATV Music administered by EMI April Music
Inc. and Welbeck Music Corp.

'Flight of the Bumblebee'
Composed by Nicolai Rimsky-Korsakov
Performed by Jascha Heifetz
Courtesy of the RCA Victor Red Seal
a Division of BMG Classics

'Theme De Camille'
From the motion picture *Le Mepris* (*Contempt*)
Composed by Georges Delerue
Courtesy of Sidomusic/B. Liechti & Co.

'Whip It'
Written by Mark Mothersbaugh and Gerald Casale
Performed by Devo
Courtesy of Warner Bros. Records Inc.
by Arrangement with Warner Special Products
and Courtesy of Virgin Records Ltd.
Published by EMI Virgin Songs, Inc.

'Ain't Got No Home'
Written and Performed by Clarence Henry
Courtesy of MCA Records
Published by ARC Music Corporation

'I'm Sorry'
Written by Ronnie Self and Dub Albritten
Performed by Brenda Lee
Courtesy of MCA Records
Published by Champion Music Corporation

'Harbor Lights'
Written by Jimmy Kennedy and Hugh Williams
Performed by The Platters
Courtesy of Mercury Records
by Arrangement with PolyGram Film & TV Licensing
Published by Chappell & Co. o/b/o Peter Maurice Music

'The House of the Rising Sun'
Written by Alan Price
Performed by The Animals
by Arrangement with ABKCO Records
and EMI Records Ltd.
Published by EMI Al Gallico Music Corp.